Arduino Data Communications

Learn how to configure databases, MQTT, REST APIs,
and store data over LoRaWAN, HC-12, and GSM

Robert Thas John

BIRMINGHAM—MUMBAI

Arduino Data Communications

Copyright © 2023 Packt Publishing

Group Product Manager: Preet Ahuja

Publishing Product Manager: Suwarna Rajput

Book Project Managers: Ashwini Gowda & Sean Lobo

Senior Editor: Sayali Pingale

Technical Editor: Irfa Ansari

Copy Editor: Safis Editing

Proofreader: Safis Editing

Indexer: Tejal Daruwale Soni

Production Designer: Alishon Mendonca

Marketing Coordinator: Rohan Dobhal

First published: November 2023

Production reference: 1031123

Published by Packt Publishing Ltd.

Grosvenor House

11 St Paul's Square

Birmingham

B3 1RB, UK

ISBN 978-1-83763-261-9

www.packtpub.com

To my wife, Patience, for supporting me whenever I need time to acquire new knowledge or to travel. Thank you. I wouldn't have finished this book without your support. Thank you for your support whenever I wasn't there to do something you needed. Thank you for your love and patience. You are the best.

– Robert Thas John

Contributors

About the author

Robert Thas John is a data engineer with a career that spans two decades. He manages a team of data engineers, analysts, and machine learning engineers – roles that he has held in the past. He leads a number of efforts aimed at increasing the adoption of machine learning on embedded devices through various programs from Google Developers and ARM Ltd, which licenses the chips found in Arduinos and other microcontrollers.

He started his career as a software engineer with work that has spanned various industries. His first experience with embedded systems was in programming payment terminals.

I would like to thank Stephen Ozoigbo for getting me interested in machine learning on microcontrollers and providing a lot of the hardware that I have worked with; the team at Edge Impulse for supporting my TinyML efforts and supplying hardware; and the Google Developers team for providing me with Cloud credits.

About the reviewer

Alfredo Moreno has over 18 years of experience in designing and developing large-scale, distributed, and complex systems, having collaborated with clients in multiple countries. He has a solid academic background with a degree in computer engineering and a master's in software architecture. He's achieved certifications in AWS, Azure, TOGAF, and IASA.

Currently, he holds a key position at Iberia, Spain's leading airline and one of the most significant worldwide. Alfredo oversees the technical architecture in three critical areas: airline operations, airport operations, and aircraft and engine maintenance.

He's authored about 15 books on software development and Arduino, with several titles becoming best-sellers.

From the bottom of my heart, I want to thank my daughter for her energy and joy, which have inspired me in the most intense moments; my wife, for being my rock and encouraging me at every step; and my parents, for always believing in me and showing me the value of perseverance. Thank you for standing by my side!

Table of Contents

3

Prototyping with Shields   35

4

Storing Data Collected from Sensors   51

5

Implementing REST and MQTT Protocols for Communication   75

Part 2: Sending Data

6

Utilizing Various Communication Technologies   109

10

Communicating via HC-12   187

11

Managing Communication with RS-485   195

Part 3: Miscellaneous Topics

12

Enhancing Security for Reducing Risk   213

13

Scaling for High Availability   229

14

Building and Manufacturing Hardware   239

Preface

I spent nearly two decades of my life writing software, training and deploying machine learning models, and speaking and teaching about these topics. I got introduced to Stephen Ozoigbo at ARM, who asked whether I had any experience speaking about ML on microcontrollers. I didn't, but I was willing to look into that. That was the beginning of my journey into TinyML. He sent me some kits from SparkFun Electronics, which I used for a 20-person workshop in 2021. I spent the next 12 months talking to developer communities in Sub-Saharan Africa about ML on the Arduino Nano RP2040 Connect. I also organized something I called the Embedded Learning Challenge, with microcontrollers paid for by ARM. All this exposed a knowledge gap on the continent when it comes to a basic understanding of microcontrollers. This book is meant to serve as an introduction to programming Arduinos. The choice of the Arduino MKR is because of the existence of certain shields that are good for learning how to work with these components without learning how to solder. My hope for you is that you will use this as a stepping stone toward solving real-world problems.

Who this book is for

If you have never programmed a microcontroller and you are wondering what all the buzz is about, especially around the **Internet of Things** (**IoT**), then this book is a great starter. If you have programmed microcontrollers but don't know about the infrastructure that stores data, this book will serve as an introduction to databases and data storage.

What this book covers

Chapter 1, *Getting Started with Arduino*, introduces you to the Arduino ecosystem and teaches you how to write your first lines of code.

Chapter 2, *Leveraging Various Sensors for Data Acquisition*, looks at various categories of sensors that exist within the Arduino ecosystem for reading data from the environment.

Chapter 3, *Prototyping with Shields*, gives an introduction to shields, which extend microcontrollers with various capabilities without requiring soldering knowledge.

Chapter 4, *Storing Data Collected from Sensors*, shows how to store data in files on a micro-SD card.

Chapter 5, *Implementing REST and MQTT Protocols for Communication*, teaches you how to set up REST APIs to read from and write to databases.

Chapter 6, Utilizing Various Communication Technologies, gives a brief overview of various communication options and which ones to consider based on the distance you need to cover.

Chapter 7, Communicating with LoRaWAN, shows how to set up a gateway and send data to The Things Network.

Chapter 8, Working with Ethernet, shows how to read data from a weather API over Ethernet and use that to make decisions when the situation doesn't allow for wireless communications.

Chapter 9, Leveraging Cellular Communication Technology, looks at how to choose a cellular radio, send and receive data over SMS and GPRS, and make phone calls.

Chapter 10, Communicating via HC-12, shows how to set up HC-12 modules, and how to send and receive data using them.

Chapter 11, Managing Communication with RS-485, looks at communicating over RS-485 and Modbus in an environmental setting.

Chapter 12, Enhancing Security for Reducing Risk, explains the threat that exists when you transmit or store data, and how you can reduce such risks.

Chapter 13, Scaling for High Availability, explores why you need to ensure that the systems that collect and store your data are available a majority of the time and strategies to consider in order to make that happen.

Chapter 14, Building and Manufacturing Hardware, discusses going from solutions based on breadboards and shields to products that you can take out into the field and test.

To get the most out of this book

You will need a version of the Arduino IDE installed on your computer. All code examples have been tested with Arduino IDE 2.2.1 running on a MacBook Pro with Intel Core but should work on other operating systems and future versions of the Arduino IDE.

Software/hardware covered in the book	Operating system requirements
Arduino IDE 2.2.1	Windows, macOS, or Linux
Python 3.7	
JavaScript	
Arduino MKR WiFi 1010	

You will need an Arduino Portenta together with an Arduino Portenta Vision Shield – Ethernet for the code examples in *Chapter 8*. A little knowledge of either JavaScript or Python will help you understand the code examples in *Chapter 5*.

If you are using the digital version of this book, we advise you to type the code yourself or access the code from the book's GitHub repository (a link is available in the next section). Doing so will help you avoid any potential errors related to the copying and pasting of code.

Download the example code files

You can download the example code files for this book from GitHub at `https://github.com/PacktPublishing/Arduino-Data-Communications/`. If there's an update to the code, it will be updated in the GitHub repository.

We also have other code bundles from our rich catalog of books and videos available at `https://github.com/PacktPublishing/`. Check them out!

Code in Action

The Code in Action videos for this book can be viewed at `https://packt.link/fglee`.

Conventions used

There are a number of text conventions used throughout this book.

`Code in text`: Indicates code words in text, database table names, folder names, filenames, file extensions, pathnames, dummy URLs, user input, and Twitter handles. Here is an example: "The first section, `void setup() {}`, holds code that will be run exactly once when the microcontroller boots up."

A block of code is set as follows:

```
#include "Display.hpp"

    void setup() {
    Display::initialize();
    Display::print_lcd("Hello, world", "of embedded");
}

void loop() {

}
```

When we wish to draw your attention to a particular part of a code block, the relevant lines or items are set in bold:

```
#include "MyEnv.hpp"

#include "MyNTPClient.hpp"
#include <Arduino_MKRENV.h>
#include <SPI.h>
#include <SD.h>
```

Any command-line input or output is written as follows:

```
mkdir MyAPI
cd MyAPI
```

Bold: Indicates a new term, an important word, or words that you see onscreen. For instance, words in menus or dialog boxes appear in **bold**. Here is an example: "Click on **Install**, below the library provided by DFRobot."

> **Tips or important notes**
> Appear like this.

Get in touch

Feedback from our readers is always welcome.

General feedback: If you have questions about any aspect of this book, email us at customercare@packtpub.com and mention the book title in the subject of your message.

Errata: Although we have taken every care to ensure the accuracy of our content, mistakes do happen. If you have found a mistake in this book, we would be grateful if you would report this to us. Please visit www.packtpub.com/support/errata and fill in the form.

Piracy: If you come across any illegal copies of our works in any form on the internet, we would be grateful if you would provide us with the location address or website name. Please contact us at copyright@packt.com with a link to the material.

If you are interested in becoming an author: If there is a topic that you have expertise in and you are interested in either writing or contributing to a book, please visit authors.packtpub.com.

Share Your Thoughts

Once you've read *Arduino Data Communications*, we'd love to hear your thoughts! Scan the QR code below to go straight to the Amazon review page for this book and share your feedback.

https://packt.link/r/1837632618

Your review is important to us and the tech community and will help us make sure we're delivering excellent quality content.

Download a free PDF copy of this book

Thanks for purchasing this book!

Do you like to read on the go but are unable to carry your print books everywhere?

Is your eBook purchase not compatible with the device of your choice?

Don't worry, now with every Packt book you get a DRM-free PDF version of that book at no cost.

Read anywhere, any place, on any device. Search, copy, and paste code from your favorite technical books directly into your application.

The perks don't stop there, you can get exclusive access to discounts, newsletters, and great free content in your inbox daily

Follow these simple steps to get the benefits:

1. Scan the QR code or visit the link below

https://packt.link/free-ebook/9781837632619

2. Submit your proof of purchase
3. That's it! We'll send your free PDF and other benefits to your email directly

Part 1:
Introduction to Arduino and Sensor Data

In this section, you will get an introduction to the Arduino ecosystem, as well as how to collect data using sensors. You will learn about some options for storing data and also learn about writing APIs so you can send data from your microcontroller to your database.

This section has the following chapters:

- *Chapter 1, Getting Started with Arduino*
- *Chapter 2, Leveraging Various Sensors for Data Acquisition*
- *Chapter 3, Prototyping with Shields*
- *Chapter 4, Storing Data Collected from Sensors*
- *Chapter 5, Implementing REST and MQTT Protocols for Communication*

1
Getting Started with Arduino

This chapter will provide a quick introduction to the Arduino ecosystem and enable you to pick boards for your projects. You will learn about the various board families and how they are positioned, and you will pick a board and write your first few lines of code to blink the RGB LED.

Arduinos are popular with students and within the maker community. However, for those who are not part of this community or for students working with Arduinos, it can be challenging to determine the right board to choose.

By the end of this chapter, you will have a solid understanding of the Arduino ecosystem and be equipped to make informed decisions when selecting Arduino boards for your projects. The knowledge you gain in this chapter will help you with picking the right boards for your project.

In this chapter, we're going to cover the following main topics:

- Learning about Arduino – the company
- Learning about Arduino – the hardware
- Learning about the Arduino IDE – the software
- Learning about the Arduino programming language
- Writing the first lines of code – Hello World

Let's get started!

Technical requirements

Some of the requirements for this chapter, such as the Arduino IDE and the board of choice, will be covered before you get to the point where you need to write and run code.

You will require the following:

- A computer capable of running the Arduino IDE
- The Arduino IDE
- The Arduino MKR WiFi 1010
- A USB data cable

All the code examples for this chapter can be found on GitHub at `https://github.com/ PacktPublishing/Arduino-Data-Communications/tree/main/chapter-1/ hello_world_mkr_wifi_1010`. You can clone the repo or download the code and open the `.ino` file with the Arduino IDE.

Learning about Arduino – The company

Arduino is an open source hardware and software company that was set up to simplify how embedded systems engineering is taught to students at a tertiary level. It began as a project in 2005, designed and soldered on a **printed circuit board** (**PCB**) using an ATmega8 chip from Atmel. This was an 8-bit chip. While the particular chip on an Arduino board isn't frequently brought up, the significance cannot be overstated.

The company provided both a board and a way to flash firmware onto the board. This simplified the process of getting machine code onto the chip that was put onto the board.

Over the years, Arduino has released additional boards with different chips and other peripherals on them, aimed at different users. It has made enhancements to the IDE, making it possible to support boards from other manufacturers. The Arduino programming language makes it possible to use one language to program different boards without dealing with the underlying differences. Finally, the Arduino Cloud provides an IoT interface for compatible boards.

Learning about Arduino – The hardware

Arduino provides various **microcontroller unit** (**MCU**) development boards. When Arduino is mentioned, a lot of users think of the Arduino Uno, which is arguably the most popular board from Arduino, as well as the most popular one manufactured by other companies based on the reference designs available from Arduino. These clones aren't called Arduino, but something similar, such as the SparkFun RedBoard manufactured by SparkFun Electronics. The following photo shows various Arduino MCUs.

Figure 1.1 – Various Arduino MCUs

We will be using official Arduino boards in this book. By using an official Arduino board, you will be helping to support the company and its open source efforts.

You might start a conversation about boards with the question, "*What is the best board for…?*". The answer, as to most questions, is, "*It depends!*"

In the world of microcontrollers, the best board is the one that gets the job done while consuming the least amount of resources (power, memory, etc.). Power consumption ties right back to the chip. The greater the capability of a chip, the more complex it is, and the greater the power consumption, normally.

During development, it is normal to pick a board at random, complete the setup, ensure it is working, and then try to downsize the board. What this means is that, at first, you might not know how large your firmware will be, or what code will need to run on it. As a result, you could pick any medium-range board.

After you are done with development, you will know the exact size of your firmware, as well as the number of pins you have utilized and the communication protocols. Then, you can pick a smaller board that supports everything you need and deploy it for production. Or, even better, you could pick the chip and sensors that you need and design a new PCB!

The first place to find Arduino hardware is on the website: `https://www.arduino.cc/en/hardware`. You can find the complete list of boards, and, as of this writing, attempts to classify them into three categories:

- **Nano Family**: Boards with a small footprint, some embedded sensors, and support for **machine learning (ML)**.
- **MKR Family**: Boards equipped with a low-power chip, a communication chip, a cryptographic chip, and support for various shields that make it possible to prototype without additional circuit work. These boards feature a 32-bit SAMD21 (ARM Cortex-M0+) chip from Microchip Technologies (`https://ww1.microchip.com/downloads/en/DeviceDoc/SAM_D21_DA1_Family_DataSheet_DS40001882F.pdf`).
- **Classic Family**: The older, more popular boards and their shields.

The second place to find Arduino hardware is on the *Pro* website: `https://www.arduino.cc/pro`. This website exists because Arduino wants to be reclassified from just something that is meant for learning to something that can be put to industrial use. Prior to this time, people would learn on an Arduino board but use a board from a competitor for the final product. The *Pro* website lists hardware in six categories (`https://www.arduino.cc/pro/hardware`):

- **Portenta Family**: Boards with the highest-rated chips for their generation, with carriers and shields that make edge deployments possible. Connectivity is provided via shields. The chip on these is a 32-bit dual-core STM32H747 (ARM Cortex-M7 and ARM Cortex-M4) from STMicroelectronics (`https://www.st.com/en/microcontrollers-microprocessors/stm32h747-757.html`).

- **Edge Control**: Remote monitoring and control carrier boards, optimized for outdoor environments. These boards feature a 32-bit nRF52840 (ARM Cortex-M4) chip from Nordic Semiconductors (`https://www.nordicsemi.com/Products/nRF52840`). Edge control boards come with two additional slots for MKR boards that let you extend functionality.

- **Nicla Family**: Thumb-sized boards with industrial-grade sensors and battery connectors. These are the smallest boards available from Arduino.

- **MKR Family**: The same as the MKR family from the main website.

- **Nano Family**: The same as the Nano family from the main website.

- **Gateways**: Devices for LoRaWAN connectivity. We will discuss these in more detail in *Chapter 7, Communicating with LoRaWAN*.

Let's proceed to consider how to pick a board for the projects you will be tackling in this book.

Choosing your board – The Arduino MKR family

The board of choice for this book will be the Arduino MKR family, an example of which is the Arduino MKR WiFi 1010 (`https://docs.arduino.cc/hardware/mkr-wifi-1010`). The MKR family of boards is targeted at makers or tinkerers, has a popular form factor that is forward compatible with the newer and more powerful Arduino Portenta family of Pro boards, and has a number of shields that minimize the need for solderless breadboards and soldering.

Rather than picking up this board alone, I would recommend purchasing a kit that comes with other components that you can utilize for projects in this book. This kit is the Arduino Oplà IoT Kit, which you can find at this URL: `https://store.arduino.cc/products/arduino-opla-iot-kit`.

You will get to work with other boards as the need for different communication methods arises. All MKR family boards utilize the same chip: the SAMD21 chip from Microchip Technologies running a 32-bit ARM Cortex-M0+.

The MKR family is made up of various boards with different capabilities, some of which are listed here:

- **Arduino MKR WiFi 1010**: This board provides WiFi and Bluetooth connectivity

- **Arduino MKR FOX 1200**: This board provides SigFox connectivity

- **Arduino MKR WAN 1310**: This board provides LoRaWAN connectivity

- **Arduino MKR GSM 1400**: This board provides GSM connectivity

Don't worry if one or more of the communication options aren't familiar right now, as we will cover them in a later chapter.

The boards have the following general features:

- 8 digital I/O pins

- 13 PWM pins

- 7 analog input pins

- 1 analog output pin

- 1 each of UART, SPI, and I2C

- 256 KB of CPU internal memory

- 32 KB of SRAM

- Onboard WiFi and Bluetooth connectivity

- Onboard RGB LED

Make sure you refer to the documentation for any board that you are working with, from the manufacturer's website. This will save you a lot of stress and time.

Every board has a pinout diagram. This document provides information on what capabilities each pin on the board has. You can find the pinout diagram for the MKR WiFi 1010 here: `https://content.arduino.cc/assets/Pinout-MKRwifi1010_latest.pdf`.

Next, let's discuss the **IDE**, which provides assistance when you write your code.

Learning about the Arduino IDE

By definition, an IDE is a software application that provides facilities for software development; it normally consists of a source code editor and may include a debugger and build automation tools.

The Arduino IDE brings together a collection of tools and interfaces that make it easier to develop your firmware. The IDE is available for various operating systems from the following URL: `https://www.arduino.cc/en/software`.

A visit to the preceding URL will show you that there is a Cloud IDE and a Desktop IDE. Let's take a closer look at each one.

Arduino Cloud IDE

The Cloud IDE complements the Arduino IoT Cloud that is available from the company. You can access the Cloud IDE from the following URL: `https://create.arduino.cc/editor`.

The Cloud IDE has a limit to how often you can compile code and deploy firmware, and is most useful in the following scenarios:

- Your computer or operating system is unable to support an official version of the Arduino Desktop IDE

- You would like to update the firmware on a device that is connected to the Arduino Cloud

The following screenshot shows a sample of what the IDE looks like. Note the items numbered **1** through **5** in the figure.

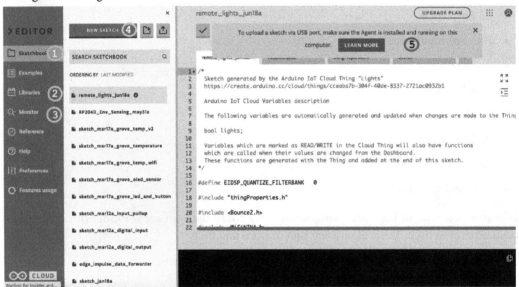

Figure 1.2 – The Arduino Cloud IDE

The large white section on the right is your code editor. The black section underneath provides output information when you perform operations such as code compilation and deployment.

The numbered sections provide certain functionality or information as follows:

1. **Sketchbook**: This lets you manage your sketches (Arduino code is called a sketch). You can see a list of sketches in the middle section.

2. **Libraries**: This lets you manage various libraries. These are code packages that let you work with some sensors, displays, or actuators, or that let you simplify complex tasks.

3. **Monitor**: This lets you view output from your serial port, an interface that lets the board communicate with computers and other devices. It is frequently used for debugging purposes.

4. **SketchBook**: This lets you create new sketches, upload sketches from your computer, or manage folders. This is only visible when you choose **Sketch** from the panel on the left.

5. **Notice pane**: This only pops up to warn you that you need the Arduino Create Agent in order for the browser to communicate with your board. The Cloud IDE requires the Chrome browser.

Arduino Desktop IDE

If you haven't already, you can get a copy of the Arduino Desktop IDE from the following URL: `https://www.arduino.cc/en/software`. After downloading and installing the appropriate version for your computer, you will be met with an interface similar to the one shown next. Please note the numbered sections.

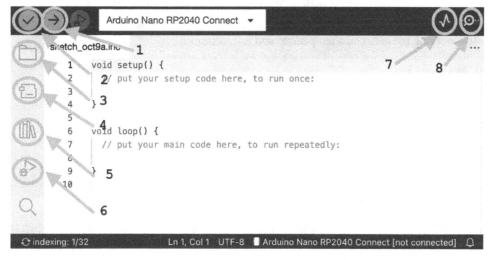

Figure 1.3 – The Arduino Desktop IDE

The white drop-down component at the top of the IDE lets you choose the board you are working with. Don't worry if you can't find your board; you can install it from **Boards Manager**. Let's take a closer look at the numbered sections:

1. This button deploys firmware to the selected board.

2. This button verifies that the code will compile for the selected board. This does a few things, including checking for syntax errors and confirming that all libraries are certified to work for your chosen board/chip.

3. **Sketch Manager**: This lets you view other sketches and open them for editing.

4. **Boards Manager**: This lets you install definitions for additional supported boards.

5. **Library Manager**: This lets you find and install libraries.

6. **Debug**: This lets you step through your code and set breakpoints that make it easier to debug.

7. **Serial Plotter**: This lets you plot numbers that are being written out to the serial console.

8. **Serial Console**: This lets you inspect output being written to the serial console.

Let's discuss the programming language next.

Learning about the Arduino programming language

The Arduino programming language is a subset of the C/C++ programming language. It's okay if you haven't written C/C++ before now, as getting started with Arduino is pretty straightforward.

Getting started with Arduino

The quickest way to get started is to click on the **File** menu on the Arduino IDE, then choose **New**. Doing that will give you a new file with a structure similar to the one in the following code block, which does nothing but give you a template to add instructions in:

```
void setup() {

}

void loop() {

}
```

The preceding code is made up of two sections:

- The first section, void setup() {}, holds code that will be run exactly once when the microcontroller boots up. The code that gets executed is contained within the opening and closing curly brackets. Here is the code again:

  ```
  void setup() {

  }
  ```

- The next section of code, void loop() {}, holds code that is executed repeatedly as long as the microcontroller is powered up. The code is also contained within the curly brackets. Here is the code again:

  ```
  void loop() {

  }
  ```

Let's proceed to discuss GPIO pins.

General purpose input and output

A lot of the interaction that happens on a microcontroller is through the **general purpose input and output (GPIO)** pins. There are two categories of pins: *digital* and *analog*. The following pinout diagram for the MKR WiFi 1010 shows the pins.

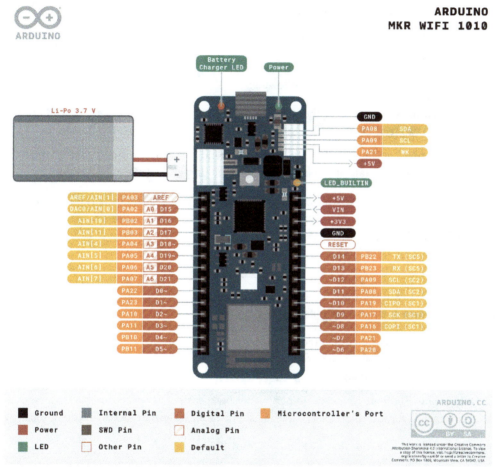

Figure 1.4 – Arduino MKR WiFi 1010 pinout diagram (source – https://docs.arduino.cc/static/9d6534bb9783a42e3527a8c03472ad10/ABX00023-full-pinout.pdf)

The pin labels are color-coded to make it easier to identify pins by their function. Some pins have only one use, such as the **Power** and **Ground** pins. Other pins have multiple uses. Pay attention to the labels that are closer to the board on the left and right. You will see that 22 pins can be used as digital pins, while 7 of those can be used as analog pins in addition. However, no pins are labeled as input or output.

Let's discuss how to configure pins for input or output depending on whether the pin is digital or analog.

Digital pins

Digital pins represent a state that depends on the amount of electricity flowing through them. There are two states:

- **Low state**: This represents an OFF state or a FALSE state. This is set when the amount of electricity is below a certain reference.

- **High state**: This represents an ON state or a TRUE state. This is set when the amount of electricity is above a certain reference.

A digital pin is configured as either of the following:

- **An input pin**, used for reading the state of a peripheral attached to it. An example of this is a button. You can read the state of an input pin using the digitalRead() function.

- **An output pin**, used to control the state of a peripheral attached to it. An example of this is an LED. You can set the state of an output pin using the digitalWrite() function.

You can configure a digital pin using the pinMode() function. The first parameter is the pin number, and the second is one of INPUT, OUTPUT, or INPUT_PULLUP. You will see this used in the Hello World example very soon.

Analog pins

Analog pins can hold a state between 0 and 1023, which is proportional to the voltage passing through the pin. There are two possible directions:

- **Input pins**: These are connected to peripherals that send a voltage value over a range. This is how peripherals such as sensors work. You can read the value of the pin using the analogRead() function.

- **Output pins**: These are connected to peripherals that can operate over a variable range, such as electric motors and actuators. You can set the value of the pin using the analogWrite() function.

You are now ready to write your first Arduino program.

Writing the first lines of code – Hello World

The first code that is introduced in programming is called Hello World. In microcontrollers, the first code blinks an LED. This is usually an onboard LED if one is present.

You will need your MKR board, a micro-USB cable, and the Arduino IDE to get started.

Installing the board

Use the following steps to set up your board:

1. Launch the Arduino IDE, if it's not running.

2. Connect one end of the micro-USB cable to your computer.

3. Remove the Arduino MKR board from its packaging and any black foam that it's sitting on. Failure to do so will result in some unexpected behavior.

4. Connect the MKR board to the other end of the micro-USB cable.

5. A green power LED should light up to show that the board is now powered on.

6. Select **Arduino MKR WiFi 1010** from the board selector dropdown at the top of the IDE. If the board isn't listed, go to **Board Manager** on the left, search for SAMD, and click **Install** under **Arduino SAMD Boards**.

We are now ready to program the MKR board. The IDE should look similar to the following figure.

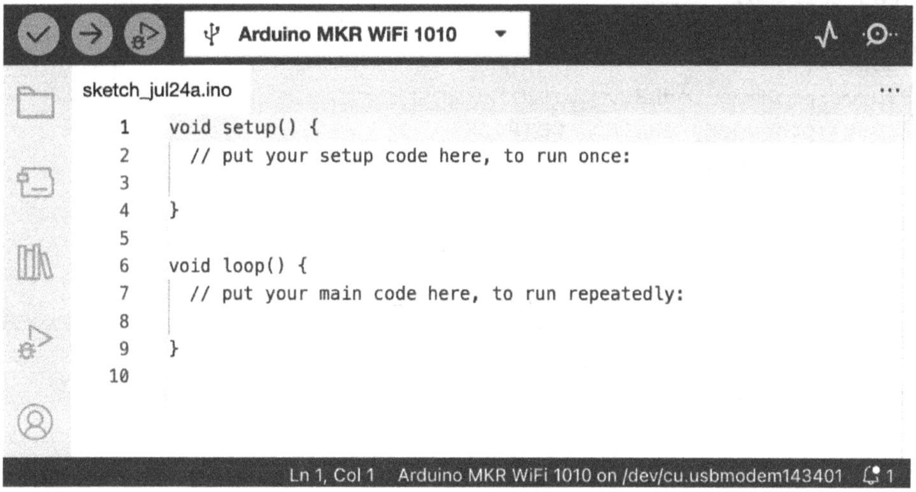

```
sketch_jul24a.ino
     1    void setup() {
     2    |  // put your setup code here, to run once:
     3    |
     4    }
     5
     6    void loop() {
     7    |  // put your main code here, to run repeatedly:
     8    |
     9    }
    10
```

Ln 1, Col 1   Arduino MKR WiFi 1010 on /dev/cu.usbmodem143401   ⌷ 1

Figure 1.5 – The IDE in the ready state

Blinking the onboard LED

The MKR board has an onboard RGB LED. **RGB** stands for **Red, Green, and Blue**. The RGB LED is connected to three pins, as follows:

*   **Green**: pin 25

*   **Red**: pin 26

*   **Blue**: pin 27

The three pins let you control the three colors independently, control the intensity, and mix the colors to produce other colors.

Let's write code to blink one or more of the LEDs. To do this, we will count from 0 to 7 in binary. This will give us three digits ranging from 000 to 111. If the digit is 0, we will turn off the corresponding LED, and if it's 1, we will turn it on. We can do this using the pins in digital mode, which will not control the intensity of the light.

The code that does this follows. You can find this code in the GitHub repository for this book, or you can type it out:

```
#include <WiFiNINA.h>
#include <utility/wifi_drv.h>

#define redLED 25
#define greenLED 26
#define blueLED 27
byte counter = 0;

void setup() {
  WiFiDrv::pinMode(redLED, OUTPUT);
  WiFiDrv::pinMode(greenLED, OUTPUT);
  WiFiDrv::pinMode(blueLED, OUTPUT);
}

void loop() {
  WiFiDrv::digitalWrite(blueLED, bitRead(counter, 0));
  WiFiDrv::digitalWrite(greenLED, bitRead(counter, 1));
  WiFiDrv::digitalWrite(redLED, bitRead(counter, 2));
  counter > 6 ? counter = 0 : counter++;
  delay(1000);
}
```

The explanation for the code is as follows:

- The first two lines include the libraries that are necessary for us to address the onboard LEDs. The LEDs on the MKR WiFi 1010 must be addressed via the WiFi library.

- The next three lines define three constants that reflect the pins we would like to address. This isn't mandatory, but it makes it easier for us to know what pins we are addressing in our code.

- The next line defines a variable called counter, which defaults to 0.

- Within the setup() function, we set all three LEDs to output mode.

- Within the `loop()` function, we do three things:

  - The first three lines set the state of each of the LEDs by using the `digitalWrite()` function that is found within the `WiFiDrv` library. This function takes two parameters: the pin and the state. The pin is specified using one of the constants we declared earlier, and the state is obtained by using the `bitRead()` function. This function, in turn, takes two parameters: the number we would like to read and the index of the least significant bit we would like to read. For example, `bitRead(6, 1)` would first convert the decimal number 6 into the binary number 110, then it would read the second rightmost digit (it uses a 0-based index). The result would be 1.

  - The next line increases our counter using a ternary operator. It is basically an `if-else` statement that sets the counter to 0 if the value is greater than 6 or increases it if it isn't.

  - The final line introduces a delay of a second (1,000 milliseconds) so that the human eye can see the LED that is lit.

Give the code a try and see how it runs on the board. The lights should range from off to blue and through a range all the way to white. There is a total of seven colors represented in this loop.

You will find the light to be too bright unless it is behind something such as a handkerchief that serves to dull the brightness. You can fix this by using `analogWrite()` and setting the value to 64 for a quarter of the brightness.

There is a second advantage to using `analogWrite()`. You can mix different ratios of the three primary colors to arrive at a lot more colors.

Summary

Throughout this chapter, you have gained knowledge about Arduino and its ecosystem, including its components and different board options. You have also selected a board to begin your journey. Furthermore, you have successfully installed the Arduino IDE and written your initial lines of code.

Moving forward to *Chapter 2, Leveraging Various Sensors for Data Acquisition*, you will delve into the realm of sensors. This chapter will explore the diverse range of sensors available and how they can be utilized to collect data. You will gain experience working with both standalone sensors and shield-mounted sensors by connecting them to the MKR board and writing code to extract data from these sensors.

2

Leveraging Various Sensors for Data Acquisition

In the previous chapter, you learned how to blink an LED. Doing that lets the microcontroller interact with its environment. You were using the LED as an actuator to control the environment. With Arduino, you can also read the environment using sensors. Sensors convert the state of the environment into an electrical signal. You can read these signals using input and output pins.

In this chapter, we are going to cover the following main topics:

- Learning about microcontroller input and output pins
- Discovering sensors

By the end of this chapter, you will have learned about various sensors and the various ways in which you can collect data. You will find this knowledge to be useful when you encounter new sensors as you go about your daily activities. The knowledge you will acquire in this chapter will come in handy for collecting data in future projects.

Technical requirements

All the code examples for this chapter can be found on GitHub at `https://github.com/PacktPublishing/Getting-Started-with-TensorFlow`. You will also need the following:

- Arduino MKR WiFi 1010
- Micro-USB cable
- LCD 1602
- Arduino Sensor Kit
- Arduino IDE

Learning about input and output pins

The first time we looked at the pinout diagram of the MKR WiFi 1010, we only discussed the digital and analog pins. Let's revisit that diagram so that we can consider the other communication technologies that are available on the MKR board:

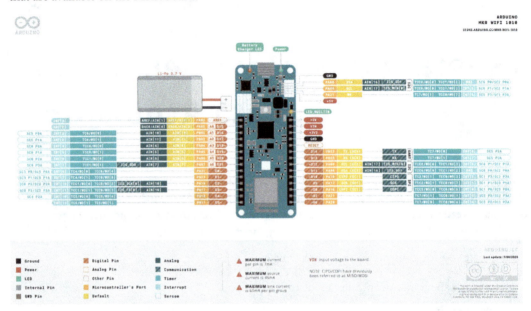

Figure 2.1 – Arduino MKR WiFi 1010 pinout diagram (source: https://docs.arduino.cc/static/9d6534bb9783a42e3527a8c03472ad10/ABX00023-full-pinout.pdf)

The preceding figure has some pins labeled in dark green. Take a look at the pins on the right-hand side of the board; you will see that they are grouped into three. These are communication protocols that are supported by the pins. We'll discuss them next.

UART

Digital pins 13 and 14 work together in tandem to support a protocol that is commonly called **Serial**. In Serial communications, data is transmitted one bit at a time. **UART** is short for **Universal Asynchronous Receiver/Transmitter**. The "Asynchronous" part in the name implies that this doesn't require the use of an external clock as a timing source. This minimizes the number of wires required for communication but requires some extra work to ensure that the communication works properly. You can use UART for communication between two microcontrollers, or between a microcontroller and a device pump. This works using two pins – one for transmitting data and a second for receiving data. The two devices communicating using serial need to agree on a data speed, called a baud rate. The data is transmitted one bit at a time.

The MKR board has two serial ports, called **Serial** and **Serial1**:

- **Serial** is used for communicating with a computer when connected using a USB cable. You can use this to output information to a console on the host computer, as well as to read input from the console. The microcontroller sends text messages over the serial interface.

- **Serial1** is used for communicating with digital pins 13 and 14. It works the same way as Serial.

You can only use UART to communicate between two devices. Let's discuss something that supports more devices concurrently.

SPI

The **Serial Peripheral Interface (SPI)** uses four wires to communicate with a peripheral, in addition to two wires for power and ground. This lets it implement synchronous communication, in which all devices communicate using a common clock, along with a chip select pin that lets it choose the peripheral that it would like to communicate with. Pins D8, D9, and D10 are used for SPI on the MKR board. These pins behave as follows:

- **COPI**: This is controller out, peripheral in. This is the pin/wire over which the microcontroller sends data out to the attached peripheral. This is pin D8 on the MKR.

- **SCK**: This is the serial clock. It is the pin that the controller uses to control timing between itself and the peripheral. This is pin D9 on the MKR.

- **CIPO**: Controller in, peripheral out. This is the pin that the controller uses to receive data from the peripheral. This is pin D10 on the MKR.

You will need four wires to work with each SPI device, plus an additional **chip select** (**CS**) pin for each peripheral, in addition to two cables for power. This could quickly become a problem. Let's look at the third communication protocol, which requires only two wires/pins for communications.

I2C

With **inter-integrated circuit communication (I2C)**, the microcontroller acts as either a controller or a peripheral. It is usually a controller.

The MKR board has two I2C channels, represented by pins D11 and D12, as well as PA08 and PA09. You will be using D11 and D12 more often. The two wires function as follows:

- **SDA**: This is the data channel and is handled by pin D11.

- **SCL**: This is the clock channel and handles the timing. It is on pin D12.

You will also need to provide power to the peripheral, so two extra wires are required for power and ground. These are as follows:

- **+5V**: The power pin, which is colored red in the diagram. You might see this pin labeled as VCC on some peripherals.

- **GND**: The ground pin, which is colored black.

You can use I2C with both sensors and actuators. Also, you can connect a whopping 128 devices to one I2C channel, so long as they have different addresses. You might come across several displays that utilize the I2C communication protocol. One of those displays is the LCD1602, which is available from Waveshare, Seeed Studio, and a host of other vendors. Let's learn how to work with one such display.

Project 1 – setting up an LCD

Follow these steps to complete this project. The code is available online at `https://github.com/PacktPublishing/Arduino-Data-Communications/tree/main/chapter-2/LCD1602-HelloWorld`:

1. Connect the MKR board and the LCD, as shown in the following figure:

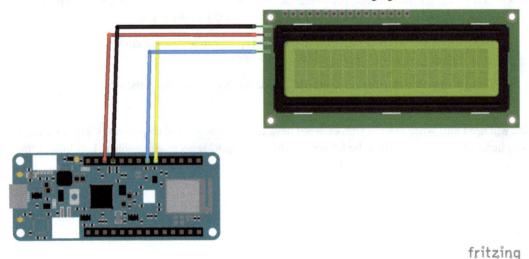

fritzing

Figure 2.2 – Connecting an LCD1602 display to the MKR WiFi 1010

2. Launch the Arduino IDE.
3. Go to **Library Manager**.
4. Type LCD1602 into the search bar.
5. Click on **Install**, below the library provided by DFRobot.

6. From the IDE, choose **File | New**, and replace the code in the `.ino` file with the following:

```
#include "DFRobot_RGBLCD1602.h"

#define red 0
#define green 0
#define blue 255

DFRobot_RGBLCD1602 lcd(16, 2);

void setup() {
    lcd.init();
    lcd.setRGB(red, green, blue);
    print_lcd("Hello, world", "of embedded");
}

void loop() {

}

void print_lcd(String l1, String l2) {
  lcd.clear();
  lcd.setCursor(0, 0);
  lcd.print(l1);
  lcd.setCursor(0, 1);
  lcd.print(l2);
}
```

Let's discuss the code:

- The first line includes the DFRobot library, which is required for communicating with the display. This library encapsulates the I2C communication, but you still need to know that the display uses I2C so that you can wire it up correctly. If you would like to see the code implementation that does the I2C addressing, you can right-click on the name of the header file and choose **Go to Definition**.

- In the next three lines, you define the brightness of the red, green, and blue channels. The LCD has three color channels. By setting red and green to 0, you turn them off, effectively setting the display to use only blue.

- In the next line, you define an instance of the DFRobot_RGBLCD1602 class. You pass in two parameters, specifying the number of columns and rows supported by the display. You are now ready to address the display.

- In the `setup()` function, you do three things:

  I.   First, you initialize the display.

  II.   Next, you set the display color.

  III. Finally, you call a custom function called `print_lcd()` that takes two parameters and prints them out on different rows. We will discuss the implementation of the `print_lcd()` function shortly.

- We leave the `loop()` function empty. If you would like to update the display continuously or periodically, you can program that in the `loop()` function.

- Finally, we come to the `print_lcd()` function. First, the function clears the display. Then, it moves the cursor to the first column and first row and prints the first parameter. Finally, it moves to the first column and second row and prints the second parameter. We made use of a function because it helps us keep the main loop smaller and neater, and we can call a function multiple times. It's also easier to edit the function whenever the need arises without changing our mail function drastically.

Congratulations – you now have code that you can utilize to display information whenever you use this particular display! Click on the **Upload** button to place the firmware onto the MKR board. You can watch a video recording of the Code in Action at `https://packt.link/chG0p`.

Let's do one more thing that will make our lives easier: we will make the code modular. This code for displaying things on the LCD will not change and doesn't need to be in our `.ino` file. Making the code modular makes it easier to swap out the LCD for something else without having to change the code too much. Let's do just that.

Project 2 – making the LCD code modular

Follow these steps to make the code modular. The code for this project is available at `https://github.com/PacktPublishing/Arduino-Data-Communications/tree/main/chapter-2/LCD1602-Modular`:

1. Begin by adding a new file to the project you are working on. In the Arduino IDE, on the bar where you have the name of the file we have been working with, click on the ellipses (three dots). This is illustrated here:

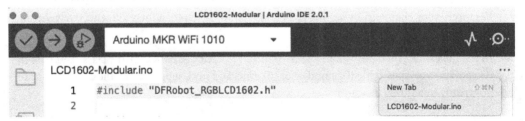

Figure 2.3 – Adding a new tab

2. A new interface will pop up, asking for a name for the new file. Type in `Display.hpp` and hit **OK**.

3. Place the following code into the newly created header file. This code defines a namespace called `Display`, which we will use to access the functions we need. We will introduce one new function header, called `initialize()`, and maintain the old `print_lcd()` header. Note that the parameter names have been changed to make them more descriptive:

```
#pragma once

#include <Arduino.h>

namespace Display {
  #define red 0
  #define green 0
  #define blue 255

  void initialize();

  void print_lcd(String line1, String line2);
}
```

4. Repeat *Steps 1* and *2* to add a new file. Call this file `Display.cpp`.

5. Paste the following code into the new file. This code implements the headers that you previously defined in `Display.hpp`:

```
#include "Display.hpp"
#include "DFRobot_RGBLCD1602.h"

namespace Display {
  DFRobot_RGBLCD1602 lcd(/*lcdCols*/16,/*lcdRows*/2);  //16
characters and 2 lines of show

  void initialize() {
    lcd.init();
    lcd.setRGB(red, green, blue);
  }

  void print_lcd(String line1, String line2){
    lcd.clear();
    lcd.setCursor(0, 0);
    lcd.print(line1);
    lcd.setCursor(0, 1);
    lcd.print(line2);
  }
}
```

6. You can now go back to your main Arduino `.ino` file and replace the code there with the following, much shorter, code, which does the same thing:

```
#include "Display.hpp"

void setup() {
    Display::initialize();
    Display::print_lcd("Hello, world", "of embedded");
}

void loop() {

}
```

As you can see, you are now doing much less in the main file, and the code has better readability. Let's discuss what is going on:

- You begin by importing `Display.hpp`. You don't need to worry about what gets imported into the implementation.

- Within the `setup()` function, you call the `initialize()` function to start up the LCD and set the desired color, and then you call the `print_lcd()` function to display what you want.

- You leave the `loop()` function empty because there is nothing to do for now.

Great – you now have a setup that you can use with various sensors to display information about what is going on with your code! Click on the **Upload** button to place this code onto the MKR board. You can watch a video recording of the Code in Action at `https://packt.link/chG0p`.

Now, let's talk about sensors.

Discovering sensors

Sensors convert external readings into electrical signals. There are so many sensors that it would be impossible to list them all here. You can find sensors in three different implementations:

- **On-board sensors**: These come integrated with the microcontroller development board. MKR boards don't come with those, but other Arduino Pro boards do.

- **Breakout boards**: These provide an interface such as a single pin, UART, SPI, or I2C for connecting to and communicating with a microcontroller.

- **Shields**: These are boards that are meant to attach to the top or bottom of a microcontroller and either integrate sensors or provide interfaces for connecting breakouts. We will discuss shields in the next chapter.

Let's discuss some sensor categories.

Motion sensors

Motion sensors try to answer one or more of the following questions:

- Is this item in motion?

- What direction is this item headed in?

- Is this item being held upward or sideways?

You will frequently find these sensors called **Inertial Measurement Units** (**IMUs**). There are three types:

- **Accelerometers**: These measure motion in three dimensions, called axes. An item that is moving straight up might have a change in only one direction, while an item that is moving inside a vehicle on a bumpy road could experience a change in all directions. These sensors are found in phones, smartwatches, activity trackers, and other devices that need to determine what the wearer (or bearer) is up to.

- **Gyroscopes**: These measure angular momentum in three axes. You can use gyroscopes to measure device orientation, such as in a phone or a smartwatch.

- **Magnetometer**: These measure the direction relative to magnetic north, similar to a compass.

You will frequently find IMUs being labeled with a certain number of axes, such as 3-axis, 6-axis, or 9-axis. Since each sensor measures three axes, dividing the number of axes on an IMU will give you the number of sensors it contains. For example, a 6-axis IMU has two sensors, usually an accelerometer and a gyroscope.

Let's look at an example project where we collect accelerometer data using a 3-axis IMU called the **LIS3DHTR**. This accelerometer is available as part of the Arduino Sensor Kit from Seeed Studio, and it uses I2C to communicate with the microcontroller. This kit is available at `https://store.arduino.cc/products/arduino-sensor-kit-bundle`.

Project 3 – reading accelerometer data

Follow these steps to get your project up and running. The code for this project is available at `https://github.com/PacktPublishing/Arduino-Data-Communications/tree/main/chapter-2/Accelerometer`:

1. Set up your microcontroller, LCD, and accelerometer, as shown in the following figure. You will notice that both the accelerometer and the LCD utilize the same I2C pins on the MKR board, but we break these out on a breadboard to make connectivity easier:

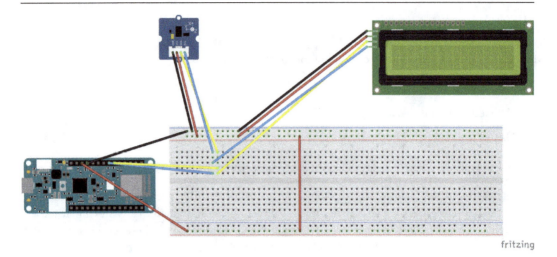

Figure 2.4 – Connecting the accelerometer and LCD to the MKR board

2.   Launch the Arduino IDE.

3.   Open the last project where you made the LCD code modular. You can find it at `https://github.com/PacktPublishing/Arduino-Data-Communications/tree/main/chapter-2/LCD1602-Modular`.

4.   From the IDE menu bar, click on **File** | **Save As** and name the new project `Accelerometer`.

5.   Open **LIBRARY MANAGER**.

6.   Search for `LIS3DHTR` and locate the library named **Grove-3-Axis-Digital-Accelerometer-2g-to-16g-LIS3DHTR by Seeed Studio**:

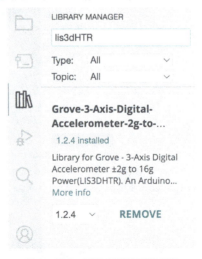

Figure 2.5 – LIBRARY MANAGER

7. Install this library.

8. Create a new file and name it `Accel.hpp`. Copy the following code into this new file. This code defines the header file with a namespace and functions for initializing and controlling the accelerometer:

```
#pragma once

#include <Arduino.h>

namespace Accel {
  void initialize();
  bool lisAvailable();
  float getAccelerationX();
  float getAccelerationY();
  float getAccelerationZ();
}
```

In this code, we include `Arduino.h`, and then we declare `namespace`. By declaring a namespace, we can work with functions, variables, and classes that have the same name as other functions, variables, and classes in another namespace with a different name. For example, we could have the `initialize()` function in multiple namespaces within our code base. We then proceed to declare five function headers within the namespace:

- `initialize()`: This will let us initialize the accelerometer

- `lisAvailable()`: This will let us check whether the accelerometer was initialized

- `getAccelerationX()`: This will let us get the acceleration along the *x-axis*

- `getAccelerationY()`: This will let us get the acceleration along the *y-axis*

- `getAccelerationZ()`: This will let us get the acceleration along the *z-axis*

9. Create a new file and name it `Accel.cpp`. Copy the following code into it. This code declares a namespace and implements functions for initializing the accelerometer, as well as returning the accelerometer values for the *x*, *y*, and *z* axes:

```
#include "Accel.hpp"
#include "LIS3DHTR.h"
#include <Wire.h>

namespace Accel {
  LIS3DHTR<TwoWire> LIS;
  #define WIRE Wire

  void initialize() {
    LIS.begin(WIRE, LIS3DHTR_ADDRESS_UPDATED);
```

```
    delay(100);
    LIS.setOutputDataRate(LIS3DHTR_DATARATE_50HZ);
}

bool lisAvailable() {
    if (!LIS) {
        return false;
    }
    return true;
}

float getAccelerationX() {
    return LIS.getAccelerationX();
}

float getAccelerationY() {
    return LIS.getAccelerationY();
}

float getAccelerationZ() {
    return LIS.getAccelerationZ();
}
}
```

Let's review the code:

- You begin by including the necessary libraries. The second library lets you interact with the accelerometer by reading its registers. The third library, `Wire.h`, lets you work with I2C devices.

- Next, you declare the namespace.

- Within the namespace, you declare an instance of the accelerometer class, called `LIS`, as well as a constant called `Wire`, which lets you interact over I2C.

- Next, you implement the `initialize()` function. This does two things – it starts up the accelerometer by calling `LIS.begin()`, passing in the `Wire` instance, and also specifies the I2C address of the accelerometer. Then, you introduce a 100 millisecond `delay()` so that the accelerometer has time to start up properly. After the delay, you proceed to set the output data rate of the accelerometer to 50 Hz.

- The `lisAvailable()` function lets you know whether or not the accelerometer was initialized successfully.

- The next three functions return the acceleration on the respective axes.

10. Update the `.ino` file so that it looks as follows. This code is responsible for importing the LCD and `Accel` namespaces, reading values from the accelerometer, and controlling the LCD:

```
#include "Display.hpp"
#include "Accel.hpp"

void setup() {
  Serial.begin(115200);
  Accel::initialize();
  Display::initialize();
  if (Accel::lisAvailable()) {
    Display::print_lcd("Accel Demo", "Open serial mon");
    Serial.println("LIS3DHTR connected.");
  } else {
    Display::print_lcd("Accel Demo", "Couldn't Start");
    Serial.println("LIS3DHTR didn't connect.");
    while (1)
      ;
    return;
  }

}

void loop() {
  Serial.print(Accel::getAccelerationX());
  Serial.print("\t");
  Serial.print(Accel::getAccelerationY());
  Serial.print("\t");
  Serial.println(Accel::getAccelerationZ());
  delay(1000);
}
```

Let's review the code:

- You begin by including `Display` and `Accel`.

- In the `setup()` function, you start the `Serial` interface by specifying the baud rate. Don't forget, Serial is the same as UART. Here, you will be communicating with the computer, not another microcontroller. Afterward, you initialize the accelerometer and the display. Then, you check whether the accelerometer was successfully initialized and output the result to both the display and the `Serial` terminal. You output to the terminal by using the `Serial.println()` function.

- In the `loop()` function, you collect the acceleration along all three axes and output them to the `Serial` terminal. You wait 1,000 milliseconds, or 1 second, so that you can read the output on the terminal comfortably.

11. Deploy the firmware to the MKR board.

After a few minutes, the board will reboot. You can open **Serial Monitor** to see the accelerometer values scrolling by. You will need to set the **baud rate** to **115200**. The display will look similar to the following:

Figure 2.6 – Serial Monitor output showing accelerometer data

This isn't a lot of fun though, so open **Serial Plotter** to see the three values plotted on a chart. The output will look similar to the following:

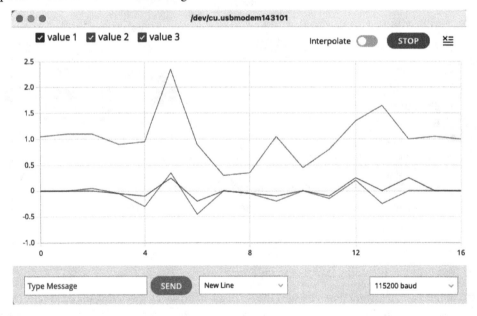

Figure 2.7 – Serial Plotter showing the output of the accelerometer readings

If you haven't tried to already, begin shaking the accelerometer and the values will change!

Congratulations – you have successfully read data from an IMU! You can watch a video recording of the Code in Action at `https://packt.link/chG0p`.

Now, let's discuss more sensors.

Acoustic sensors

Acoustic sensors measure things based on sound. A microphone is probably the most popular type of acoustic sensor, which you could use to capture speech. Another popular sensor in this category is an ultrasonic sensor, which you can use to measure the distance of one object to another. This is the sensor used in vehicles for parking distance control.

Environmental sensors

These sensors measure the environment. Some of the things you can measure with this class of sensors include the following:

- **Temperature**: How hot or cold the environment is.
- **Humidity**: Relative humidity is a measure of how much moisture is in the air.
- **Air pressure**: This is a measure of the amount of force that the air is exerting.
- **Gases**: These are either toxic gases or particulate matter such as smoke.
- **Liquid level**: This is a measure of the height of liquid in a container. With a knowledge of the diameter of the container, it's easy to calculate the total volume of liquid within the container.
- **Moisture**: This is a measure of how much moisture there is in a soil sample. This is useful for precision agriculture.
- **Hall effect**: This is useful for detecting electrical energy based on magnetic force fields.
- **Flame**: This is useful for detecting fire outbreaks.
- **Color**: This is useful for detecting the presence of certain colors.

Let's move on to vision sensors.

Vision sensors

These sensors deal with light. Here are some examples:

- **Camera**: These imaging sensors let you take photographs and are useful in settings where you need to either monitor activity without putting a sensor on the subject or would like to take photographs when an event is detected.
- **Thermal**: These detect variations in heat within an environment
- **Light**: These detect light intensity and are useful for controlling other devices based on the output
- **Laser sensors**: These are useful for measuring distance by emitting light and measuring how long it takes to travel back
- **PIR sensors**: Passive infrared sensors measure movement within the field of view

Biometric sensors

You can utilize biometric sensors to take measurements of the human body. Here are some examples of these:

- **Pulse sensor**: This uses a **Photoelectric Pulse Wave Method (PPWM)** to measure the change in the volume of a blood vessel as the heart pumps blood

- **Heart rate sensor**: This measures the heart rate using either the electrical pulses generated during each cardiac cycle or by measuring changes in vascular pressure during heart contractions

- **Temperature sensor**: This measures the temperature of the wearer

- **Fingerprint sensor**: This takes a photo of a finger and extracts a template that can be stored, retrieved, and used for comparison

- **Muscle sensor**: This measures muscle activity by measuring electrical signals

- **EMG/ECG/EKG sensor**: This measures muscle activity with an **electromyography (EMG)** or heart rhythm with an **electrocardiogram (ECG or EKG)**

Force

These sensors measure the amount of force being applied on a surface. Examples of these sensors are as follows:

- **Pressure sensor**: This measures the amount of force required to prevent a liquid or gas from expanding. They can also be used to measure the level of fluid in a container.

- **Strain sensor**: This measures the external force that is being applied to a stationary object.

- **Flow sensor**: This measures the rate at which liquids and gasses move through a pipe.

Rotation

This class of sensors is also called encoders, or rotary encoders. One common example of this is a knob. You can utilize them to take a reading based on how far the knob has been rotated.

Summary

In this chapter, you learned some more about the capabilities of the I/O pins on the MKR board and wrote code to interact using Serial and I2C. You also interacted with an IMU sensor and observed the output using both the Serial terminal and the plotter.

In *Chapter 3*, you will learn about shields, which let you create prototypes without having to use a breadboard and wires while still giving you access to some common sensors.

Further reading

To learn more about the topics that were covered in this chapter, take a look at the following resources:

- *Serial communications from SparkFun Electronics*: `https://learn.sparkfun.com/tutorials/serial-communication/all`

- *SPI*: `https://learn.sparkfun.com/tutorials/serial-peripheral-interface-spi/all`

- *Inter-integrated circuits*: `https://learn.sparkfun.com/tutorials/i2c`

- *C++ namespaces*: `https://learn.microsoft.com/en-us/cpp/cpp/namespaces-cpp?view=msvc-170`

3

Prototyping with Shields

In this chapter, you will learn about the sensors that you can work with without having to use a solderless breadboard and cables. When working with breadboards and cables, you might find that something has stopped working because of a loose cable connection. You might also find that you have run out of space on a breadboard. This is where shields come in handy. You will create a project that works with one of these shields: the environment shield. You will also get an introduction to carrier boards and will build a project that makes use of the MKR IoT Carrier. The projects will help build your confidence in collecting data without using breadboards and give you a strong foundation for adding complexity to your setups without worrying about debugging faulty cable connections. By the end of this chapter, you will have written different projects that collect environment data for later use.

In this chapter, we are going to cover the following main topics:

- What is a shield?
- Working with sensor shields
- Discovering other types of shields
- Working with the MKR IoT Carrier

Technical requirements

The code examples used in this chapter can be found at `https://github.com/PacktPublishing/Arduino-Data-Communications/tree/main/chapter-3`.

You will also require the following:

- Arduino MKR WiFi 1010
- Arduino MKR ENV Shield (`https://docs.arduino.cc/hardware/mkr-env-shield`)
- Arduino MKR IoT Carrier (`https://docs.arduino.cc/hardware/mkr-iot-carrier`)

- Micro-USB cable
- Arduino IDE

What is a shield?

A **shield** is a **printed circuit board** (**PCB**) that attaches to a microcontroller and gives it additional capabilities that it doesn't natively ship with. Most shields are the same size as the microcontroller they are meant to work with. An example shield for the Arduino Portenta H7 microcontroller is shown in the following figure:

Figure 3.1 – Arduino Portenta Vision Shield – Ethernet

Shields are meant to be mounted on top of the microcontroller. They receive power from the microcontroller, so they don't have a power connector. Most shields have stacking headers, so you can mount other shields on top of them.

There is another group of PCBs called carriers.

What are carriers?

Carriers are boards, but they do not mount onto a microcontroller. Instead, the microcontroller mounts onto the carrier. Carriers provide connectors for plugging other devices into the microcontroller. Arduino currently provides the following carriers for working with the MKR:

- **MKR Motor Carrier**: You can connect up to four servo motors and four DC motors to this carrier using screw terminals that hold your cables firmly in place. This carrier also comes with an onboard microcontroller so you can offload some processing from the MKR board.

- **MKR Connector Carrier**: You can connect up to six analog and six digital peripherals to this carrier using Grove connectors. The Grove system was pioneered by Seeed Studio.

- **MKR IoT Carrier**: You can make use of this carrier to rapidly prototype using a number of onboard sensors. We will make use of this carrier in a project.

Let's proceed to work with some shields.

Working with sensor shields

We will work on two projects that measure environmental data and motion data. We will do two new things in these projects:

- Get time from an NTP server so that we have a sense of when exactly we are taking sensor readings. This is useful because it's important to assign a date and time to any reading that we will be storing.

- Learn to put readings into a format called JSON. **JSON** is short for **JavaScript Object Notation** and is a useful format for sending data over the internet.

Project 1 – Working with the MKR ENV Shield R2

In this project, you will learn to take sensor readings from the Arduino MKR ENV Shield R2. This shield has the following onboard sensors:

- **LPS22HP**: Atmospheric pressure sensor from ST Microelectronics

- **HTS221**: Temperature and humidity sensor from ST Microelectronics

- **TEMT6000**: Light intensity sensor from Vishay

The code for this project is available in the following GitHub repository: `https://github.com/PacktPublishing/Arduino-Data-Communications/tree/main/chapter-3/Arduino%20MKR%20WiFi%201010%20ENV%20Shield`.

Follow the next steps to attach the shield to the MKR board and read the various sensors:

1. Attach the shield on top of the MKR board while taking care to align the pins.
2. Launch the Arduino IDE.
3. Open the library manager.
4. Search for `MKR ENV`.
5. Install `Arduino_MKRENV by Arduino`.
6. Search for and install the `UnixTime` library.
7. Search for and install the `Arduino_JSON` library.
8. Search for and install the `RTCZero` library.
9. Clone the GitHub repository for this project.
10. Open the `arduino_secrets.h` file. This file contains the credentials for connecting to a wireless network and looks like the following:

```
#define SECRET_SSID ""
#define SECRET_PASS ""
```

The first line is the name of the network that you would like to connect to. Put the name between the quote marks.

The second line is the password of the network that you would like to connect to. Put that in between the quote marks.

11. You are ready to verify the code and upload it to the board. Upload the code to the board.

12. Open the Serial terminal and set the baud rate to 115200. You will see output similar to the following after a few seconds:

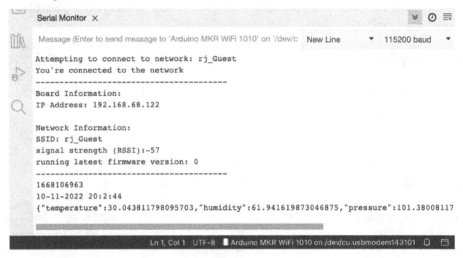

Figure 3.2 – The output of the firmware

The video showing the code in action is available at https://packt.link/sfncm.

Let's dissect the output:

- The first line informs you that the MKR board is trying to connect to a Wi-Fi network, and also tells you the name of the network.

- The second line notifies you when the connection is successful.

- The lines between the two dashed lines give you some information about the wireless network that the board is connected to.

- The line showing **1668106963** displays the Unix time or epoch. This is the number of seconds since 1970.

- The next line shows the date and time obtained by converting the Unix time from the previous line.

- The last line shows you all of the environmental readings from the ENV shield. These readings have been put into a JSON object and are subsequently displayed in String format.

Let's discuss the code in some of these files.

Understanding Arduino MKR WiFi 1010 ENV Shield.ino

Let's look at the first 40 lines in this file. As you would expect, this file imports the necessary libraries that will let the microcontroller connect to the Wi-Fi network to read the current time from a server and also take various readings from the ENV shield. The microcontroller outputs all of this information via `Serial`, and that is what you see in the Serial terminal. Let's review the code:

1. You will start by importing four header files. All four files are locally defined, and you can inspect their source codes. The code for this is shown here:

    ```
    #include "MyWireless.hpp"
    #include "MyNTPClient.hpp"
    #include "MyEnv.hpp"
    #include "MyClock.hpp"
    ```

    *   `MyWireless.hpp` gives you the functions required to initialize the Wi-Fi radio and to connect to a wireless radio.

    *   `MyNTPClient.hpp` gives you the functions required to read time from an NTP server.

    *   `MyEnv.hpp` gives you the functions required to read the sensor values from the ENV shield.

    *   `MyClock.hpp` gives you a real-time clock. This will let you set and keep the time and is useful for knowing when exactly you are taking a reading.

2. In the next line, we define a variable, `status`, which keeps track of the connection status of the Wi-Fi module. This is shown in the code section here:

    ```
    int status = MyWireless::getIdleStatus();
    ```

3. Next, we define `lastMillis` with a type of `auto`. The type will be inferred from the return type of `millis()`, which tells us how many milliseconds the microcontroller has been running for and is useful for measuring intervals. We also define a constant, `myDelay`, which determines how many seconds our interval will last. These two lines are shown here:

    ```
    auto lastMillis = millis();
    const int myDelay = 5000;
    ```

4. Next, we define an instance of `MyClock`, which we call `rtc`. This instance, or object, will let us set the current time and then get the time whenever we need it. This line of code is shown here:

    ```
    MyClock::MyClock rtc = MyClock::MyClock();
    ```

5. Within the `setup()` function, we connect to the `Serial` terminal and specify a baud rate of `115200`. The function will pause until the terminal is opened from the Arduino IDE. This code snippet is shown here:

    ```
    Serial.begin(115200);
      while (!Serial);
    ```

6. Still within the `setup()` function, after the `Serial` terminal has been opened, the function proceeds to attempt a connection to the wireless network. It tries this every 10 seconds until the connection succeeds. This code snippet is shown here:

```
while (status != MyWireless::getConnectedStatus()) {
    Serial.print("Attempting to connect to network: ");
    Serial.println(MyWireless::get_ssid());
    status = MyWireless::initialize();
    delay(10000);
}
```

7. After establishing a connection, the microcontroller will attempt to initialize the NTP client and get the current time from an NTP server. This is shown in the following lines of code:

```
MyNTPClient::initialize();
    unsigned long currentTime = MyNTPClient::getUnixTime();
    if(!rtc.initialize(currentTime)) {
        Serial.println("Unable to initialize the Realtime Clock,
aborting ...");
        while(1);
    }
```

8. After getting the current time, the microcontroller will attempt to initialize the ENV shield:

```
if(!MyEnv::initialize()) {
    Serial.println("Couldn't initialize the ENV Shield,
halting");
    while(1);
}
```

9. If the microcontroller succeeds in all of the preceding steps, it will proceed to print out information to the `Serial` terminal. This code snippet is shown here:

```
Serial.println("You're connected to the network");
    Serial.println("------------------------------------------");
    printData();
    Serial.println("------------------------------------------");
    Serial.print("NTP Unix Time: ");
    Serial.println(currentTime);
  Serial.println(MyNTPClient::getTimeFromUnix(currentTime));
    Serial.print("RTC Unix Time: ");
    Serial.println(rtc.getEpochs());
    Serial.println(rtc.getWATDateTime());
    lastMillis = millis();
    Serial.println(MyEnv::getReadings(currentTime));
```

Understanding MyWireless.hpp

This header file defines functions that make it possible to control the Wi-Fi module on the microcontroller. Here is a quick look at the code:

```cpp
#pragma once

#include <Arduino.h>

namespace MyWireless {
  int initialize();
  int getStatus();
  int getIdleStatus();
  int getConnectedStatus();
  IPAddress getLocalIp();
  String getSSID();
  String get_ssid();
  long getRSSI();
  bool isOnLatestFirmware();
}
```

Here is a brief explanation of the functions:

- `initialize()`: Use this function to initiate a connection to the wireless network.
- `getStatus()`: This returns the status of the Wi-Fi module, whether it is connected or not.
- `getIdleStatus()`: This returns the value of an IDLE status, so we can check whether the Wi-Fi module is not connected.
- `getConnectedStatus()`: This returns the value of a CONNECTED status, so we can check whether the Wi-Fi module is connected to a wireless network.
- `getLocalIp()`, `getSSID()`, and `getRSSI()`: These return details from the Wi-Fi module such as the IP address that was assigned to the microcontroller and the signal strength.
- `isOnLatestFirmware()`: This informs the user whether the MKR board is running the latest Wi-Fi firmware. This is useful for knowing when to update the firmware.

The Wi-Fi module has many capabilities, but we will not be exploring them for now.

Understanding MyNTPClient.hpp

This header file defines functions that are useful for getting the time from a **Network Time Protocol (NTP)** server. The time is sent back as the number of seconds since 1900. We then subtract 70 years in seconds from this value to get Unix time, also known as epochs. This operation is handled by the getUnixTime() function. Unix time is a popular format and there are websites that you can use to convert Unix time to date and time. In our code, the getTimeFromUnix() function gives us this information. The Unix time, or date and time, is useful for knowing when you collected sensor data. The code in the header file is shown here:

```
#pragma once

#include <Arduino.h>

namespace MyNTPClient {
  void initialize();
  unsigned long getUnixTime();
  unsigned long sendNTPpacket(IPAddress& address);
  String getTimeFromUnix(unsigned long unixTime);
}
```

Understanding MyEnv.hpp

This header file provides functions for reading sensor data. The initialize() function starts the sensors, while getTemp(), getHumid(), getPressure(), and getLux() return the temperature, humidity, pressure, and illuminance, respectively. The getJSONReadings() function returns all of the readings for temperature, humidity, pressure, and illuminance as a JSON object. The JSON object that is returned looks like the following:

```
{
    "unixTime": 1668205306,
    "temperature": 27.833511352539062,
    "humidity": 53.654937744140625,
    "pressure": 101.5428237915039,
    "illuminance": 12.903225898742676
}
```

The final function, getReadings(), returns the result in the String format. This time, the result is returned on one line, as you would have seen in *Figure 3.2*.

Discovering other types of shields

Arduino provides various shields. Let's place some of these in categories.

Providing additional connectivity

MKR boards come in different variants, providing different connectivity options. One popular connectivity option is Wi-Fi. There are other connectivity options that you will not find as MKR boards, but you can get a shield for some of these:

- The **MKR ETH Shield** will let you plug an Ethernet cable into your MKR board. This is useful for environments where wireless signals would interfere with the operation of other machinery, such as in a medical setting. This shield also provides an SD card slot for data logging purposes.

- The **MKR 485 Shield** will let you connect to a legacy industrial system and communicate with it. This shield lets you implement communications using the serial protocol.

Communicating with automobiles

The **MKR CAN Shield** will let you connect to the brains of an automobile using something called a **Controller Area Network**. You can make use of this connection to control sensors and displays, or to read data from sensors within the automotive space.

Outputting information

The **MKR RGB Shield** provides a dense way of outputting information in the absence of an actual screen. It comes with an array of RGB LEDs arranged in 7 rows and 12 columns.

Providing expansion

A number of shields will let you expand the storage on the MKR board or solder additional components. These include the following:

- The **MKR MEM Shield** provides an additional 2 MB flash memory as well as SD card storage for any MKR board. It also provides a prototyping area, so you can solder on sensors, actuators, or motors.

- The **MKR SD Proto Shield** provides an SD card slot as well as the prototyping area, without the flash storage.

- The **MKR Proto Shield** provides a prototyping area, so you can solder on any sensors, actuators, or screens.

Motion sensing

The **MKR IMU Shield** provides a nine-axis inertial measurement unit for measuring accelerometer, gyroscope, and magnetometer information. This is useful for measuring different things from activity on a shipping crate to earth tremors at a location of interest. You can also use this to build a motion controller.

Geolocation

The **MKR GPS Shield** utilizes various satellites to provide location information. This shield is useful in applications where you need to track the location of items such as vehicles and shipping containers.

We have had a brief discussion of shields, so let's proceed to discuss the MKR IoT Carrier, which provides additional capabilities.

Working with the MKR IoT Carrier

The **MKR IoT Carrier** is designed for the MKR board to be attached on top of it. It comes with the following sensors:

- Five capacitive touch sensors
- A temperature, humidity, and barometric pressure sensor
- A six-axis inertial measurement unit
- A color detection sensor
- A gesture sensor

It also has an OLED display, two onboard relays, two analog Grove connectors, and one I2C Grove connector. You can see the MKR IoT Carrier in this video: `https://packt.link/sfncm`.

Let's work with the MKR IoT Carrier to collect sensor data.

Project 2 – Collecting sensor data with the Arduino MKR IoT Carrier

In this project, we will use the **MKR WiFi 1010** to connect to a wireless network and then fetch the time from an NTP server when the microcontroller starts up. Afterward, every minute, we will read the temperature, humidity, and pressure and display those on the OLED display. The code for this project is available on GitHub at the following URL: `https://github.com/PacktPublishing/Arduino-Data-Communications/tree/main/chapter-3/Arduino-MKR-WiFi-1010-Carrier`.

Please follow these steps to complete this project:

1. Attach the MKR WiFi 1010 board to the MKR IoT Carrier, making sure the pins are aligned according to the labels.
2. Launch the Android IDE.
3. Open the Library Manager.

4. Search for and install the following libraries: MKRIoTCarrier, RTCZero, UnixTime, and Arduino_JSON.

5. Clone the project from the GitHub repository and open it in the Arduino IDE.

6. Open arduino_secrets.h and fill in your Wi-Fi credentials.

7. Upload the sketch onto the MKR board.

A video showing the code in action is available at https://packt.link/sfncm. Let's discuss some of the code.

Understanding the .ino file

This file controls the entire operation of the microcontroller and the carrier. We begin by importing all of the libraries that we need. Four of these are defined in the project, while the last one is required for starting the MKR carrier. The code follows next:

```
#include "MyWireless.hpp"
#include "MyNTPClient.hpp"
#include "MyClock.hpp"
#include "MyCarrier.hpp"

#include <Arduino_MKRIoTCarrier.h>
```

Next, we create some variables and a constant. We set the status variable to IDLE because that is the initial state of the Wi-Fi radio until it has connected to a network. We use the lastMillis variable to track the last time that we did something, and we use it in the loop() function in place of the delay() function. We use the myDelay constant to only do something after a set interval in conjunction with the lastMillis variable. We also define an instance of the clock, called rtc here, so that it can keep track of time once we set it. We define two instances of Carrier: one in a custom class so we can encapsulate a lot of the display logic away from our .ino file, and a second one that we need to initialize the carrier within the .ino file. The code is shown here:

```
int status = MyWireless::getIdleStatus();
auto lastMillis = millis();
const int myDelay = 60000;
MyClock::MyClock rtc = MyClock::MyClock();
MyCarrier::MyCarrier myCarrier = MyCarrier::MyCarrier();
MKRIoTCarrier carrier;
```

We do a few things within the setup() function:

1. We wait a second and a half, then we set a CARRIER_CASE variable to false. This adjusts the sensitivity of the capacitive touch buttons when we aren't using the outer case. Then, we start the carrier by calling carrier.begin(). We need to do this within our setup() function. Finally, we pass the address of the carrier object to our custom class instance when we call myCarrier.initialize(&carrier). This lets us reuse the same carrier instance without creating a second from inside our custom object. We do all this with the following lines of code:

    ```
    delay(1500);
    CARRIER_CASE = false;
    carrier.begin();
    myCarrier.initialize(&carrier);
    ```

2. Once our carrier has been initialized, we display some information on the screen to show that it's starting. We also start Serial and set the baud rate. This happens in the following lines of code:

    ```
    display("Starting ..");
    Serial.begin(115200);
    ```

3. Next, we display information on the screen showing that we are trying to connect to the network. The microcontroller will loop until the connection is successful because we can't get time from the internet if the connection does not succeed. We proceed to do that with the following lines of code:

    ```
    while (status != MyWireless::getConnectedStatus()) {
        display("Network ..");
        status = MyWireless::initialize();
        delay(10000);
    }
    ```

4. Next, we initialize the NTP client, fetch the current time from a server, and then instantiate an RTP clock that will keep time as long as the microcontroller is powered. This happens with the following code:

    ```
    MyNTPClient::initialize();
    unsigned long currentTime = MyNTPClient::getUnixTime();
    if(!rtc.initialize(currentTime)) {
        display("RTC Fail!");
        while(1);
    }
    ```

5. The last thing that we do within our `setup()` function is display the current time and sensor readings on the OLED display, and then take note of when we called this function. The code for this is shown here:

```
myCarrier.displaySensors(rtc.getWATTime());
lastMillis = millis();
```

6. The entirety of our `loop()` function is concerned with whether 60 seconds have elapsed since we last displayed the time and sensor readings. If so, the screen is refreshed with new information. Note that we avoid using the `delay()` function because we don't want the microcontroller to go to sleep. This way, it can respond to any interrupts that might arise. That section of code is shown here:

```
void loop() {
  if( (millis() - lastMillis >= myDelay)) {
    myCarrier.displaySensors(rtc.getWATTime());
    lastMillis = millis();
  }
}
```

7. We defined a helper function to render text on the screen during the setup sequence. The code for that is shown here:

```
void display(String text) {
  carrier.display.fillScreen(0x0000);
  carrier.display.setCursor(25, 100);
  carrier.display.setTextSize(3);
  carrier.display.print(text);
}
```

8. The other new code that you might find interesting is in `MyCarrier.hpp` and `MyCarrier.cpp`.

Understanding MyCarrier.hpp

This header file contains the custom class definition that we will use to manage the carrier. The one thing you might find to be new is the class definition within the namespace. This will let us create an instance that will remain in memory as long as the microcontroller is powered. The `initialize()` function takes a **pointer** to the carrier that we instantiated in `setup()`. This pointer lets us work with the same instance of the carrier. The code is shown here:

```
#pragma once

#include <Arduino.h>
#include <Arduino_MKRIoTCarrier.h>
```

```
namespace MyCarrier {
  class MyCarrier {
    public:
      void initialize(MKRIoTCarrier* carrier);
      float getTemperature();
      float getPressure();
      float getHumidity();
      void displaySensors(String time);
  };
}
```

Understanding MyCarrier.cpp

This file implements the code for `MyCarrier`. It includes a file, `logos.h`, that contains character arrays that represent the bitmap images for the icons we use for temperature, humidity, and pressure. We are making use of Google's Material Design icons, which you can find at the following URL: `https://fonts.google.com/icons`. You can convert any icon of your choice into an array at this URL: `https://javl.github.io/image2cpp/`.

Within `MyCarrier.cpp`, we implement a namespace. We then create a pointer to the carrier from our `setup()` function and then implement the `initialize()` function of the `MyCarrier` class. Don't confuse the class with the namespace; it's contained within the namespace. The implementation looks like the following code:

```
MKRIoTCarrier* myCarrier;

void MyCarrier::initialize(MKRIoTCarrier* carrier) {
  myCarrier = carrier;
}
```

In the preceding code, `myCarrier` is a pointer. `MyCarrier` refers to the class. This is how you implement the code for a class in C++. The `initialize()` function takes a pointer as an argument and stores it in `myCarrier`, our local instance. The pointer is created by adding `*` to any type.

Let's consider the implementation of `getTemperature()`. Here, we use an arrow function. The arrow, `->`, lets us access the element of a pointer. You will see that this is different from how we have done in the past where we used a dot operator. In the code, we use the arrow on the first part to access an element, then we use the dot to access the element of that element. The code for this appears here:

```
float MyCarrier::getTemperature() {
  return myCarrier->Env.readTemperature();
}
```

The rest of the implementation code is similar to what we have just seen.

Summary

In this chapter, you learned about shields and carriers, and then worked on some projects using both a shield and a carrier. This was important because you got to focus on the code that you needed to write to collect data without having to fiddle with breakout boards, breadboards, and wires that could come loose and lead to a lot of time spent debugging your code. With the MKR IoT Carrier, you were also able to display the readings on the OLED screen. This is useful for communicating information to users without asking them to connect the device to a computer for serial output. We are collecting data but not storing it.

In the next chapter, we will discuss various strategies for storing this data locally, especially given that the MKR IoT Carrier and the MKR ENV Shield both come with SD card slots.

Further reading

To learn more about the topics covered in this chapter, you can visit the following links:

- *MKR Motor Carrier*: https://docs.arduino.cc/hardware/mkr-motor-carrier
- *Arduino MKR Shields*: https://www.arduino.cc/en/hardware#shields
- *How to clone a GitHub repo*: https://github.com/git-guides/git-clone

4

Storing Data Collected from Sensors

In the previous two chapters, we learned how to collect data from various sensors. However, the best we have done is display the information on a screen. It's a waste to collect all of that data and not store it. Let's look at how we can store the data that we are collecting. By the end of this chapter, you will know how to store data in files and various file formats that are in common use, set up a database, and write queries to read data out of a database. The data that you store will be useful for analysis in the future, usually by data analysts. For example, if you collect and store temperature and humidity data from different weather stations over a certain period, then that data can be used to analyze weather patterns.

In this chapter, we are going to cover the following main topics:

- Storing data
- Working with flat files
- Working with databases

We'll start by listing what you will need to complete this chapter.

Technical requirements

You will require the following to complete this chapter:

- The Arduino IDE
- Arduino MKR WiFi 1010
- A micro-USB cable
- Arduino MKR ENV Shield or MKR IoT Carrier
- A micro-SD card

- An SD card reader

- A Raspberry Pi 3 or 4, or a virtual machine

If you have got everything you need, then let's proceed to collect and store some data.

The source code for this chapter can be found in this book's GitHub repository: `https://github.com/securetorobert/Arduino-Data-Communications/tree/main/chapter-4/`.

Storing data

The easiest way to store data is offline, where a connection to the internet or a local network is not required. Where a small amount of data is concerned, this might be done on the memory of the device, the **Electronic Erasable Programmable Read-Only Memory (EEPROM)**. However, we will be dealing with a lot of data, so we need to store it somewhere with a reasonable amount of space. Also, while some microcontrollers have an EEPROM, the MKR board doesn't.

MKR boards do not have expandable storage but some shields do. The MKR ENV Shield is one of them. We will attach a micro-SD card to the MKR ENV shield and store data on it.

We store data in files. Each file has a format. One quick way of knowing what format a file is stored in is by looking at the name of the file and the extension.

In the following project, we will create a sketch that will write temperature and humidity readings to a file. To make it fun and easy to read the file, we will use the TSV format.

> **Note**
> The TSV file format will be covered in depth in the upcoming section.

We want the information to be useful, so we will output the Unix time along with each of the readings. Unix time is the number of seconds that have elapsed since January 1, 1970. The time is recorded relative to **Coordinated Universal Time (UTC)**. The final output will be a file where each line has three values: the Unix time, the temperature, and the humidity. We will take readings once each minute and update the file. This approach is called **appending the file**.

There are 60 minutes in each hour and 24 hours in a day. If we decide to store all of the readings for 1 year in a file, we will end up with 525,600 lines in that file. We could store the readings for an entire year in one file, or we could choose to store the readings for only a month in a file, which would range between 40,320 and 44,640 lines in the file, depending on the month. We could also choose to store one file per day, which would have 1,440 lines in it. The approach that we choose will depend on how we intend to process those files further down the road.

For this project, we'll store 1 day's worth of data per file. To do this, we will create a folder for each year, and a folder for each month, and then name the file according to the day.

We have everything that we need to get the current time and date from previous examples, and we already know how to read the temperature and humidity. So, let's proceed with the project.

Project 1 – Storing temperature and humidity in a file

The source code for this project is available at `https://github.com/securetorobert/Arduino-Data-Communications/tree/main/chapter-4/Arduino-MKR-WiFi-1010-ENV-Shield-SD-Card`.

Follow these steps to get the code that will write the temperature and humidity to a file:

1. Clone the source code from this book's GitHub repository.
2. Launch the Arduino IDE.
3. Open the files in the downloaded repository.
4. Edit the `arduino_secrets.h` file and fill in your network credentials.
5. Place the micro-SD card into the appropriate slot on the MKR ENV Shield.
6. Attach the MKR ENV Shield to the MKR WiFi 1010.
7. Connect the MKR board to your computer.
8. Upload the sketch to the MKR board.
9. Open **Serial Monitor**.
10. Observe the output and ensure there are no errors.
11. Wait a few minutes and turn off the power to the MKR board.
12. Remove the SD card and plug it into your computer. You might need an adapter.
13. Browse to the SD card from your file manager.
14. You should see a folder named after the current year. Open this.
15. You should see a folder named after the current month. Open this.
16. You should see a file named after the current day. Open this with a text editor of your choice. It should look similar to the following screenshot:

Figure 4.1 – Logging temperature and humidity to a file

Let's go back and look at some of the code.

Analyzing the .ino file

The `Arduino-MKR-WiFi-1010-ENV-Shield-SD-Card.ino` file begins with several includes and only two of them are new to you:

- `SPI.h` makes it possible to communicate using the SPI protocol. This is the SD card interface that the MKR ENV board uses.

- `SD.h` provides functions for reading from SD cards and writing to them.

We also declare a constant, `chipSelect`, that sets the PIN that the card reader will use. The code for all of these is shown here:

```
#include "MyWireless.hpp"
#include "MyNTPClient.hpp"
#include "MyClock.hpp"
#include "MyEnv.hpp"

#include <Arduino_MKRENV.h>
#include <SPI.h>
#include <SD.h>

float temp, humid;
const int chipSelect = 4;
unsigned long lastRead = millis();
const int myDelay = 60000;
int status = MyWireless::getIdleStatus();
MyClock::MyClock rtc = MyClock::MyClock();
```

We do a bunch of things within the setup() function:

1. We begin by opening a serial port so that we can log information. This is useful since we don't have a screen attached to this MKR board. This is shown in the following snippet:

    ```
    Serial.begin(115200);
    ```

2. Next, we check that the MKR ENV board is attached and working properly. If it isn't, we pause the execution:

    ```
    if (!ENV.begin()) {
        Serial.println("Failed to initialize MKR ENV shield!");
        while (1);
    }
    ```

3. Next, we check that an SD card is attached and that we can read it:

    ```
    Serial.print("\nInitializing SD card...");
      if (!SD.begin(chipSelect)) {
        Serial.println("initialization failed. Things to check:");
        Serial.println("* is a card inserted?");
        Serial.println("* is your wiring correct?");
        Serial.println("* did you change the chipSelect pin to match
    your shield or module?");
        while (1);
      }
      Serial.println("Card detected.");
    ```

4. Next, we connect to the wireless network:

    ```
    while (status != MyWireless::getConnectedStatus()) {
        Serial.print("Attempting to connect to network: ");
        Serial.println(MyWireless::get_ssid());
        status = MyWireless::initialize();
        delay(10000);
    }
    ```

5. Next, we initialize the NTP client and get the time from a server:

    ```
    MyNTPClient::initialize();
      unsigned long currentTime = MyNTPClient::getUnixTime();
      if(!rtc.initialize(currentTime)) {
        Serial.println("Unable to initialize the Realtime Clock,
    aborting ...");
        while(1);
      }
    ```

6. Within the `loop()` function, we wait every 60 seconds to update the temperature and humidity, log this over serial, and write this out to file. The function for writing to file is in the `MyEnv` namespace. The code within the `loop()` function is listed here:

```
void loop() {
  if (millis() - lastRead > myDelay) {
    lastRead = millis();
    readEnv();
    Serial.print("T: ");
    Serial.println(temp);
    Serial.print("H: ");
    Serial.println(humid);
    String y = rtc.getYear();
    String m = rtc.getMonth();
    String d = rtc.getDay();
    unsigned long epochs = rtc.getEpochs();
    MyEnv::writeTSVToFile(y, m, d, epochs);
  }
}
```

7. The `readEnv()` function updates the temperature and humidity reading and is simple:

```
void readEnv() {
  temp = MyEnv::getTemp();
  humid = MyEnv::getHumid();
}
```

Here, we made use of several functions from the `MyEnv` namespace. Now, let's take a look at the header file.

Analyzing the MyEnv.hpp file

This header file defines a namespace and some functions inside it. We worked with this file in a previous project, but this version of the file has some different functions.

We are only working with the temperature and humidity sensors, so we have removed the capability to read the pressure and luminance.

We have added two new functions that will return a string in both CSV and TSV format. We have also added a function that will write the TSV string to a file. This header file definition is shown here:

```
#pragma once

#include <Arduino.h>
#include <Arduino_JSON.h>
```

```
namespace MyEnv {
  bool initialize();
  float getTemp();
  float getHumid();
  JSONVar getJSONReadings(unsigned long unixTime);
  String getCSVReadings(unsigned long unixTime);
  String getTSVReadings(unsigned long unixTime);
  void writeTSVToFile(String y, String m, String d, unsigned long
unixtime);
}
```

The functions defined in the header file are implemented in the MyEnv.cpp file. Let's take a look at that.

Analyzing MyEnv.cpp

We have two new header files in the #include section. You have seen these previously: SPI and SD. The code for this is as follows:

```
#include "MyEnv.hpp"

#include "MyNTPClient.hpp"
#include <Arduino_MKRENV.h>
#include <SPI.h>
#include <SD.h>
```

Within the namespace, we implement the new functions. Let's take a look at the function that returns String in tab-delimited format. It's simply a concatenated string with tabs (\t) between every value. Here is the code:

```
String getTSVReadings(unsigned long unixTime) {
    String readings = String(unixTime);
    readings.concat("\t");
    readings.concat(getTemp());
    readings.concat("\t");
    readings.concat(getHumid());
    return readings;
}
```

Finally, let's take a look at the function that writes to file. This function initializes the SD card reader, constructs a folder structure, and then opens a file for writing. If the file is opened successfully, the microcontroller writes the data to the file, ending the entry with a newline character. Finally, it closes the file. The code for this is as follows:

```
void writeTSVToFile(String y, String m, String d, unsigned long
unixtime) {
    SD.begin(4);
    String f = String("/");
    f.concat(y);
    f.concat("/");
    f.concat(m);
    if(!SD.exists(f)) {
       SD.mkdir(f);
    }
    f.concat("/");
    f.concat(d);
    f.concat(".tsv");

    File myFile = SD.open(f, FILE_WRITE);
    if(myFile) {
       myFile.println(getTSVReadings(unixtime));
       myFile.close();
    }
}
```

You now have everything it takes to write sensor data to a file on an SD card. The Code in Action video is available at https://packt.link/Gksf0.

The data we have stored is in what is called a **flat file**. Let's consider flat files in more detail.

Understanding flat files

A flat file contains all of the information in one file. We saw this example of how all of the temperature and humidity information is stored in one file. Let's consider some formats for storing data in a flat file.

Getting to know the TXT file format

One common file format is **TXT**. This format represents a text file. This simply means that the file is not specially formatted, and you can read it using a bunch of tools and editors. If you are on **Microsoft Windows**, you can read this type of file using an application called **Notepad**. On **Mac**, you can use **TextEdit**. On **Linux**, you can use **Nano**, **Vim**, **Emacs**, and a host of other editors.

This file can hold any body of text without any special formatting.

Getting to know the CSV file format

Another common file format is **Comma-Separated Values (CSV)**. It is used to store information in which the different values are separated by a comma and are all stored on one line. Every line is terminated with a **newline character** (\n).

A lot of data is shared in CSV format. This format can be read by simple text editors because the files are also TXT files. Even more importantly, this format can be read by spreadsheet applications such as Microsoft Excel and Google Sheets. These applications can read the file and separate the data into different columns, presenting it in a tabular format.

Getting to know the TSV file format

A third and popular file format is **Tab-Separated Values (TSV)**. It uses tabs (\t) to separate values instead of commas. This is useful because the output appears more columnar, with more space between the values, when viewed by the human eye. It is also useful in places where the values being stored have commas in them.

When a file is in CSV format, it becomes difficult to store anything that has a comma in it, such as street addresses. With CSV, the workaround for this is to wrap such values within quotation marks. Reading such values back out requires some string manipulations that are easier in some programming languages than others. TSV format solves this problem by separating the values using tabs. Of course, you will need to worry about values that have tabs in them, but this isn't common.

Getting to know the JSON file format

JavaScript Object Notation (JSON) stores data as objects. These objects are encapsulated in curly brackets with the data stored as key-value pairs. The JSON file could contain one or more objects. If the file contains one object, the file begins with { and ends with }. If the file contains more than one object, the objects are held in an array, and the file begins with [and ends with].

JSON files and objects have the advantage of being self-contained. Because each object contains a name-value pair, different objects can contain different types of information. For example, you could begin collecting information from a weather station that only has temperature and humidity readings. After a few months, the station has a pressure sensor installed, so you start to capture that as well. The JSON file will capture the new information without any new preparation. If you tried that with a CSV or TSV file, you would suddenly have new columns that could cause problems when the data is being read.

There are other file formats, but we don't need to get into those at the moment. Instead, let's consider the situation in which the MKR board is placed in a position that is hard to reach. If we placed MKR boards in a thousand weather stations, we would be required to visit each one to retrieve the data. This is less than ideal. We would also lose data in the interval required to swap out one SD card for another. Thirdly, regardless of the location of our files, how could we find a certain value inside a file? For example, how would we know what the hottest hour was on a particular day, or the hottest day of the year at a particular station?

The answer lies in databases.

Working with databases

You can use a database to keep information organized. Databases are frequently backed by an engine called the **database server**. How a Database server does its job is not as important as what a database server empowers you to do.

While we have been able to store data on a file, we need to ask ourselves, "*What happens if the file gets corrupted? How do we provide backup for this data?*" database servers can provide redundancy, replication, and high availability for our data when we need it.

You can use a database server to store and retrieve information when you need to. When you retrieve information from a database, you specify what you want and not how to get it. This is different from how we have done things so far, where we have to program the microcontroller to do exactly what we want the way we want it. When we tell a microcontroller how to do something, that style of programming is called **imperative**. When we let the database determine how to do what we want, that style of programming is called **declarative**.

Here are some of the things that a database server makes possible:

- Returning limited results from the entire data
- Running statistics on numerical data
- Performing transformations on data
- Sorting the data

Just as there are different file formats, there are also different types of databases. Let's discuss a few of them.

Flat-file databases

The data that we stored in a single file could qualify as a **flat-file database**. This type of database has the advantage of being easy to understand and easy to add records to. On the other hand, it is quite difficult to make changes to this file. To make a change, you would need to write code that performs a search within the file to locate the old value, and then replace the old value with the new one. We have seen how to append data to a file, but how do you edit data on a particular line? Making changes to the records in a database is called an **update**. Also, searching for (**retrieving**) records in this type of database can be hard if we are not working sequentially. This is because a search frequently involves reading the contents of the file from the beginning to the end, or until you have located the data you are looking for. If you had a file containing all of the hourly temperatures for an entire year and you wanted to find out the number of days with an average temperature above a certain value, you would have to read through the entire file and perform some computations. You would quickly find that this isn't a trivial operation.

Despite these challenges, flat-file databases are in widespread use.

Relational (SQL) databases

A **Relational Database Management System (RDBMS)** provides a service beyond just storing and retrieving data. It makes it easy to carry out a series of operations that are important to the data management process. These include the following:

- `Create`: The process of adding new data to storage
- `Retrieve`: The process of getting either all or a subset of the data out of storage
- `Update`: The process of modifying the data that has been stored
- `Delete`: The process of removing data that was previously stored

In addition to all of this, an RDBMS takes care of how the data is stored while introducing some redundancy to the system.

RDBMS also introduces the notion of **schemas** and **tables**.

A table contains rows of data. A row of data represents a record. Each row contains all of the information required to transmit the data without repetition. If the data had information that could be repetitive, this repetitive data would be held in a second table. This process is called **normalization**, and it is this process that leads to **relationships** between tables. This relationship is what lends itself to the relational aspect of RDBMS.

Schemas group related tables together, making it possible for one RDBMS to host multiple tables with the same name but different applications. For example, the RDBMS could have a schema for weather and another schema for sales. Both of these schemas could have a table called `location`.

If we had multiple sensors collecting temperature and humidity data, one approach would be to store the information about the location of the sensor alongside the date on which the data was collected. The table that stores this information, along with the location of the sensor (latitude and longitude), the name of the station, the date on which the sensor was installed, and the altitude of installation, might look as follows:

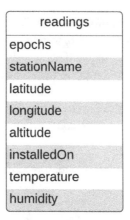

Figure 4.2 – Table structure for sensor readings

The problems with the table structure (*Figure 4.2*) are as follows:

- **Repetitive information**: All the information about the location of the sensor will be repeated every single time that we store a reading.

- **Redundant information**: If the information about the sensor changed, such as the name of the station, we would be forced to change that name in a lot of places.

- **Difficult identification**: With multiple sensors, we can expect to have multiple readings come in at the same time. As a result, we would need to specify the name of the sensor, along with the time whenever we need to retrieve the temperature and humidity readings.

We could solve this problem by introducing normalization. To normalize the table, we must introduce a new table that holds all of the information about the station, then move all of that information into this table, where we have only one record of it, along with a unique identifier, which is also called a **primary key (PK)**. The readings table will now only contain information about the temperature and humidity, along with the date and the unique identifier of the station, which is called a **foreign key (FK)**. The FK in the **readings** table creates a relationship to the PK in the **stations** table. The new table structure would look as follows:

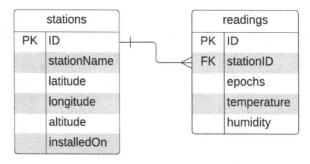

Figure 4.3 – The normalized table structure

The preceding table structure assumes that each station has only one sensor (**temperature** and **humidity**). What if each station could have multiple sensors at different locations? How would you change this table structure?

From an IoT perspective, there are three places where a database could sit:

- **On-device**: We could place a database such as SQLite on the microcontroller so that we can manage a database on the SD card. We will not go into that in this book, but it is something that you could research if you find the topic or application to be interesting.

- **On the edge**: We could set up a database server such as MySQL on a low-power device such as a Raspberry Pi. This device would be on the same network as the microcontrollers that are collecting information. These microcontrollers would then send the data that they are collecting to this RDBMS. This RDBMS then takes care of forwarding the data periodically, as network connectivity permits. The advantage of this approach is that the entire network doesn't need to have access to the internet.

- **In the cloud**: This would require us to set up an RDBMS on a powerful computer in a central location. The sensors could either write to this RDBMS, or they could write to edge instances that update the cloud instance. Amazon (AWS), Microsoft (Azure), Oracle, and Google Cloud all provide cloud platforms on which we could set up an RDBMS.

Let's proceed to configure a MySQL database server on the edge. However, before we do that, let's confirm that you have an SSH certificate on your computer (Linux or Mac). This certificate will make it possible for your computer to authenticate against the server without you having to provide a username and password, thus providing an extra layer of security. If you use Windows, please get **puttygen** from `https://www.puttygen.com/`. Follow these steps for Linux and Mac:

1. Open the Terminal window.

2. Browse to your home directory using the following command:

   ```
   cd ~
   ```

3. Search for SSH certificates by running the list (`ls`) command on a hidden directory:

   ```
   ls .ssh
   ```

4. If you see an output that lists two files, `id_rsa` and `id_rsa.pub`, then you are ready to proceed to the next section. The output should be similar to the following. Don't worry if you don't see `known_hosts` and `known_hosts.old` – they only exist if you have tunneled into another computer in the past:

```
[(base) Roberts-MacBook-Pro-2:~ robert$ ls -l .ssh
total 48
-rw-------  1 robert  staff  3243 Mar  1  2019 id_rsa
-rw-r--r--  1 robert  staff   755 Mar  1  2019 id_rsa.pub
-rw-------  1 robert  staff  7363 Nov 29 23:08 known_hosts
-rw-r--r--  1 robert  staff  6619 Nov 29 23:07 known_hosts.old
```

Figure 4.4 – SSH keys

5. If you get an error saying that the folder doesn't exist, then use the following command to generate new keys:

```
ssh-keygen -t rsa -b 4096
```

6. Follow the instructions on the screen to finish generating the SSH keys.

A video showing how to implement these steps is available at https://packt.link/Gksf0.

Let's proceed to the next project, where we'll configure a MySQL database server.

Project 2 – Configuring a MySQL database server

This project assumes that you are making use of a Raspberry Pi 3 or 4. If you are using an alternative piece of hardware or a virtual machine, please install Ubuntu 22.04 LTS or any other LTS version. Let's begin by installing Ubuntu Server on a Raspberry Pi.

Installing Ubuntu Server on a Raspberry Pi

Please follow these steps to install Ubuntu 22.04 LTS, or any other LTS version, on a Raspberry Pi:

1. Download the Raspberry Pi Imager from https://www.raspberrypi.com/software/.
2. Install the Raspberry Pi Imager.
3. Launch the Raspberry Pi Imager.
4. Insert the SD card into the reader on your computer.
5. In the **Raspberry Pi Imager** window, under **Operating System**, click **Choose OS**.
6. Choose **Other General Purpose OS | Ubuntu | Ubuntu Server 22.04.1 LTS (64-bit)**.
7. Under **Storage**, click **Choose Storage**.
8. Select your card from the options that you see.
9. Click on the *Settings* icon at the bottom right of the screen.
10. Check the box next to **Set hostname** and type in your desired name for the server. Note this name down because it makes it easy to find the server on a network with lots of devices.
11. Check the box next to **Enable SSH**.

12. Choose the radio button next to **Allow public-key authentication only**:

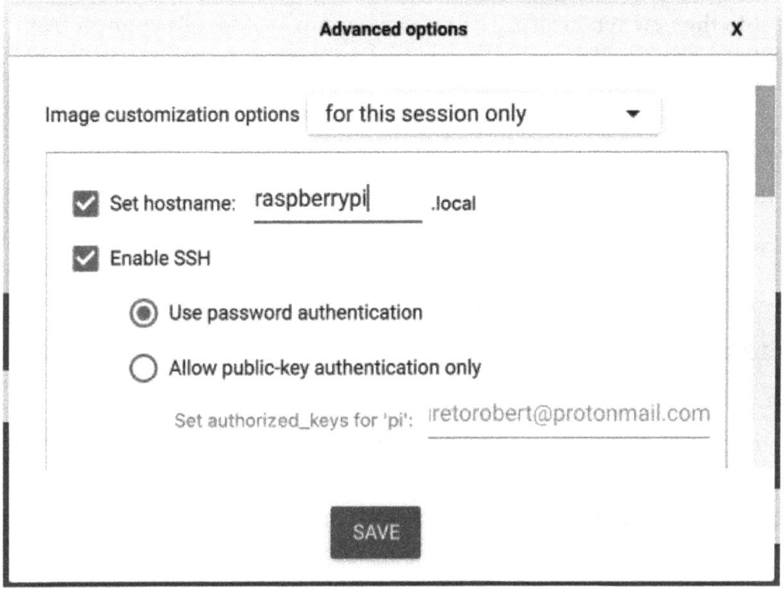

Figure 4.5 – Configuring the server

13. Check the box next to **Set username and password**. This will make it possible for you to log into the device using a keyboard and monitor.

14. Be sure to provide the username and password that you would like to use, and remember them.

15. Check the box next to **Configure wireless LAN**.

16. Fill in **SSID** with the network's name.

17. Fill in **Password**.

18. Check the box next to **Set locale settings** and fill in the settings accordingly.

19. Click **Save**.

20. Click **Write**.

21. Wait a while for the OS to be written onto the SD card.

22. Eject the card when you get the instruction to do so.

23. Insert the card into the Raspberry Pi.

24. Boot up the Raspberry Pi. You may attach a keyboard and monitor before doing so.

25. Wait a few minutes and then check your router for the IP address of the new device.

Congratulations – you have a new instance of Ubuntu Server running! A video showing these steps is available at https://packt.link/Gksf0. It's now time to connect to it remotely and issue commands.

Connecting to Ubuntu Server

You can connect to the new server using `ssh` from a Linux or Mac. To connect from Windows, please get **putty** from `https://www.putty.org/`. Follow these steps to connect to the server from Linux or Mac:

1. Open your Terminal.

2. Type in the following command:

   ```
   ssh username@192.168.68.132
   ```

3. Replace `username` with the username you chose while setting up.

4. Replace `192.168.68.132` with the IP address of the new device.

5. Hit *Enter* on your keyboard.

6. If this is the first time you are connecting to the setup, you will likely get an output similar to the following:

```
The authenticity of host '192.168.68.132 (192.168.68.132)' can't be established.
ED25519 key fingerprint is SHA256:+AkgqswbwFoWaoxbGbjmqZjm94YqbpzBv/fRW3Z1ZtQ.
This key is not known by any other names
Are you sure you want to continue connecting (yes/no/[fingerprint])? yes
```

Figure 4.6 – SSH connection screen

7. Type `yes`.

8. Hit *Enter*.

9. You will see something similar to the following when you are connected:

```
Warning: Permanently added '192.168.68.132' (ED25519) to the list of known hosts.
Welcome to Ubuntu 22.04.1 LTS (GNU/Linux 5.15.0-1012-raspi aarch64)

 * Documentation:  https://help.ubuntu.com
 * Management:     https://landscape.canonical.com
 * Support:        https://ubuntu.com/advantage

  System information as of Tue Nov 29 23:07:40 WAT 2022

  System load:  0.224609375      Temperature:           46.7 C
  Usage of /:   32.9% of 6.96GB  Processes:             153
  Memory usage: 5%               Users logged in:       0
  Swap usage:   0%               IPv4 address for wlan0: 192.168.68.132


113 updates can be applied immediately.
63 of these updates are standard security updates.
To see these additional updates run: apt list --upgradable


Last login: Tue Nov 29 17:07:27 2022
```

Figure 4.7 – Connected remotely

A video showing the preceding steps is available at `https://packt.link/Gksf0`.

Congratulations – you are now connected to the newly configured server! Let's proceed and install MySQL Server and the client software. All of this needs to be done while you are remotely connected to the Raspberry Pi.

Installing MySQL Server

Follow these steps to set up the server and client using the `apt` package manager:

1. Update `apt` using the following command:

   ```
   sudo apt update
   ```

2. Wait for the process to complete.

3. Install the MySQL Server software using the following command:

   ```
   sudo apt install mysql-server
   ```

4. Respond to any prompts asking for permission, then wait for the installation to complete. The screen will print out a lot of output; you should read it if you can.

5. Start the MySQL database server using the following command:

   ```
   sudo systemctl start mysql.service
   ```

The system doesn't print anything to show that the command succeeded, but it worked if you didn't get an error message. A video showing the preceding steps is available at `https://packt.link/Gksf0`.

Congratulations – you have successfully set up MySQL Server. It's not secure, but you can log into the server.

Logging in and securing MySQL Server

Follow these steps to secure MySQL Server:

1. Ensure that you are remotely connected to the server via `ssh`.

2. Type the following command to log into MySQL as a superuser:

   ```
   sudo mysql
   ```

3. If this works, you will get the **mysql prompt**. It looks similar to the following:

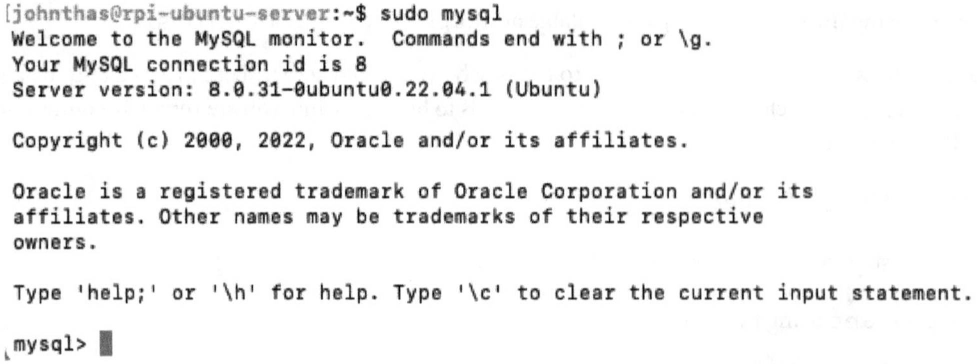

```
[johnthas@rpi-ubuntu-server:~$ sudo mysql
Welcome to the MySQL monitor.  Commands end with ; or \g.
Your MySQL connection id is 8
Server version: 8.0.31-0ubuntu0.22.04.1 (Ubuntu)

Copyright (c) 2000, 2022, Oracle and/or its affiliates.

Oracle is a registered trademark of Oracle Corporation and/or its
affiliates. Other names may be trademarks of their respective
owners.

Type 'help;' or '\h' for help. Type '\c' to clear the current input statement.

mysql>
```

Figure 4.8 – The mysql prompt

4. We need to issue a SQL command that instructs the server to change how the root user is *authenticated*. We will discuss SQL some more after we are done securing the server. Type the following command into the prompt, all on one line, and replace password with what you would like to use:

    ```
    ALTER USER 'root'@'localhost' IDENTIFIED WITH mysql_native_
    password BY 'password';
    ```

5. If you didn't make any errors in typing, the prompt will output feedback similar to the following:

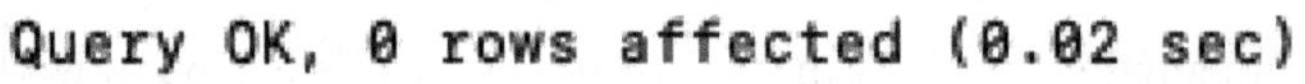

    ```
    Query OK, 0 rows affected (0.02 sec)
    ```

    Figure 4.9 – ALTER USER query result

6. You need to persist this instruction. Type in the following command:

    ```
    flush privileges;
    ```

7. With everything completed, exit MySQL for now by typing in the following command:

    ```
    exit
    ```

8. You will be taken back to the OS prompt of Ubuntu. Run the MySQL secure installation script by typing the following command into the prompt:

    ```
    mysql_secure_installation
    ```

9. Fill in the root password.

10. Follow the prompts that appear and respond accordingly.

11. Wait for the script to complete execution.

12. Back at the OS prompt, log into `mysql` with user credentials as root by typing the following command:

```
mysql -u root -p
```

13. The prompt will request a password. Type in the password that you configured for the root user.

14. Set the authentication method for the root user back to the default by typing in the following SQL command:

```
ALTER USER 'root'@'localhost' IDENTIFIED WITH auth_socket;
```

15. Hit *Enter* and look out for confirmation that the command was executed successfully.

A video showing the preceding steps is available at `https://packt.link/Gksf0`.

Congratulations – you have successfully set up a MySQL database! Let's proceed and create a database schema and a user for logging into the database.

Creating a user

Let's create a database schema:

1. While still logged in as the root user, type in the following SQL command:

```
CREATE DATABASE telemetry;
```

2. Create a user. Be sure to replace the appropriate fields in the following command:

```
CREATE USER 'username'@'localhost' IDENTIFIED BY 'password';
```

3. Confirm that the command was executed correctly.

4. This command grants the newly created user permission to log in locally. We also need the user to log in remotely, so execute the following command, making sure you replace `username` and `password` appropriately:

```
CREATE USER 'username'@'%' IDENTIFIED BY 'password';
```

5. Confirm that the command was executed correctly.

6. Commit the changes by running the following command:

```
flush privileges;
```

7. Grant the newly created user permissions to connect to this database by running the following SQL command:

```
GRANT ALL ON telemetry.* TO username;
```

8. Exit MySQL by typing the following command:

    ```
    exit
    ```

9. Connect as the newly created user, making sure you replace `username` with the correct one:

    ```
    mysql -u username -p
    ```

10. Type in the correct password and confirm that you can log in.

A video showing the preceding steps is available at `https://packt.link/Gksf0`.

Congratulations – you have set up a new user! We will be doing some more work with this database server later. For now, let's discuss other database types.

Document-oriented databases

Document-oriented databases are also called **NoSQL** databases because you don't need to use SQL to interact with them. They do not have schemas. Instead, they have **collections** that hold **documents** in them. These documents are in JSON format and do not need to conform to the same structure. However, it is best practice to place documents with the same structure in a collection.

These databases are best for rapid experimentation where you are not sure of what data you would like to store. You can set up a database and begin storing data, and the structure of this data (fields) can change as you continue to experiment with your application. This isn't something you can do easily with relational databases because you will need to alter your table structure whenever you decide to do this.

NoSQL databases do not require normalization, and some users frequently nest necessary information within the document. Writing to these databases can be fast. While you can read data from these databases, the structure of these databases isn't suited to data analysis. You will frequently need to move the data out into a more appropriate database before you can extract insights.

One popular NoSQL database is **MongoDB**. It is easy to set up on your device, although we won't be doing that in this book. Getting started with MongoDB is easy because there are several books available to teach you how to get started on a lot of platforms. MongoDB has a version that is free to use, similar to MySQL. You can learn more by visiting `https://www.mongodb.com/home`.

Another NoSQL database is **Cloud Firestore**. Cloud Firestore is available on the Firebase platform, which is also called a **mobile backend as a service** (**MBaaS**) because it provides not only a database but an entire suite of products that makes it easy for mobile application developers to get started without having to set up a database and an application layer. You can learn more by visiting `https://firebase.google.com/`.

NoSQL databases have their uses, but when collecting sensor data, the schema doesn't change often. One thing that is common when collecting sensor data is that the data is collected at an interval. You could collect temperature readings every minute, every 5 minutes, or every 60 minutes. The sequence of this data makes it possible for you to track changes over time. This sort of data is frequently called a **time series**. Let's look at databases that are optimized for storing this sort of data.

Time series databases

Time series databases introduce the notion of **measurements** in place of tables. Technically speaking, these are the same. However, while tables in an RDBMS introduce keys or indexes, measurements introduce a **timestamp**.

If we have a sensor that collects temperature and humidity readings at regular intervals, we will have a measurement with *fields* called **temperature** and **humidity**. The structure would look similar to the following:

timestamp	fields	
	temperature	humidity
11:00	32.1	65
11:05	32.1	66

Figure 4.10 – Time series measurements

If we have more than one sensor, such as in a bedroom and a kitchen, then we will need to introduce a **tag** called **location** to tell us where this sensor is located. The new structure would look similar to the following:

timestamp	fields		tags
	temperature	humidity	location
11:00	32.1	65	kitchen
11:00	29.0	50	bedroom
11:05	32.1	66	kitchen
11:05	28.8	49	bedroom

Figure 4.11 – Time series measurements with tags

Time series databases introduce some features that make them stand apart from other databases:

- Data life cycle management
- Summarization
- Large range scans

When working with time series, it is important to understand **granularity**. Granularity refers to the level of precision of the available data. For example, if you collect data every minute, you could return the data every minute, every hour, every day, every week, and so on. As you move from the level of the minute to the level of the week and month, your granularity reduces. However, the data you return becomes a statistical measure, such as the average monthly temperature or the maximum monthly temperature for the period under consideration.

Going back to our example of collecting measurements every minute, that would be 525,600 records for each sensor every year. This doesn't appear to be a large number, but consider storing this much data for 8,000 sensors. That becomes a whooping 4.2 billion records. How do you manage that in one table?

This is where **retention policies** come into play. This states how long you need to keep data within the database for either business or compliance reasons.

When working with an RDBMS, the usual approach is to introduce **partitioning**. Partitioning forces the **database management system** (**DBMS**) to physically separate how the data is stored, and the table doesn't read a partition unless it is specifically instructed to do so.

One advantage of partitioning is that it makes it easy to remove from a table. For this reason, date partitions are frequently implemented in tables. Does this remind you of our timestamps?

What exactly do we use data for? We frequently utilize data for two purposes:

- **Analysis**: Looking back at trends to try to identify patterns
- **Forecasting**: Using the identified patterns to make predictions

We might be interested in how the weather was changing every minute yesterday, but we rarely make predictions at the level of the minute. What this means is that even though we have collected data for every minute, after a certain period, we might not be interested in that level of granularity.

Time series databases make it possible to implement a retention policy that will automatically reduce the level of granularity after a certain period, reducing the amount of data that is being stored.

We typically do not update or delete data in a time series database manually because it doesn't make any sense to do so.

Let's set up one popular time series database called InfluxDB. Here is a quick comparison of the terms before we get started:

Relational Database	Document Database	Time Series Database
Schema	Collection	Bucket
Table	Document	Measurement
Column	Field	Field
N/A	N/A	Tag
PK/Index	Index	Timestamp
Record	Document	Point

Let's set up InfluxDB so that we can utilize it to store measurements.

Project 3 – Configuring an InfluxDB server

This project assumes that you are making use of a Raspberry Pi 3 or 4. If you are using an alternative piece of hardware or a virtual machine, please install Ubuntu 22.04 LTS or any other LTS version. If you didn't install Ubuntu on the Raspberry Pi, please refer to the first section of *Project 2 – configuring a MySQL database server*, to learn how to do that. Afterward, please proceed to the next section.

Installing InfluxDB

Follow these steps to install the DBMS on your existing Ubuntu installation:

1. Connect to your Ubuntu Server instance from a Terminal.
2. Go to `https://portal.influxdata.com/downloads/`.
3. Scroll down to the **Platform** selector.
4. Choose **Ubuntu & Debian (ARM 64-bit)**.
5. Copy the output.
6. Return to the remote Terminal.
7. Paste the output into the Terminal and hit *Enter*.
8. Follow the prompt to complete the setup.
9. Type the following command to start up the InfluxDB service:

    ```
    sudo service influxdb start
    ```

10. Disconnect from the remote Terminal.

A video showing the preceding steps is available at `https://packt.link/Gksf0`.

Congratulations – you have installed InfluxDB! Now, you need to configure it.

Configuring InfluxDB

Follow these steps:

1. Go to `http://192.168.68.112:8086`, making sure you replace the IP address with that of your Ubuntu Server.
2. Click **Get Started**.
3. Fill in the form on the next page with the appropriate data.
4. Click **Continue**.

A video showing the preceding steps is available at `https://packt.link/Gksf0`.

Congratulations – you have successfully set up a time series database that you can utilize to store sensor data!

There are other types of databaseMSs that we have not discussed, such as graph databases for managing relationships, and key-value stores for state management. We haven't looked at them in detail because you don't need them at this point.

Congratulations on making it to the end of this chapter.

Summary

In this chapter, you learned about different approaches and formats for storing data and learned how to store data in a flat file on the MKR board. You also learned about databases and set up two different DBMSs: an RDBMS called MySQL and a time series DBMS called InfluxDB. The skills you have learned will come in handy when you set up databases that you can use to store data.

In *Chapter 5*, you will learn how to move data into and out of the DMBSs that you've configured.

Further reading

You can learn about a library for working with SQLite on an Arduino at `https://github.com/siara-cc/sqlite_micro_logger_arduino`.

5

Implementing REST and MQTT Protocols for Communication

Database management systems (**DBMSs**) are good at storing and retrieving data, but they are not normally designed for communicating over the internet. Furthermore, while they can handle large amounts of data, they are not designed to handle this from thousands of sources. This is where **REpresentational State Transfer** (**REST**) and **Message Queueing Telemetry Transport** (**MQTT**) come in handy. These two protocols make it possible for us to build third-party applications to communicate with a DBMS at scale. You will be setting up REST and MQTT services in this chapter.

In this chapter, we are going to cover the following main topics:

- Working with RESTful APIs in Node.js and JavaScript

- Working with RESTful APIs in Python

- Working with MQTT

By the end of this chapter, you will have set up infrastructure that makes it possible to communicate with your DBMS over a network or the internet.

Technical requirements

You will be working with **Structured Query Language** (**SQL**), Python, and JavaScript in this chapter. The code for this chapter is available at the following GitHub URL: https://github.com/ PacktPublishing/Arduino-Data-Communications/tree/main/chapter-5.

Working with REST

Most DBMSs will ship with an interface that makes it possible to interact with the server, type in commands, and get responses. You have seen this at play when logging into the server remotely and typing in mysql from the command line.

REST makes it possible to communicate with an application server over **HyperText Transfer Protocol (HTTP)**, which, in turn, communicates with a DBMS using any native technology that is supported. **HTTP** and **HTTPS** are normally the first part of most URLs that you type into the address bar of a browser. HTTPS is HTTP with a secure component.

Both HTTP and HTTPS tell the browser how to communicate with the server that it is connecting to. Most DBMSs are not designed to work with HTTP or HTTPS, so we will need to set up a separate component (called middleware) that will communicate with the DBMS while exposing an HTTP or HTTPS interface.

Before we do that, let's set up some tables within the telemetry schema in our MySQL database. These tables will be based on the design shown in the following figure:

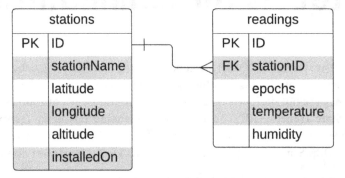

Figure 5.1 – The tables we will be creating

On to the project!

Project 1 – Defining tables within MySQL

In this project, you will connect to the MySQL DB instance and create two tables. The SQL script we will be working with is available at https://github.com/PacktPublishing/Arduino-Data-Communications/tree/main/chapter-5/MySQL-Create-Tables.

Follow these steps to connect to the remote server, clone the GitHub repository, and then execute a SQL file to create the tables:

1. Connect to the remote server using the following shell command, making sure you replace both the username and the IP address with the correct values for your setup:

    ```
    ssh username@192.168.68.127
    ```

2. Clone the GitHub repository using the following command:

    ```
    git clone https://github.com/PacktPublishing/Arduino-Data-
    Communications.git
    ```

3. Use the following command to navigate to the folder that contains the script for this project:

```
cd Arduino-Data-Communications/chapter-5/MySQL-Create-Tables/
```

4. Use the following command to replace the username with what you set up:

```
mysql telemetry -u username -p < ./create_tables.sql
```

5. Type in your password at the prompt; it will look similar to the following.

```
Enter password:
```

Figure 5.2 – The MySQL password prompt

6. The MySQL client will return you to the command line. Log into MySQL using the following command:

```
mysql -u username -p
```

7. Type in the correct password at the next prompt.

8. You will now be at the mysql prompt. Change to the telemetry schema using the following command.

```
use telemetry;
```

You will get a response similar to the following, showing that you have successfully changed schemas:

```
mysql> use telemetry;
Reading table information for completion of tab
le and column names
You can turn off this feature to get a quicker
startup with -A

Database changed
```

Figure 5.3 – Schema change confirmation

9. Use the following command to list the tables within the schema:

```
show tables;
```

The output will be similar to the following:

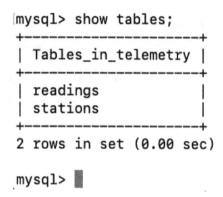

```
mysql> show tables;
+---------------------+
| Tables_in_telemetry |
+---------------------+
| readings            |
| stations            |
+---------------------+
2 rows in set (0.00 sec)

mysql>
```

Figure 5.4 – The output of the show tables command

Congratulations, you have successfully created two related tables within the telemetry schema and also confirmed that the tables were created!

The steps for this workshop are shown in the code video available at https://packt.link/OSzj4.

Let's analyze the script contained within the create_tables.sql file that we used in the project. The extension of the file shows us that it contains SQL. There are three instructions in this file. Each instruction is terminated with a semi-colon, and an instruction in SQL can span multiple lines, although that's just for readability. When you type SQL into a command line, you will typically type everything on one continuous line.

The first instruction causes the interpreter to change schemas. It's like what you used on line 8 in *Project 1 – defining tables within MySQL*. Here it is:

```
USE telemetry;
```

SQL is not case-sensitive. The keywords in uppercase are just there to help you tell the keywords apart from the values that we are passing in.

The second instruction creates the table called stations. This instruction will only run if the table doesn't exist in the schema. This way, you can avoid losing data if the table already exists. Here is the instruction:

```
CREATE TABLE IF NOT EXISTS stations (
    id INT NOT NULL AUTO_INCREMENT PRIMARY KEY,
    stationName VARCHAR(255),
    lat FLOAT,
    lon FLOAT,
    alt FLOAT,
    installedOn DATE DEFAULT(CURRENT_DATE)
);
```

We created this table first because, logically speaking, we can't collect readings until we have set up stations. We discussed normalization in *Chapter 4*, and the column named `id` introduces the properties we need to enforce uniqueness within this table. The column named `stationName` is set up to hold a string value, while `lat`, `lon`, and `alt` are set up to hold floating-point numbers. The names have been shortened to make them easier to work with, but they represent latitude, longitude, and altitude, respectively. The column named `installedOn` holds a date value. We want to know when this station was set up. If we don't supply a value, the date on which we make this entry is assumed to be the date on which the station was set up.

The final instruction creates the table called `readings`. The code is shown here:

```
CREATE TABLE IF NOT EXISTS readings(
    id INT NOT NULL AUTO_INCREMENT PRIMARY KEY,
    stationID INT,
    epochs TIMESTAMP DEFAULT(CURRENT_TIMESTAMP),
    temperature FLOAT,
    humidity FLOAT,
    FOREIGN KEY (stationID) REFERENCES stations(id) ON UPDATE RESTRICT
ON DELETE RESTRICT
);
```

In this instruction, we introduce a foreign key constraint (`stationID`) that points to the `id` column within the `stations` table. This is what introduces the relationship between tables. The foreign key constraint also prevents you from either changing a station ID or deleting a station after you have inserted data that pertains to that station into the `readings` table.

We have set up two tables, but they are empty. Let's look at how to get data into those tables using SQL before we set up a REST layer.

Working with SQL

Creating tables in SQL falls into a class of operations called **data definition language** (DDL). However, working with data falls into a class called **data manipulation language** (DML). DML falls into four categories that are frequently called **create, retrieve, update, and delete** (CRUD). Let's take a brief look at CRUD.

Project 2 – Inserting data into a MySQL table

We must create operations and insert data into a table. This uses an `INSERT` statement in SQL. The script for this project is available at `https://github.com/PacktPublishing/Arduino-Data-Communications/blob/main/chapter-5/MySQL-Create-Tables/insert_data.sql`.

Follow these steps to insert data into the tables:

1. Log into the remote server using the following shell command, making sure you replace the IP address with your server's:

    ```
    ssh username@192.168.68.127
    ```

2. Log into MySQL using the following shell command, making sure you replace the username with the appropriate value:

    ```
    mysql -u username -p
    ```

3. Provide the correct password at the next prompt.

4. Change to the telemetry schema using the following statement on the MySQL prompt:

    ```
    USE telemetry;
    ```

5. Create a station by using the following insert statement. You should type everything on one line:

    ```
    INSERT INTO stations (stationName, lat, lon, alt)
    VALUES ('Station 1', 3.3, 0.0, 100);
    ```

6. The prompt should output a result similar to the following:

    ```
    mysql> INSERT INTO stations (stationName, lat, lon, alt)
    [    -> VALUES ('Station 1', 3.3, 0.0, 100);
    Query OK, 1 row affected (0.01 sec)
    ```

    Figure 5.5 – The insert was successful

7. Simulate readings from this station by using the following insert statements:

    ```
    INSERT INTO readings (stationid, epochs, temperature, humidity)
    VALUES (1, NOW(), 11.6, 66);
    INSERT INTO readings (stationid, epochs, temperature, humidity)
    VALUES (1, TIMESTAMPADD(MINUTE, 1, NOW()), 11.6, 65);
    INSERT INTO readings (stationid, epochs, temperature, humidity)
    VALUES (1, TIMESTAMPADD(MINUTE, 2, NOW()), 11.6, 64);
    ```

8. You will get a confirmation from the prompt showing that each insert was successful.

When inserting data into the readings table, we specify the stationid parameter that the record is for. In this case, the value is 1. We know this because of how our stations table is defined, and the fact that the **primary key** auto-increments.

A recording showing the previous steps is available at https://packt.link/OSzj4.

You can confirm what the stations table contains by proceeding to the next project.

Project 3 – Retrieving data from a MySQL table

In this project, you will learn how to retrieve or fetch data from a table using SQL. The scripts we'll be using are available at `https://github.com/securetorobert/Arduino-Data-Communications/blob/main/chapter-5/MySQL-Create-Tables/retrieve_data.sql`.

Follow these steps to retrieve data from the tables used in the previous project:

1. Log into the remote server using the following shell command, making sure you replace the IP address with your server's:

    ```
    ssh username@192.168.68.127
    ```

2. Log into MySQL using the following shell command, making sure you replace the username with the appropriate value:

    ```
    mysql -u username -p
    ```

3. Provide the correct password at the next prompt.

4. Change to the `telemetry` schema by using the following statement on the MySQL prompt:

    ```
    USE telemetry;
    ```

5. Use the following statement to read all of the data contained in the `stations` table:

    ```
    SELECT * FROM stations;
    ```

    The result from the prompt will look similar to the following:

    ```
    [mysql> SELECT * FROM stations;
    +----+-------------+------+------+------+-------------+
    | id | stationName | lat  | lon  | alt  | installedOn |
    +----+-------------+------+------+------+-------------+
    |  1 | Station 1   | 3.3  |   0  | 100  | 2023-01-04  |
    +----+-------------+------+------+------+-------------+
    1 row in set (0.00 sec)
    ```

    Figure 5.6 – The result of the SELECT statement

6. Similarly, you can retrieve all of the data in the `readings` table using the following statement:

    ```
    SELECT * FROM readings;
    ```

7. The result will be three records. You can filter records to meet certain criteria. For example, you can filter your results to only readings with humidity below 66% by using the following statement:

    ```
    SELECT * FROM readings WHERE humidity < 66;
    ```

The result will be similar to the following:

```
[mysql> SELECT * FROM readings WHERE humidity < 66;
+----+-----------+---------------------+-------------+----------+
| id | stationID | epochs              | temperature | humidity |
+----+-----------+---------------------+-------------+----------+
|  2 |         1 | 2023-01-04 23:18:44 |        11.6 |       65 |
|  3 |         1 | 2023-01-04 23:19:47 |        11.6 |       64 |
+----+-----------+---------------------+-------------+----------+
2 rows in set (0.00 sec)
```

Figure 5.7 – The result of using a filter

Congratulations – you have successfully retrieved data from a MySQL table! A video showing the preceding steps is available at https://packt.link/OSzj4.

Updating and deleting data might not be something that you do often, but let's proceed to learn those skills. In the next project, we will update the data in a table.

Project 4 – Updating data in a MySQL table

In this project, you will learn how to update data in a table using SQL. The scripts we'll be using are available at https://github.com/securetorobert/Arduino-Data-Communications/tree/main/chapter-5/MySQL-Create-Tables.

Follow these steps to complete this project:

1. Log into the remote server using the following shell command, making sure you replace the IP address with your server's:

    ```
    ssh username@192.168.68.127
    ```

2. Log into MySQL using the following shell command, making sure you replace the username with the appropriate value:

    ```
    mysql -u username -p
    ```

3. Provide the correct password at the next prompt.

4. Change to the telemetry schema by using the following statement on the MySQL prompt:

    ```
    USE telemetry;
    ```

5. Use the following statement to insert a new record:

    ```
    INSERT INTO stations (stationName, lat, lon, alt)
    VALUES ('Station 4', 3.4, 0.1, 90);
    ```

6. Use the following statement to read all of the data contained in the stations table:

    ```
    SELECT * FROM stations;
    ```

7. The result from the prompt will look similar to the following. Please take note of the newly inserted record:

```
mysql> SELECT * FROM stations;
+----+-------------+------+------+------+-------------+
| id | stationName | lat  | lon  | alt  | installedOn |
+----+-------------+------+------+------+-------------+
|  1 | Station 1   | 3.3  |    0 | 100  | 2023-02-28  |
|  2 | Station 4   | 3.4  | 0.1  |  90  | 2023-03-03  |
+----+-------------+------+------+------+-------------+
2 rows in set (0.00 sec)
```

Figure 5.8 – Fetching the records in the table

8. Use the following statement to update the altitude of Station 4 from 90 to 92. To accomplish this, we will refer to the station using its ID, which is 2 in this case:

```
UPDATE stations SET alt = 92 WHERE id = 2;
```

You should get an output similar to the following:

```
mysql> UPDATE stations SET alt = 92 WHERE id = 2;
Query OK, 1 row affected (0.02 sec)
Rows matched: 1  Changed: 1  Warnings: 0
```

Figure 5.9 – The result of a successful update statement

9. Use the following SELECT statement to confirm that the changes were successful:

```
SELECT * FROM stations;
```

Congratulations – you have successfully updated a record in a SQL table! These steps are available in a screen recording at https://packt.link/OSzj4.

Relational databases also support deleting data, although that is something you should consider carefully because you can't recover your data after deletion. We'll learn how to delete data in the next project.

Project 5 – Deleting data from a MySQL table

In this project, you will learn how to delete data from a table using SQL. The scripts we'll be using are available at https://github.com/securetorobert/Arduino-Data-Communications/tree/main/chapter-5/MySQL-Create-Tables.

Follow these steps to complete this project:

1. Log into the remote server using the following shell command, making sure you replace the IP address with your server's:

```
ssh username@192.168.68.127
```

2. Log into MySQL using the following shell command, making sure you replace the username with the appropriate value:

```
mysql -u username -p
```

3. Provide the correct password at the next prompt.

4. Change to the `telemetry` schema by using the following statement on the MySQL prompt:

```
USE telemetry;
```

5. Use the following statement to read all of the data contained in the `stations` table:

```
SELECT * FROM stations;
```

The output should look similar to the following.

```
mysql> SELECT * FROM stations;
+------+--------------+-------+-------+-------+--------------+
| id   | stationName  | lat   | lon   | alt   | installedOn  |
+------+--------------+-------+-------+-------+--------------+
|    1 | Station 1    |   3.3 |     0 |   100 | 2023-02-28   |
|    2 | Station 4    |   3.4 |   0.1 |    92 | 2023-03-03   |
+------+--------------+-------+-------+-------+--------------+
2 rows in set (0.01 sec)
```

Figure 5.10 – The result of the SELECT statement

6. Use the following statement to delete `Station 4` from the table:

```
DELETE FROM stations WHERE id = 2;
```

7. The output of this command should look similar to the following.

```
mysql> DELETE FROM stations WHERE id = 2;
Query OK, 1 row affected (0.03 sec)
```

Figure 5.11 – The result of the DELETE statement

8. Use the following statement to confirm that the record is no longer in the table:

```
SELECT * FROM stations;
```

Congratulations – you have successfully deleted a record from a SQL table! These steps are available in a screen recording at https://packt.link/OSzj4.

With that, we have learned about CRUD and how to write statements using SQL. Let's proceed to implement a REST API for our MySQL database.

Implementing a REST API using JavaScript

So far, we have learned about creating tables, as well as inserting, updating, and deleting data using a relational database and a terminal. However, we do not have access to this terminal from our microcontrollers. To communicate with our database server from the microcontrollers, we will introduce a middleware, called an API server. There are various types of APIs but we will utilize **REST**.

We will implement a REST API using a server-side version of JavaScript called Node.js. From the website, it is described as an asynchronous, event-driven JavaScript runtime that lets you run JavaScript code outside of a web browser. You can learn more about it at `https://nodejs.org/en`. Let's begin by installing the Node.js CLI from the Ubuntu CLI.

Installing Node.js

Follow these steps to install Node.js on your instance of Ubuntu Server:

1. Log into the remote server using the following shell command, making sure you replace the IP address with your server's:

    ```
    ssh username@192.168.68.127
    ```

2. Use the following command to install Node.js:

    ```
    sudo snap install node –classic
    ```

    A successful installation will print an output similar to the following:

```
node (18/stable) 18.12.0 from OpenJS Foundation (iojs✓) installed
```

Figure 5.12 – The output of the Node.js installation

Congratulations – you now have Node.js installed. Next, we need to set up an application structure using a Node.js framework called Express. Express is a backend web application framework that provides a robust set of features for web and mobile applications, as well as APIs. You can learn more at `https://expressjs.com/`.

Setting up an application structure

Follow these steps to set up an application structure:

1. Create a new folder called `MyAPI` by using the following command:

    ```
    mkdir MyAPI
    ```

2. Navigate into that folder by using the following command:

    ```
    cd MyAPI
    ```

3. Generate the application structure by using the following command:

```
npx express-generator
```

4. If you get a prompt stating that you need to install `express-generator`, choose to install it and continue:

```
Need to install the following packages:
  express-generator@4.16.1
[Ok to proceed? (y)
```

Figure 5.13 – A prompt to install express-generator

5. Wait for the process to complete execution. You should see an output similar to the following:

```
create : routes/index.js
create : routes/users.js
create : views/
create : views/error.jade
create : views/index.jade
create : views/layout.jade
create : app.js
create : package.json
create : bin/
create : bin/www

install dependencies:
  $ npm install

run the app:
  $ DEBUG=myapi:* npm start
```

Figure 5.14 – The output of setting up an Express application

6. The basic application structure has been created, but you need to install dependencies. You can do that by running the following instruction from the command line:

```
npm install
```

7. Wait for the instruction to finish executing.

8. You are now ready to start the server for the first time. Run the following command to do so:

```
DEBUG=myapi:* npm start
```

You should get the following output from the command line:

```
> myapi@0.0.0 start
> node ./bin/www

  myapi:server Listening on port 3000 +0ms
```

Figure 5.15 – The Express application is running

Congratulations – you have successfully set up a Node.js application and started it! You can check this application out by browsing to the IP address of your server on port 3000. The URL will be similar to `http://192.168.68.127:3000` but be sure to replace the IP address with that of your server. All of these steps are shown in the video available at `https://packt.link/OSzj4`.

When you browse to the server URL on the appropriate port number, the server assumes that you are human and sends out a response in a human-readable format. However, what we want to implement is machine-to-machine communication, where a sensor can send out data to this application. For this to happen, we need to implement **routes**.

Understanding routes and routing

When you type a URL into a browser, you specify a route. If you type `http://192.168.68.127:3000`, then the route is said to be the **root**, specified by `/`. You also implicitly specify a **method**. That method is called **GET**. There are four methods that you can map to **CRUD** operations and that you can use to implement database operations. The relationship between these is shown in the following table:

REST Method	HTTP Method	Database Statement
Create	POST	INSERT
Retrieve	GET	SELECT
Update	PUT	UPDATE
Delete	DELETE	DELETE

In addition to the method, we will need to implement routing to implement the REST API. Since we have two tables, we will need to implement two routes:

- `/stations`: For CRUD operations on the `stations` table
- `/readings`: For CRUD operations on the `readings` table

The full URL for a route to the stations would be similar to `http://192.168.68.127:3000/stations`.

The Express application that we generated has a structure similar to the following:

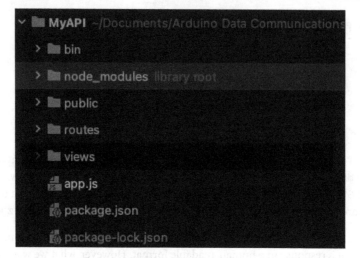

Figure 5.16 – The application folder's structure

Here is a brief explanation of what you can see:

- `bin`: This is a folder.

- `node_modules`: This folder contains all the modules that are installed by the Node.js interpreter. You normally don't need to transport this folder between deployments.

- `public`: This folder contains the resource files that are used by web pages for rendering purposes, such as images and stylesheets.

- `routes`: This folder contains the implementation of routes.

- `views`: This folder contains the implementation of web pages.

- `app.js`: This file contains the definition code for your application.

- `package.json`: This file contains metadata information about your application, as well as the names of versions of any dependency packages.

- `package-lock.json`: Ignore this file.

Within the `app.js` file, you will find two lines that define routers for the index path and users. The code snippet looks similar to the following:

```
var indexRouter = require('./routes/index');
var usersRouter = require('./routes/users');
```

The `var` keyword declares a **variable**, `indexRouter` is the name of the variable, and the `require()` function is similar to the `#include` directive. The parameter that's passed to `require()` is the name of a module in the `routes` directory.

The actual routing happens further down in the file. Here is the code snippet for that:

```
app.use('/', indexRouter);
app.use('/users', usersRouter);
```

Armed with this information, you are now ready to set up a router for stations.

Project 6 – Defining a route

In this project, we will create a route for stations that lets us define a REST API. The code for this project is available at `https://github.com/securetorobert/Arduino-Data-Communications/tree/main/chapter-5/MyAPI`.

Follow these steps to add a route for stations:

1. Edit the `package.json` file so that it looks as follows. It includes the `mysql` module as a dependency:

    ```
    {
      "name": "myapi",
      "version": "0.0.0",
      "private": true,
      "scripts": {
        "start": "node ./bin/www"
      },
      "dependencies": {
        "cookie-parser": "~1.4.4",
        "debug": "~2.6.9",
        "express": "~4.16.1",
        "http-errors": "~1.6.3",
        "jade": "~1.11.0",
        "morgan": "~1.9.1",
        "mysql2": "~2.3.3"
      }
    }
    ```

2. From the command line, run the following command to install the new module:

    ```
    npm install
    ```

3. Create a new file called `stations.js` in the `routes` folder.

4. Edit the file and add the following lines to include the necessary modules:

    ```
    var express = require('express');
    var router = express.Router();
    var mysql = require('mysql2');
    ```

5. Add the following lines to configure a connection to your server, making sure you edit the file to use the correct IP address, username, and password:

```
var conn = mysql.createConnection({
    host: '192.168.68.127',
    user: 'username',
    password: 'password',
    database: 'telemetry'
});
```

6. Add the following lines to create a route that implements the GET method:

```
router.get('/', function(req, res, next) {
    conn.connect();
    const query = 'SELECT * FROM stations';
    conn.query(query, function(error, results, fields) {
        if (error) throw error;

        res.send(results);
    });
    conn.end();
});
```

7. Add the following line to export the file as a module:

```
module.exports = router;
```

8. Save and close the file.

9. Open the app.js file for editing.

10. Add the following code below the line that starts with var usersRouter:

```
var stationsRouter = require('./routes/stations');
```

11. Add the following code after the code on line 24 – that is, app.use('/users', usersRouter);:

```
app.use('/stations', stationsRouter);
```

12. Save and close the file.

13. Run the following instruction from the command line:

```
DEBUG=myapi:* npm start
```

14. Open a browser and paste in the following URL, making sure you edit the IP address to reflect the one in use by your server: http://192.168.68.127:3000/stations.

You should get a result similar to the following:

```
[{"id":1,"stationName":"Station 1","lat":3.3,"lon":0,"alt":100,"installedOn":"2023-01-03T23:00:00.000Z"}]
```

Figure 5.17 – The output from the GET request

The content in the browser is in JSON format, although it isn't formatted for human readability.

Congratulations on completing this project. You have successfully added a route to retrieve data contained within the stations table. The rest of the code for create, update, and delete is contained within the stations module.

You can watch a step-by-step video detailing the instructions at https://packt.link/OSzj4.

Testing REST APIs isn't done by browsing them. Instead, you want to use a tool such as Postman for that. You can find a link to this in the *Further reading* section of this chapter.

You can watch a video of using Postman to test the APIs at https://packt.link/OSzj4.

So far, we have set up a REST API using JavaScript and Node.js. Let's do the same thing using Python, which is a different programming language.

Implementing a REST API using Python

If you are familiar with Python programming, then you might find yourself wondering whether you can write your APIs using Python instead of JavaScript. The answer is in the affirmative, and we are going to do just that.

We will make use of Python 3 and FastAPI to create the REST API that we need. FastAPI is a Python framework for building APIs. Python can be downloaded at https://www.python.org/downloads/.

Follow these steps to confirm that you have Python installed:

1. The first thing that you need to do is confirm that you have a version of Python installed that is at least 3.7. You can do that by running the following command from your CLI:

    ```
    python -V
    ```

    You should get an output similar to the following if you have Python installed:

    # Python 3.7.1

    Figure 5.18 – The result of checking the Python version

2. If you don't have Python installed, please visit the Python downloads page to get the right version for your operating system.

3. Install a virtual environment. You need to do this to avoid package conflicts. You can run the following command to install a virtual environment:

    ```
    pip3 install virtualenv
    ```

4. Wait for the command to complete.

5. Create a virtual environment for working with FastAPI by running the following command:

    ```
    virtualenv my_fast_api
    ```

6. Run the following command to activate the virtual environment:

    ```
    source my_fast_api/bin/activate
    ```

Once you have Python installed and the environment activated, you may proceed to install the two dependencies that we need.

Installing dependencies

Follow these steps to install the necessary dependencies:

1. The first dependency that we need is **FastAPI**. You can install it by running the following command from the terminal:

    ```
    pip3 install fastapi
    ```

    You should get an output similar to the following:

```
Collecting fastapi
  Downloading fastapi-0.92.0-py3-none-any.whl (56 kB)
    |████████████████████████████████| 56 kB 449 kB/s
Collecting pydantic!=1.7,!=1.7.1,!=1.7.2,!=1.7.3,!=1.8,!=1.8.1,<2.0.0,>=1.6.2
  Downloading pydantic-1.10.5-cp37-cp37m-macosx_10_9_x86_64.whl (2.8 MB)
    |████████████████████████████████| 2.8 MB 1.2 MB/s
Collecting starlette<0.26.0,>=0.25.0
  Downloading starlette-0.25.0-py3-none-any.whl (66 kB)
    |████████████████████████████████| 66 kB 1.9 MB/s
Collecting typing-extensions>=4.2.0
  Downloading typing_extensions-4.5.0-py3-none-any.whl (27 kB)
Collecting anyio<5,>=3.4.0
  Downloading anyio-3.6.2-py3-none-any.whl (80 kB)
    |████████████████████████████████| 80 kB 2.1 MB/s
Requirement already satisfied: idna>=2.8 in /Users/robert/anaconda3/lib/python3.7/site-packages (from anyio<5,>=3.4.0->starlett
e<0.26.0,>=0.25.0->fastapi) (2.8)
Collecting sniffio>=1.1
  Downloading sniffio-1.3.0-py3-none-any.whl (10 kB)
Installing collected packages: typing-extensions, sniffio, anyio, starlette, pydantic, fastapi
Successfully installed anyio-3.6.2 fastapi-0.92.0 pydantic-1.10.5 sniffio-1.3.0 starlette-0.25.0 typing-extensions-4.5.0
```

Figure 5.19 – Installing FastAPI

2. The next dependency that we need to install is a server application. We will make use of **Uvicorn**. Use the following CLI command to install it:

    ```
    pip3 install uvicorn[standard]
    ```

Wait for the installation to complete, then proceed to the next section, where we'll create a folder and start writing our API in Python.

Creating the application structure

Follow these steps to create the application structure:

1. Create a folder using the following command.

    ```
    mkdir MyFastAPI
    ```

2. Navigate into the folder by using the following command:

    ```
    cd MyFastAPI
    ```

3. Use the following command to create a file:

    ```
    touch main.py
    ```

4. Open the main.py file with any editor of your choice to begin writing code.

5. Paste the following code into the main.py file:

    ```
    from fastapi import FastAPI
    app = FastAPI()
    @app.get("/")
    def read_root():
        return {"App": "MySQL API using FastAPI"}

    @app.get("/stations")
    def read_stations():
        return {"stations": []}
    ```

6. Save the file.

7. Run the following command from the terminal to start the server:

    ```
    uvicorn main:app -reload
    ```

8. You should get an output similar to the following:

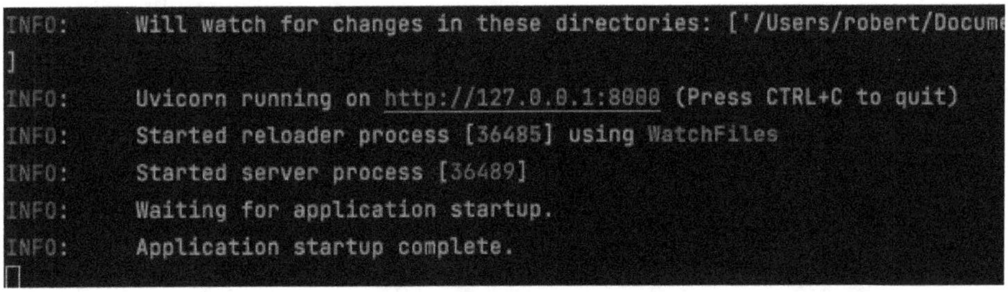

```
INFO:      Will watch for changes in these directories: ['/Users/robert/Docume
]
INFO:      Uvicorn running on http://127.0.0.1:8000 (Press CTRL+C to quit)
INFO:      Started reloader process [36485] using WatchFiles
INFO:      Started server process [36489]
INFO:      Waiting for application startup.
INFO:      Application startup complete.
```

Figure 5.20 – Running the server

9.   Browse to the following URL, making sure you replace the IP address with that of your server: `http://127.0.0.1:8000/`.

10. You should see a familiar JSON output.

Congratulations – you now have a stub for a REST API that you created using Python! The preceding steps are illustrated in a video available at `https://packt.link/OSzj4`. You will find a more featureful implementation at `https://github.com/PacktPublishing/Arduino-Data-Communications/tree/main/chapter-5/MyFastAPI`.

With that, we have implemented a REST API for MySQL, which is a relational database. Let's look at what is needed for InfluxDB, the time series database that we set up in a previous chapter.

REST API for InfluxDB

InfluxDB has an API baked in that makes it possible to make CRUD calls without having to implement a separate application.

Let's begin by getting some sample data into our instance of InfluxDB.

Getting sample data into InfluxDB

Follow these steps to create a bucket and populate it with some sample data:

1.   Browse to the URL of the server that hosts your InfluxDB instance. The format of the URL is `http://192.168.68.127:8086/`. Ensure that you replace the IP address in the URL with the one for your server.

2.   Sign in with your **username** and **password**.

3.   Use the menu on the left to navigate to the **Buckets** screen, as shown in the following screenshot:

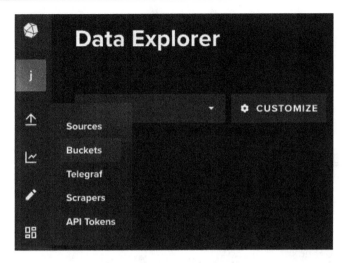

Figure 5.21 – Navigating to the Buckets screen

4. Click on the + **CREATE BUCKET** button on the right of the screen, then fill in noaa in the **Name** field. Since this is a private server, I will set **Delete Data** to **NEVER**. If you would like to have InfluxDB manage your data over time, use the **OLDER THAN** option. This information is shown in the following screenshot:

Figure 5.22 – Creating a bucket

5. Click on the **CREATE** button.

6. Navigate to the **Data Explorer** page.

7. Click on the **SCRIPT EDITOR** button on the right of the page.

8. Paste the following script into the editor:

```
import "experimental/csv"

relativeToNow = (tables=<-) => tables
    |> elapsed()
    |> sort(columns: ["_time"], desc: true)
    |> cumulativeSum(columns: ["elapsed"])
    |> map(fn: (r) => ({r with _time: time(v: int(v: now())) -
r.elapsed * 1000000000)}))
csv.from(url: "https://raw.githubusercontent.com/securetorobert/
Arduino-Data-Communications/main/chapter-5/InfluxDB-Sample-Data-
NOAA/noaa.csv")
    |> relativeToNow()
    |> limit(n: 100)
    |> to(bucket: "noaa")
```

The page should look as follows:

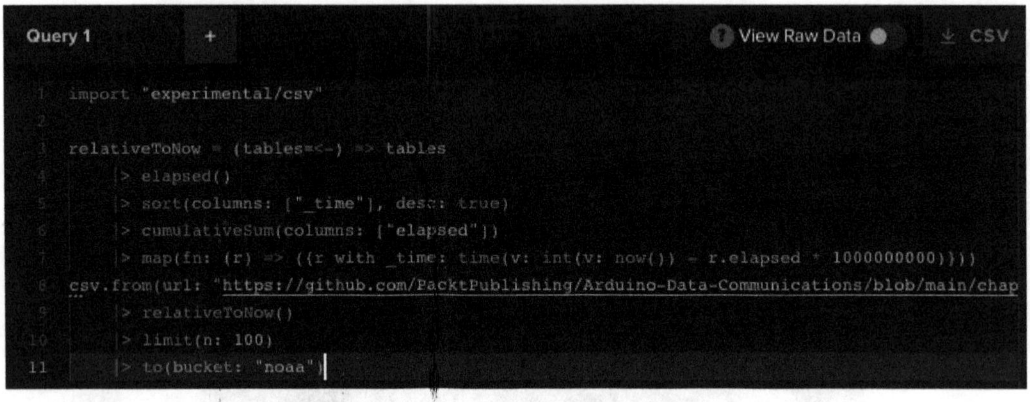

Figure 5.23 – Loading data into a bucket

9. Click on the **SUBMIT** button and wait for the operation to complete.

You can view these steps in a Code in Action video at https://packt.link/OSzj4.

Congratulations – you have data in InfluxDB, and we are almost ready to connect via an API to read it back out! But before we do that, we need to generate an API token.

Generating an API token

Follow these steps to generate an API token:

1. Use the menu on the left to navigate to the **API Tokens** page.
2. Click on the **+ GENERATE API TOKEN** button.
3. Choose **All Access API Token** from the dropdown.
4. Fill in the **Description** field.
5. Click **Save**.
6. Copy the displayed token and store it somewhere safe. A password manager is a good place to do this.

Congratulations – you now have an API token that you can utilize for API calls! Let's proceed and make some API calls.

Making an API call

Follow these steps to fetch data from the **noaa** bucket using Postman:

1. Launch Postman. You can install it from the following URL if you don't have it installed: `https://www.postman.com/downloads/`.
2. Set the HTTP method to `GET`.
3. Set the URL to `http://192.168.68.127:8086/api/v2`.
4. Replace the URL with the correct IP address of your server.
5. Switch to the **Authorization** tab and set **Type** to **API Key**.
6. Set **Key** to **Authorization**, **Value** to your API token, and **Add to** to **Header**.
7. Switch to the **Headers** tab and add a new entry with **Key** set to **Content-Type** and **Value** set to **application/json**.
8. Switch to the **Body** tab.
9. Choose the radio button beside **x-www-form-urlencoded**.
10. Set **Key** to `db` and **Value** to `noaa`.
11. Set **Key** to `q` and **Value** to the following query:

    ```
    SELECT * FROM average_temperature
    ```

    Your screen will look similar to the following:

Figure 5.24 – Making an API call

12. Click on the **Send** button. You will get an output at the bottom of the screen similar to the following:

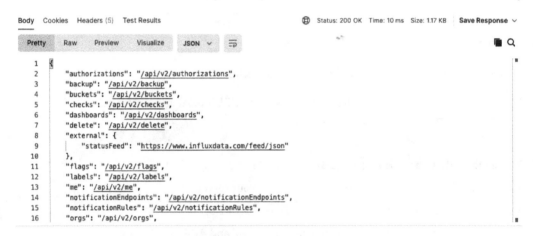

Figure 5.25 – The response from the API call

Congratulations – you have made a successful API call! You can see these steps in action in the following video: https://packt.link/OSzj4.

There is just one problem with our query: it doesn't return the data contained in the bucket!

Let's return to the InfluxDB web console and look at what's going on in the **Data Explorer** area. Take a look at the following screenshot, where we are using **Query Builder**:

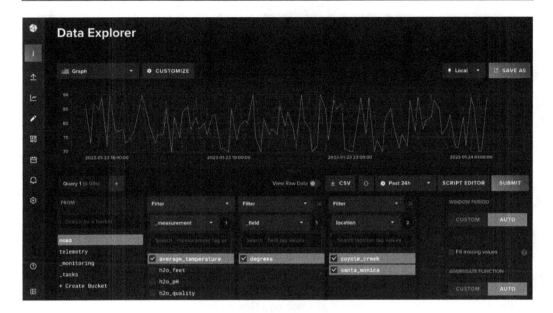

Figure 5.26 – InfluxDB's Query Builder

We can see that the upper half of the window is taken up by a chart, while the lower half is taken up by a series of windows. These can be broken down as follows:

- **FROM**: This is where we select our bucket, similar to a database schema
- **Filter**: This is where we select our measurement, similar to a table
- **Filter**: This is where we select our field
- **Filter**: This is where we select any tags that we want to filter by
- **WINDOW PERIOD**: This is where we want to set our granularity

There is also a window that lets us set how far back we want to fetch data from. InfluxDB works with a custom language called Flux. We can write Flux by switching to **Script Editor**, which provides a code window on the left and a filter on the right that makes it easy to find what we need. The following screenshot shows an example Flux query:

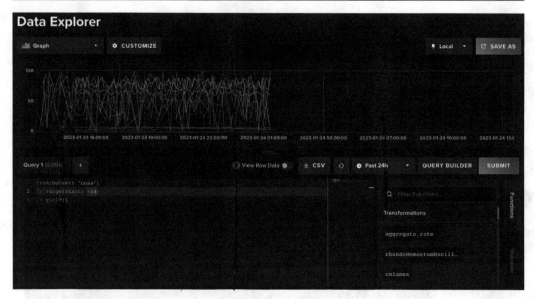

Figure 5.27 – Writing a Flux query

Flux can generally be divided into three parts:

- **Source**: Defined with a `from()` function, this generally contains the name of the bucket to read data from

- **Filters, ranges, aggregates**: These are functions that limit the volume of data that gets returned

- **Yield**: This returns the results to the user

All functions are separated by a **pipe-forward operator** (| >). Armed with this information, let's pass the following query to our API:

```
from(bucket: "noaa")
        |> range(start: -24h, stop: -12h)
        |> filter(fn: (r) => r._measurement == "average_temperature")
        |> yield()
```

To run this query, we will need to make a few changes to our settings in Postman. These are detailed here:

1. Change the HTTP method to POST.

2. Change the URL so that it looks like `http://192.168.68.127:8086/api/v2/query?orgID=organization`.

3. In **Headers**, change **Content-Type** to `application/vnd.flux`.

4. Generate a custom API token that can read and write to all buckets and Telegraf. Copy this token and replace what you have in the **Authorization** window with **Token** and a space followed by the token.

5. Type the Flux query into the **Body** tab as raw. Make sure you use two tabs before each pipe-forward.

The following screenshot shows the output of this API call:

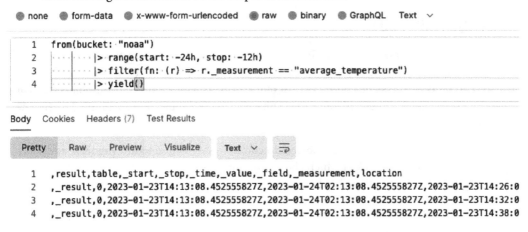

Figure 5.28 – The Flux query in the API call

Congratulations – you have finally fetched data from InfluxDB! These steps are shown in the Code in Action video available at `https://packt.link/OSzj4`.

With InfluxDB, as with most time series databases, you typically want to perform two operations: create and retrieve. These are represented by two different URLs, as shown here:

Action	URL	Method
Create	/api/v2/write	POST
Retrieve	/api/v2/query	POST

When you communicate with a REST API, the server you are communicating with needs to allocate resources for this. Let's use an analogy of the server being a house, and the requests being sent to the house being packages. In this scenario, every package that gets sent to the house needs to be received by someone in the house. As a result, there is a limit to the number of packages that can be processed at any given point in time.

Sometimes, the API server runs out of resources, encounters an error, needs to restart, or is unable to write to the DB. The problem with all of these scenarios is that REST is stateless, so once the function's execution completes, you no longer have the information that was sent to it.

One solution to these problems is to introduce a queue. This way, the messages wait until resources are available.

As an analogy, instead of packages getting delivered to your house and hoping that someone is available to receive them, the post office could hold your packages in a box and you could go over whenever you are free to retrieve as many as you can carry at once. That way, you could set up a schedule for retrieving your packages.

This is where **MQTT** comes in.

Working with MQTT

MQTT implements publish-subscribe **machine-to-machine** (**M2M**) communications in a lightweight manner. This makes it possible to communicate over limited bandwidth. It implements a **broker**, which you can think of as a stand-in for the post office. Brokers have **topics**, and endpoints **publish** *messages* into these topics. Other endpoints then **subscribe** to these topics and are notified when new messages are published.

MQTT brokers make it possible for IoT devices to communicate without knowing their addresses using topics. They also keep track of which clients are connected to the network using a keep-alive messaging system. MQTT has three key benefits:

- **Efficiency**: The implementation uses the least amount of energy and data to send messages across
- **Reliability**: The implementation has various quality-of-service levels that determine how messages are stored by the broker and either sent to clients or received by clients
- **Flexibility**: The implementation lets developers choose their message expiration settings

MQTT certainly has its disadvantages, which include the following:

- **Latency**: The MQTT broker introduces some delays in communications
- **Security**: MQTT lacks encryption by default

There are numerous MQTT brokers, but we will be working with an open source broker called **Mosquitto**. It's hosted at `https://mosquitto.org/`. Let's look at the architecture that we need to configure to support sending data into our database (InfluxDB) using MQTT:

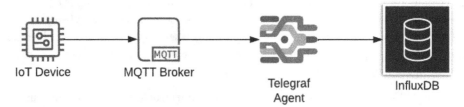

Figure 5.29 – The MQTT broker architecture

We will need to configure both an MQTT **broker** (Mosquitto) as well as a Telegraf **agent** for our sensor readings to end up in our database.

Installing the Mosquitto MQTT broker

Follow these steps to install the MQTT broker on your Ubuntu Server installation:

1. Open a terminal on your computer.

2. Connect remotely to the Ubuntu Server instance using the following command-line instruction. Make sure you replace the IP address with the correct one:

    ```
    ssh username@192.168.68.127
    ```

3. Use the following command-line instruction to install Mosquitto:

    ```
    sudo apt install mosquitto
    ```

4. Use the following command to install additional tools for managing and testing:

    ```
    sudo apt install mosquitto-clients
    ```

5. Use the following commands to stop and start the broker:

    ```
    sudo systemctl stop mosquito
    sudo systemctl start mosquito
    ```

Congratulations – you now have an MQTT broker up and running! You can see these steps in the following video: https://packt.link/OSzj4.

Now, let's install the Telegraf agent.

Installing the Telegraf agent

Follow these steps to install Telegraf:

1. Open a terminal on your computer.

2. Connect remotely to the Ubuntu Server instance using the following command-line instruction. Make sure you replace the IP address with the correct one:

    ```
    ssh username@192.168.68.127
    ```

3. Visit the following URL in a browser: https://portal.influxdata.com/downloads/.

4. Scroll down to the **Telegraf** section.

5. Choose a version from the first dropdown.

6. Choose a platform from the second dropdown.

7. Copy the instructions in the window.

8. Paste the instructions into the terminal window and hit *Enter*.

9.   Wait for the instruction to finish executing.

10. Log into your instance of InfluxDB.

11. Visit the **Telegraf** page and create a new configuration.

12. When you're asked where you would like to get data from, search for and choose **MQTT**.

13. Proceed to save the configuration, then follow the instructions to copy the newly generated token and paste it into the command line of your Ubuntu server.

14. Start Telegraf as instructed. The configuration page looks similar to the following:

Figure 5.30 – The Telegraf configuration page

As usual, you should save the token and instructions somewhere safe.

Congratulations – you have installed the Telegraf agent! You can see these steps in a video at https://packt.link/OSzj4.

Summary

In this chapter, you learned how to configure a REST API layer so that you can communicate with an RDBMS over the internet. You also learned how to communicate with InfluxDB over a REST API. Finally, you learned about MQTT and also configured an MQTT broker and Telegraf so that data sent over MQTT can end up in the database.

In the next chapter, we will discuss the various communication technologies that you can utilize to move data from your Arduino board into these databases.

Further reading

To learn more about the topics that were covered in this chapter, take a look at the following resources:

- *MySQL statements*: `https://dev.mysql.com/doc/refman/8.0/en/sql-statements.html`

- *Node.js*: `https://nodejs.org/en/`

- *Express.js framework*: `https://expressjs.com/`

- *Postman*: `https://www.postman.com/`

- *Flux*: `https://docs.influxdata.com/flux/v0.x/get-started/`

- *Writing data with the InfluxDB API*: `https://docs.influxdata.com/influxdb/v2.0/write-data/developer-tools/api/`

- *Retrieving data with the InfluxDB API*: `https://docs.influxdata.com/influxdb/v2.0/query-data/execute-queries/influx-api/`

- *MQTT and Mosquitto*: `https://mosquitto.org/man/mqtt-7.html`

- *FastAPI*: `https://fastapi.tiangolo.com/`

Part 2:
Sending Data

In this section, you will learn about various communication technologies and examples of how to utilize some of them.

This section has the following chapters:

- *Chapter 6, Utilizing Various Communication Technologies*
- *Chapter 7, Communicating with LoRaWAN*
- *Chapter 8, Working with Ethernet*
- *Chapter 9, Leveraging Cellular Communication Technology*
- *Chapter 10, Communicating via HC-12*
- *Chapter 11, Managing Communication with RS-485*

6

Utilizing Various Communication Technologies

We have set up infrastructure that lets us communicate with our databases over a network such as a **Local Area Network (LAN)** or over the **internet**. This chapter goes into detail about the choice of how we might communicate with these networks. You will learn about the various communication options based on the distance of your device from the closest radio antenna, and you will complete two projects that illustrate communicating over a **Wi-Fi** network to a REST endpoint.

In this chapter, we are going to cover the following main topics:

- Utilizing short-range communications
- Utilizing medium-range communications
- Utilizing long-range communications
- Communicating with REST APIs

By the end of this chapter, you will have gained clarity about what communication technology to choose based on the distance that you need to cover. You will also have taken sensor readings and sent them to a REST API endpoint over Wi-Fi.

Technical requirements

We will be making use of the following in this chapter:

- The Arduino IDE
- Arduino MKR WiFi 1010
- Arduino MKR ENV Shield
- Ubuntu Server

- MySQL database

- Node.js

The code for this chapter is available at the following GitHub URL: `https://github.com/PacktPublishing/Arduino-Data-Communications/tree/main/chapter-6`.

Utilizing short-range communications

Short-range communication typically limits itself to utilization within a building, such as a home. Technologies such as Bluetooth, Zigbee, and Wi-Fi are frequently used for short-range communication. Let's briefly consider some of these technologies.

Bluetooth

When you work with Bluetooth, the network that you set up is frequently called a **Personal Area Network (PAN)**. These networks have extremely short coverage, usually around 30 feet or 10 meters, and normally support peer-to-peer communication. You can find these frequently implemented between phones and other devices such as speakers, headsets, wearables, and automobiles. Some microcontrollers that have onboard Wi-Fi also have Bluetooth capabilities. You will need to read the documentation of the board to find this information. For example, the Arduino MKR WiFi 1010 has an onboard u-blox Nina-W10 chip that gives it Wi-Fi and Bluetooth capabilities. As a result, you can write and deploy an application that runs on a mobile device and uses Bluetooth to communicate with this microcontroller board.

Bluetooth will not work across an entire building and isn't really meant to connect multiple devices simultaneously. This brings us to the next technology.

Zigbee

When you think about connecting multiple devices in a building, Zigbee is one technology that bubbles up to the top. It doesn't consume a lot of power. It's possible to have one **controller (or coordinator)** that connects to another network, such as the internet, while **terminals** can connect to the coordinator or act as **routers** for terminals that are too far away from the coordinator. If you think of any IoT devices that need a base station before you can control them, they are most likely using Zigbee. Devices can communicate at distances up to 20 meters if there are no obstacles between them.

Let's consider one more communication technology that lets you communicate over a slightly longer distance as well as across networks.

Wi-Fi

You will need to set up a Wi-Fi **base station** or **access point** (**AP**) before you can connect other devices to it. Wi-Fi networks are so ubiquitous that we hardly think about them. This is especially true when we consider the fact that a lot of devices use Wi-Fi networks to communicate to servers over the internet, and not to other devices on the same network. For example, you could have many phones on the same Wi-Fi network that utilize the network to access the internet but don't communicate with each other.

We have made use of Wi-Fi networks in two ways so far. We have used a network to enable our Arduino MKR board to connect to the internet, and we have used it to connect our Ubuntu server to the internet to install software. Later on, we will utilize our Wi-Fi network to enable communication between our Arduino MKR board and our databases running on the Ubuntu server.

Wi-Fi devices can connect to a base station that is at most 100 meters away, without obstacles. However, many devices do not have radios capable of connecting beyond a few meters, and the communication quality drops at that point. Beyond this range, you will need to set up a **repeater** or multiple APs in order to maintain quality.

Wi-Fi is great when power is not an issue. If you need to utilize something that doesn't require the range that Wi-Fi provides while also requiring frugality in power consumption, then consider utilizing Zigbee.

If you have devices that need to operate outdoors within a 1 km radius, or indoors where you have interference from machinery, such as on a factory floor, then the technologies we have discussed so far will not work. Let's look at additional technologies in the next section.

Utilizing medium-range communications

While short-range communication technologies had a maximum range between 10 meters and 100 meters, medium-range communications technologies will let us communicate at a distance of up to 1 km. Let's briefly discuss two of them.

RS-485

Wireless signals are not suitable in certain situations where the signals could interfere with the operation of machines, such as in a hospital setting, or where the machines could interfere with the signals, such as in a factory. In these situations, it is normal to utilize cables. The RS-485 standard defines the electrical communications for communication between two systems without specifying the protocol to be used. The cable used in RS-485 communications may be as long as 1.2 km long while resisting electromagnetic interference from electric motors.

RS-485 isn't limited to industrial settings and is also utilized in building automation and the control of lights and security panels.

When we have open space, such as an outdoor setting, we need different technology.

HC-12

HC-12 utilizes wireless transceivers to communicate over a distance reaching up to 1 km outdoors on a 433 MHz frequency. HC-12 implements serial communications and supports 100 channels.

When we need to communicate beyond the 1 km limit, we have to look at other technologies.

Utilizing long-range communications

Beyond PANs and **Local Area Networks** (**LANs**), there are situations that require microcontrollers to communicate over longer distances. Sometimes these devices are fixed, while at other times they are in motion. The following technologies cater to these scenarios.

LoRaWAN

LoRaWAN is based on the promise of two things: *low power* and *long range*. It is not designed for transmitting at broadband speeds, but the small packets of data that it transmits can reach great distances without requiring the devices to consume a lot of power. LoRaWAN networks utilize a point-to-multipoint topology. LoRaWAN gateways are connected to power and the internet, and they relay messages from endpoint clients. LoRaWAN devices can communicate at distances reaching 16 km in open fields, and 5 km in densely populated areas.

LoRaWAN gateways come in both indoor and outdoor variants, and you can easily set one up yourself. Additionally, you can configure your gateways to be either public or private. If a public gateway is available, you can set up your devices to connect to it and start transmitting data.

LoRaWAN communicates over unlicensed frequencies but these vary across different regions of the world.

LoRaWAN requires you to set up your own infrastructure or to find a local provider that has already set up infrastructure. This arrangement might not always be suitable for you. This is where SigFox comes in.

SigFox

SigFox has operating principles that are similar to LoRaWAN. The focus is on low power consumption and low bandwidth transmission over long distances. LoRaWAN limits data transmission to 12 bytes per message, and a maximum of 140 data transmissions daily. SigFox doesn't require you to set up your own infrastructure. Instead, the company behind the technology partners with local telecoms providers to provide network coverage. SigFox is reported to be widely used in smart city applications as well as in providing communications for utilities (power or water) meters.

SigFox coverage is available in over 70 countries. But, SigFox isn't free to use since it leverages existing service providers. The communication range is between 3 km and 10 km.

If SigFox and LoRa do not meet your needs, either due to availability or due to bandwidth limitations, then consider cellular communication.

Cellular communication

Cellular communication has a number of benefits. First is the ubiquitous nature. Cellular communication technology is old and as a result, networks are available in a lot of places. While they are mostly used to transmit voice, they are quite robust at providing both text-based communications using **Short Message Services (SMS)**, as well as data transmission, with the only limitation being imposed by the generation of the cellular technology that is in use.

Cellular communication technology is widely used in IoT applications where assets are in motion but need to report telemetry. It is also used in geofencing. Cellular communication supports a maximum distance of 35 km from base stations.

Cellular communication takes place over licensed spectrum and connectivity to networks is provided by a **Subscriber Identity Module (SIM)**. This could be either physical or electronic.

With the information given in the previous section, you should be equipped to decide on which communication technology to utilize based on your specific needs.

Before we utilize any long-range communication technologies, let's test the connectivity between our microcontroller and our APIs.

Communicating with REST APIs

To test the connection between our microcontroller and our REST API, please follow these steps:

1. Log in remotely to your Ubuntu server.

2. Navigate to an empty folder.

   Clone the GitHub repository for this book using the following CLI command:

   ```
   git clone https://github.com/PacktPublishing/Arduino-Data-
   Communications.git
   ```

3. Navigate into the API project folder for this chapter using the following CLI command:

   ```
   cd Arduino-Data-Communications/chapter-6/MyAPI/
   ```

4. Inspect the folder contents using the following command:

   ```
   ls -l
   ```

You should have an output similar to the following.

```
johnthas@raspberrypi:~/Arduino-Data-Communications/chapter-6/MyAPI$ ls -l
total 100
-rw-rw-r--   1 johnthas johnthas  1253 Mar  7 12:03 app.js
drwxrwxr-x   2 johnthas johnthas  4096 Feb 25 14:29 bin
drwxrwxr-x 103 johnthas johnthas  4096 Mar  7 12:12 node_modules
-rw-rw-r--   1 johnthas johnthas 73371 Mar  7 12:12 package-lock.json
-rw-rw-r--   1 johnthas johnthas   317 Mar  7 12:03 package.json
drwxrwxr-x   3 johnthas johnthas  4096 Feb 25 14:29 public
drwxrwxr-x   2 johnthas johnthas  4096 Mar  7 12:11 routes
drwxrwxr-x   2 johnthas johnthas  4096 Feb 25 14:29 views
```

Figure 6.1 – The folder contents

5. Feel free to read through any of the files to get a sense of what is contained in them. The package.json file contains the list of modules that we need to install. Install the dependencies by running the following command:

    ```
    npm install
    ```

6. Navigate to the routes folder using the following command:

    ```
    cd routes
    ```

7. The database connection now uses connection pooling and has been moved to a new file to make it easier to edit. The last time that we worked with database connections, we opened one connection whenever we got a REST request, and we closed it afterward. With a connection pool, we establish a connection and keep it open. In this case, our pool can have up to 10 connections open, handling 10 requests simultaneously. Inspect the file and edit the necessary credentials. Here is an example of what the code looks like:

    ```
    var mysql = require('mysql2');

    var conn = mysql.createPool({
        host: '192.168.68.100',
        user: 'db_username',
        password: 'db_password',
        database: 'telemetry',
        waitForConnections: true,
        connectionLimit: 10,
        maxIdle: 10,
        idleTimeout: 60000,
        queueLimit: 0
    });

    module.exports = conn;
    ```

8. Inspect the `stations.js` file. The definition of the database connection has changed to use our new module. This is what the line reflecting the change looks like:

```
var conn = require('./dbConn');
```

9. Inspect the `readings.js` file. This file will provide the endpoints for **POST**ing readings and also **GET**ting readings. The code within the file is split into four sections: the declarations, the GET router, the POST router, and the exports. The code is as shown here:

```
var express = require('express');
var router = express.Router();

var conn = require('./dbConn');

router.get('/', function(req, res, next) {
    const query = 'SELECT * FROM readings';
    conn.query(query, function(error, results, fields) {
        if (error) throw error;

        res.send(results);
    });
});

router.post('/', function(req, res, next) {
    const query = 'INSERT INTO `readings` (`stationid`,
`epochs`, `temperature`, `humidity`) VALUES (?, ?, ?, ?)';
    conn.query(query, [req.body.stationid, new Date(), req.body.
temperature, req.body.humidity], function (error, results) {
        if (error) throw error;

        res.send(results);
    });
});

router.put('/', function(req, res, next) {
    res.send('update a reading');
});

router.delete('/', function(req, res, next) {
    res.send('delete a reading');
});

module.exports = router;
```

10. In `router.post()`, we see a new type of **SQL** query. This style uses a prepared statement to avoid excessive concatenation of strings and other data types. Instead, the variables that need to be passed into the `INSERT` statement are represented by question marks. Here is the snippet once more:

```
const query = 'INSERT INTO `readings` (`stationid`, `epochs`,
`temperature`, `humidity`) VALUES (?, ?, ?, ?)';
```

11. When we eventually execute the query, we pass in the values as an array. You can see that in the following line of code. Notice that for the second parameter, `epochs`, we pass in the current date and time on the server. This is an important concept to note, in which we will need to correlate the time at the sensor location to the time of the server:

```
conn.query(query, [req.body.stationid, new Date(), req.body.
temperature, req.body.humidity], function (error, results) {
    if (error) throw error;

    res.send(results);
});
```

12. The `function (error, results) {}` within `conn.query()` is a result handler. It returns an error if one is encountered while attempting to execute the query, otherwise, it returns a `result` object. We return this result to the function caller.

13. Return to the outer folder by using the following CLI command:

```
cd ..
```

14. Inspect the `app.js` file. We have added two lines to this file so that the `readings` router is recognized.

15. Start the server using the following CLI command:

```
DEBUG=myapi:* npm start
```

You should get an output similar to the following.

```
johnthas@raspberrypi:~/Arduino-Data-Communications/chapter-6/MyAPI$ DEBUG=myapi:* npm start

> myapi@0.0.0 start
> node ./bin/www

  myapi:server Listening on port 3000 +0ms
```

Figure 6.2 – NPM start

Congratulations, you have a REST server capable of inserting data into the MySQL database running on the server. You can find the preceding steps in a video at the following URL: https://packt.link/aQRgX.

You will need to check that things are working as expected, so let's do that using Postman.

Testing the API endpoint using Postman

If you don't have Postman installed, visit this URL to download a version for your operating system – `https://www.postman.com/`:

1. Test that you can get readings by using the `GET` handler and proving the URL in the following format, making sure to replace the IP address with the correct one for your server: `http://192.168.68.105:3000/readings`.

2. Your Postman window should look similar to the following screenshot:

Figure 6.3 – Postman GET settings

3. Click the **Send** button on the right of the screen.

4. The result at the bottom of the screen should look similar to the following screenshot.

```
Body   Cookies   Headers (7)   Test Results

  Pretty    Raw    Preview    Visualize    JSON  ∨    ⇄

   1    [
   2        {
   3            "id": 1,
   4            "stationID": 1,
   5            "epochs": "2023-02-28T03:37:08.000Z",
   6            "temperature": 11.6,
   7            "humidity": 66
   8        },
   9        {
```

Figure 6.4 – The GET response

5. Now that we are sure we can communicate with the REST server, let's post a reading to the server. Change the endpoint to `POST` and the URL to `http://192.168.68.105:3000/readings` while making sure you adjust the IP address to the correct one. The result should look similar to the following screenshot.

```
POST    ∨    http://192.168.68.105:3000/readings
```

Figure 6.5 – The Postman POST settings

6. We need to send in a **payload** along with our request. The payload contains the data that we would like inserted into the table. Our payload is a JSON object with values as shown here:

```
{
    "stationid": 1,
    "epochs": 1,
    "temperature": 30.5,
    "humidity": 65
}
```

7. The payload is contained in the **Body** tab and is specified as **raw JSON**. The setting looks similar to the following screenshot.

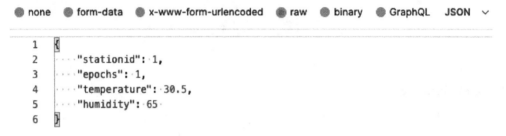

Figure 6.6 – The request body

8. Click the **Send** button.

9. The result should look similar to the following:

Figure 6.7 – The POST response

Congratulations, you have successfully tested the REST API server. The preceding steps are shown in a video at the following URL: https://packt.link/aQRgX.

Finally, let's connect our Arduino MKR WiFi 1010 to our server so that we can send sensor readings across.

Project 1 – Send sensor readings to the REST API

In this project, we will make use of the Arduino MKR WiFi 1010 and the MKR ENV Shield to collect temperature and humidity readings and send those to the REST API for storage in the MySQL database that we have been working with. The code for this project is available at the following GitHub URL: https://github.com/PacktPublishing/Arduino-Data-Communications/tree/main/chapter-6/MKR-WIFI-ENV-REST-Simple.

Please follow these steps to complete this project:

1. Launch the Arduino IDE.

2. Create a new sketch.

3. We need to include certain libraries, including the arduino_secrets.h library that we haven't created yet. Proceed to add the following to the sketch:

```
#include <Arduino_MKRENV.h>
#include <SPI.h>
#include <WiFiNINA.h>
#include <Arduino_JSON.h>
#include "arduino_secrets.h"
```

4. Let's declare some constants and variables. The following will be familiar from previous projects:

```
unsigned long lastRead = millis();
const int myDelay = 15000;

float temperature, humidity;
const int stationId = 1;

char ssid[] = SECRET_SSID;
char pass[] = SECRET_PASS;

int status = WL_IDLE_STATUS;
```

5. Let's add three new variables. We need these to communicate over HTTP to our REST API. The server variable holds the IP address, the port variable holds the port number, and the client variable will establish the connection. The declarations are shown here:

```
IPAddress server(192,168,68,120);
uint16_t port = 3000;
WiFiClient client;
```

6. We do four things within the `setup()` function: open the `Serial` interface, initialize the MKR ENV, connect to Wi-Fi, and print out a notification to `Serial`. This is all shown in the following code:

```
void setup() {
  Serial.begin(115200);
  while (!ENV.begin()) {
    Serial.println("Failed to initialive ENV Shield, waiting
...");
    delay(10000);
  }
  while (status != WL_CONNECTED) {
    Serial.println("Attempting WiFi connection ...");
    status = WiFi.begin(ssid, pass);
    delay(10000);
  }
  Serial.println("Connected to WiFi");
}
```

7. Within the `loop()` function, we set up a condition that only executes after every 15 seconds. This is shown in the following code:

```
void loop() {

  if (millis() - lastRead > myDelay) {


  }
}
```

8. Within the inner condition, we begin by reading our temperature and humidity, and then ensuring that our HTTP `client` is not connected to the server. The code is shown here:

```
lastRead = millis();
temperature = ENV.readTemperature();
humidity = ENV.readHumidity();
Serial.print("T: ");
Serial.println(temperature);
Serial.print("H: ");
Serial.println(humidity);

client.stop();
```

9. Next, we attempt to connect to our server on the given port. If we are unable to establish a connection, we simply print out a notification. This is shown in the following code:

```
if (client.connect(server, port)) {



} else {
  Serial.println("Can't connect to server");
}
```

10. If we succeed in establishing a connection, we create a JSON payload, convert it to a string, and send it to the server via HTTP POST. The code is shown here:

```
JSONVar payload;
payload["stationid"] = stationId;
payload["epochs"] = 1;
payload["temperature"] = temperature;
payload["humidity"] = humidity;

String p = JSON.stringify(payload);

Serial.println("Connected to server, posting data");
/*client.println("GET /readings HTTP/1.1");
client.println();*/
client.println("POST /readings HTTP/1.1");
client.println("Content-Type: application/json");
client.print("Content-Length: ");
client.println(p.length());
client.println();
client.println(p);
client.println("Connection: close");
client.println();
```

11. Finally, in the Arduino IDE, add a new tab and save it as `arduino_secrets.h`. Put in the following code and input the correct values for your Wi-Fi network:

```
#define SECRET_SSID ""
#define SECRET_PASS ""
```

12. Upload the sketch to your microcontroller and observe the `Serial` terminal.

Congratulations, you have successfully taken sensor readings and stored them in a database table. The preceding steps are available in the video at the following URL: `https://packt.link/aQRgX`.

Summary

In this chapter, you learned about various communication technologies, the distance they cover, the amount of data or bandwidth that they support, and any limitations that might apply to utilizing them. You also made use of Wi-Fi to transmit sensor data to a remote system.

In the next chapter, you will learn how to set up a LoRa network and transmit data over it.

7
Communicating with LoRaWAN

In this chapter, you will learn about the network implementation of LoRA, called **LoRaWAN**, and an infrastructure implementation called **The Things Network** (**TTN**). You will also learn about the hardware components that are needed to make creating LoRaWAN networks a possibility. Finally, you will learn how you can communicate with your APIs over LoRaWAN.

By the end of this chapter, you will have set up a gateway device and an end device to send data to TTN.

In this chapter, we are going to cover the following main topics:

- Introduction to LoRa and LoRaWAN
- Working with The Things Network
- Purchasing and setting up radios and gateways

Let's consider what we will need to complete this chapter.

Technical requirements

You will need the following in order to complete the tasks in this chapter:

- Arduino IDE

- Arduino MKR WAN 1310

- Arduino WisGate Edge Lite 2

- Arduino MKR ENV Shield

- Arduino Portenta H7 and Portenta Vision Shield – LoRa (optional)

The code for the exercises in this chapter can be found at the following GitHub URL: `https://github.com/PacktPublishing/Arduino-Data-Communications`.

Introduction to LoRa and LoRaWAN

A **Wide Area Network** (**WAN**) can be loosely defined as any technology that can connect devices across a large geographical area, and in some cases, even across the world. Working backward, we see that LoRaWAN is a WAN that we can set up using LoRA, which is a long-range, low-power technology. LoRaWAN is a type of **Low-Power WAN** (**LPWAN**) connectivity protocol. LoRa is the physical communication layer that powers LoRaWAN.

LPWAN setups do not provide a large bandwidth, meaning that devices can only send small amounts of data at any point in time, and usually at a periodic interval, such as hourly. It is important to note that you cannot send a continuous stream of data on a LoRaWAN network. You can't send accelerometer data, for example. You also can't send images and videos on the network. If you wish to conserve power, you will need to use a fire-and-forget methodology where you program devices to send messages without waiting for confirmation from the network.

LoRaWAN operates on an unlicensed spectrum frequency, meaning that you do not need to pay to utilize equipment that operates on this frequency. This frequency depends on the geographical region, as follows:

- **USA**: 915 MHz

- **Europe**: 868 MHz

- **Australia**: 915 MHz

- **Asia**: 433 MHz

- **Africa**: 868 MHz

You can get a lot of information about LoRaWAN from the following URL: `https://lora-alliance.org/`.

> **Note**
>
> We will be working with the Arduino MKR WAN 1310 in this chapter. The MKR WAN 1310 has the same form factor as the MKR WiFi but trades in the WiFi and Bluetooth module for a LoRa module. You can get information about this board at the following URL: `https://store-usa.arduino.cc/products/arduino-mkr-wan-1310`.
>
> If you can't get your hands on an Arduino MKR WAN 1310, then you can make use of an Arduino Portenta H7. The Portenta H7 has the same form factor as the MKR boards but comes with a much more powerful dual-core processor. All existing MKR shields work on the Portenta H7, but you will need to solder your headers yourself. There are three variants of this board, and you can get additional information at the following URL: `https://www.arduino.cc/pro/hardware-product-portenta-h7/`. The Portenta H7 supports a vision shield with LoRa connectivity, which you can find here: `https://docs.arduino.cc/hardware/portenta-vision-shield`.
>
> The Arduino MKR WAN 1310 uses the same board driver as the MKR WiFi 1010, and you will not need to configure anything differently to get the board working. Just don't try to make use of any code that relies on Wi-Fi connectivity since the radios are missing.
>
> If you are working with the Portenta H7, you will need to install the driver called **Arduino Mbed OS Portenta Boards**. The procedure for installing a board driver for the Portenta H7 is covered in the following section.

Installing a board driver for the Portenta H7

Please follow these steps to install a board driver for the Portenta H7:

1. Launch the Arduino IDE.
2. Open **Boards Manager**.
3. Search for `Arduino Portenta H7`.
4. Locate the entry for **Arduino Mbed OS Portenta Boards by Arduino**.
5. Install this driver.

Congratulations, you are now ready to program the Arduino Portenta H7! A video showing the preceding steps is available at the following URL: `https://packt.link/NsWYe`.

Working with LoRa radios from the Arduino IDE requires the installation of the LoRa library. Let's do this next.

Installing the LoRa library

Follow these steps to install the LoRa library:

1. Launch the Arduino IDE.
2. Open **Library Manager**.
3. Search for `lora`.
4. Locate the entry for **LoRa by Sandeep Mistry**.
5. Install this library.

Congratulations, you are now ready to program using LoRa. The previously mentioned steps are available in a video at the following location: `https://packt.link/NsWYe`.

There are two general methods of implementing a LoRaWAN network, as we will see.

Using point-to-point communication

In point-to-point communication, two microcontrollers with LoRa modules can communicate with each other. Technically speaking, one board is configured to listen for messages while the other board is configured to send messages. You could use this arrangement to deploy one board at a location with sensors, and another board at a distance away that controls actuators. The sender will broadcast the message using LoRa and any listeners within range will receive any message being broadcast. Let's implement a simple sender that broadcasts its station ID along with the current temperature and humidity at regular intervals.

Project 1 – sending temperature and humidity readings using LoRa

Follow these steps to program an Arduino MKR WAN 1310 with an MKR ENV Shield to send temperature and humidity readings over LoRa. The code for this project is available at the following GitHub URL – `https://github.com/PacktPublishing/Arduino-Data-Communications/tree/main/chapter-7/MKR-WAN-Simple-LoRa-Sender`:

1. Connect the Arduino MKR ENV to the Arduino MKR WAN 1310.
2. Connect the setup to your computer.
3. Launch the Arduino IDE.
4. Create a new sketch.
5. We will need to work with the ENV shield along with the LoRa radio, so include the required libraries using the following code:

```
#include <Arduino_MKRENV.h>
#include <SPI.h>
#include <LoRa.h>
```

6. Let's declare some constants and variables to hold the values of our temperature and humidity, the station ID, and the counters for the last time we sent out a message, using the following code snippet:

```
unsigned long lastRead = millis();
const int myDelay = 15000;
float temperature, humidity;
const int stationId = 1;
```

7. Let's initialize the ENV Shield and the LoRa radio module within our `setup()` function using the following code snippet. The LoRa radio is configured to communicate using 915 MHz (USA frequency), but you can set it to other supported frequencies:

```
void setup() {
  Serial.begin(115200);
  while (!ENV.begin()) {
    Serial.println("Failed to initialive ENV Shield, waiting
...");
    delay(10000);
  }
  Serial.println("Initialized ENV Shield");
  if (!LoRa.begin(915E6)) {
    Serial.println("Failed to initialize LoRa, aborting");
    while(true);
  }
}
```

8. Finally, let's define our `loop()` function. In there, we will ensure that our code only executes after a set interval. Within that interval, we will take our temperature and humidity readings and broadcast over the LoRa radio:

```
void loop() {
  if (millis() - lastRead > myDelay) {
    lastRead = millis();
    temperature = ENV.readTemperature();
    humidity = ENV.readHumidity();
    Serial.print("T: ");
    Serial.println(temperature);
    Serial.print("H: ");
    Serial.println(humidity);

    LoRa.beginPacket();
    LoRa.print(stationId);
```

```
        LoRa.print(":");
        LoRa.print(temperature);
        LoRa.print("|");
        LoRa.print("humidity");
        LoRa.endPacket();
    }
}
```

9. Upload the sketch to your board and open **Serial Monitor** to confirm that there are no errors.

Congratulations, you have set up a board to broadcast the temperature and humidity from a station over LoRa. A video illustrating the preceding code is available at the following URL: `https://packt.link/NsWYe`.

Let's configure another board to read the data that is being sent over LoRa.

Project 2 – simple LoRa receiver

Please follow these steps to program an Arduino Portenta H7 with the Portenta Vision Shield – LoRa to listen for packets using LoRA. The code for this project is available at the following GitHub URL – `https://github.com/PacktPublishing/Arduino-Data-Communications/tree/main/chapter-7/Portenta-H7-Simple-LoRa-Receiver`:

1. Connect the Vision Shield – LoRa to the Arduino Portenta H7 using the high-density connectors.

2. Connect the Arduino Portenta H7 to your computer.

3. Launch the Arduino IDE.

4. Start a new sketch.

5. Even though we are using a Portenta H7, the library we need for communicating over LoRa is MKRWAN. Let's include it using the following code snippet:

    ```
    #include <MKRWAN.h>
    ```

6. We need an instance of LoRaModem to handle our communications:

    ```
    LoRaModem modem;
    ```

7. Our `setup()` function will be responsible for initializing our radio and notifying us. We will initialize our serial port for monitoring purposes and wait for the serial monitor to be opened before our code executes:

    ```
    void setup() {
      Serial.begin(115200);
      while(!Serial);
    ```

```
    if (!modem.begin(US915)) {
      Serial.println("Failed to initialize LoRa modem, aborting");
      while(true);
    }
    Serial.println("Initialized LoRa modem");
}
```

8. In our `loop()` function, we check whether the radio has received any broadcast data. If it has, we proceed to create a character array that can hold 64 elements. We then initialize an integer to 0, thus pointing at the first element of the array. Then, we read all of the data that the radio received into the array. Finally, we print all of that out, one character at a time:

```
void loop() {
  if(!modem.available()) {
    return;
  }
  char buffer[64];
  int i = 0;
  while(modem.available()) {
    buffer[i++] = (char)modem.read();
  }
  Serial.print("Received: ");
  for (unsigned int j = 0; j < i; j++) {
    Serial.print(buffer[j] >> 4, HEX);
    Serial.print(buffer[j] & 0xF, HEX);
    Serial.print(" ");
  }
  Serial.println();
}
```

9. Upload the sketch to the Portenta H7, wait for it to complete, and then open **Serial Monitor** to observe the output.

Congratulations, you have successfully programmed a Portenta H7 with Vision Shield – LoRa to receive data over LoRa. A code-in-action video is available at the following URL: https://packt.link/NsWYe.

Point-to-point communication isn't widely used because you can't connect the microcontrollers to other networks simultaneously. Instead, a network similar to a LAN is frequently utilized. This is a WAN and it uses a **star topology** (also called a network).

Using star networks

With a star network, the microcontrollers are called **nodes**. Nodes need to connect to a **gateway**, which forwards the data packets to a **network server**. The gateway is connected to power and has a route to the network server. A lot of gateways come with an **Ethernet** port for high-speed network connectivity, and some have a port for connecting a **SIM** card for backup, or as a primary in the event of a remote deployment. A diagram of a star network is shown in the following figure.

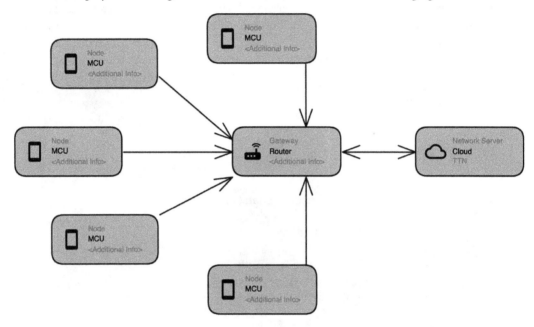

Figure 7.1 – A star network

The network server is completely different from the servers we set up in previous chapters. It is responsible for controlling the virtualized MAC layer of LoRaWAN. Gateways are frequently pre-integrated with network servers in order to simplify LoRaWAN deployments.

Both gateways and networks can be either *public* or *private*. Public networks are open to the general public, while private networks are limited to only certain users or devices.

Unlike in a LAN (e.g., Wi-Fi network) where devices are connected to only one switch, the nodes in a LoRaWAN network are not exclusively connected to one gateway. Instead, they broadcast to all gateways within range as long as those gateways are listening on that frequency. Communication between the nodes and the gateways uses LoRa. The gateways, in turn, connect to the network server using the internet.

Let's discuss one public LoRa network server that we will make use of in this chapter.

Working with The Things Network

TNN is a public LoRaWAN network server that makes it easy to register gateways, applications, and devices (nodes) and to transmit data from nodes to the network server via the registered gateways.

TTN enforces a few constraints that you need to be aware of before you start using it. These include the following:

- Only transmitting binary data
- Keeping data sizes as small as possible
- Avoiding continuous data transmission
- Utilizing an **Adaptive Data Rate (ADR)**
- Avoiding downlink messages if possible
- Avoiding confirmed uplinks

You can get started by visiting `https://www.thethingsnetwork.org/` and creating an account. When you log in, you will be met with a console that lets you manage either applications or gateways. The top of the console looks like the following.

Figure 7.2 – TTN console

Let's take a look at gateways.

Understanding gateways on TTN

When you visit the **Gateways** tab on TTN, it will ask you to register a gateway if you haven't already, and it will list all registered gateways that you might have. This is shown in the following figure.

Figure 7.3 – TTN gateways

You may click on the ID of the gateway to get additional information. Doing that will take you to a page with a menu on the left. The menu looks similar to the following figure.

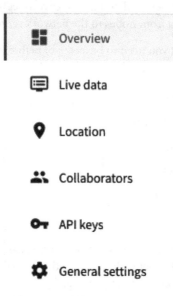

Figure 7.4 – TTN gateway menu

The **Overview** page provides various bits of information grouped into four sections, as follows:

- **General Information**: This contains details of the gateway device, when it was registered on the platform, and its gateway server address.

- **LoRaWAN Information**: This contains details about the frequency plan and a link to download the configuration data.

- **Location**: This plots the location on a map if that information was provided during setup. If this information wasn't provided, you can still plot it manually by visiting the **Location** link on the menu.

- **Live Data**: This shows any traffic passing through the gateway device.

The **Live data** link on the menu takes you to a larger view where you can see more information about traffic, and you can also inspect the data or export it as a JSON file.

The **Location** link on the menu takes you to a page where you can do the following:

- Set the location privacy, which determines whether or not that location is shown to other users of TTN.

- Set the location source, either manually or automatically from the messages that get sent to the network server.

- Set the device placement, whether indoors or outdoors. You may also choose *unknown* if you don't have that information.

- Set the location data, which is the longitude, latitude, and altitude.

- Remove location data, if you do not wish to show this device location.

The **General settings** link on the menu takes you to a page where you can manage a few other settings, as well as delete the gateway device from the network. You will need to delete the device if you want to change the registered frequency, for example.

You may register a new gateway device by clicking on the + **Register gateway** button at the top right of the screen when you are on the **Gateways** page. The page looks like the following screenshot.

Register gateway

Register your gateway to enable data traffic between nearby end devices and the network. Learn more in our guide on Adding Gateways .

Gateway EUI ⑦

| Gateway EUI | Continue without EUI |

To continue, please confirm the Gateway EUI so we can determine onboarding options

Figure 7.5 – TTN gateway registration

You will need a gateway at hand before you can proceed, so we will come back to this screen in a little bit. For now, let's look at applications.

Understanding applications on TTN

Applications on TTN group devices with the same payload together. The payload is simply the message that you wish to transmit, such as weather station, temperature, and humidity. When put together, this constitutes a payload. All of the nodes transmitting the same payload are grouped in one application on TTN. When you visit the **Applications** page, you will see a list of applications that you have created. This is shown in the following screenshot.

Figure 7.6 – TTN applications

You may click on the ID of the application to access the application details. When you do that, you will get a menu on the left side of your screen, similar to the following screenshot.

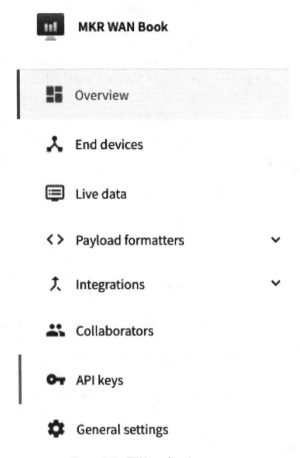

Figure 7.7 – TTN applications menu

The **Applications** overview page provides three bits of information:

- The application ID and when it was created.
- Live data showing message traffic.
- End devices showing their IDs and the last time they were active. You also have the option to add devices at this point.

The **End devices** page, which you can access from the menu, shows you the registered end devices and a link to add new devices.

The **Live data** page shows an expanded view of data traffic.

The **Payload formatters** page provides facilities to convert the payload from binary to another format that you can either read directly or pass on to an API. There are various options for specifying formatters, as you can see in the following screenshot.

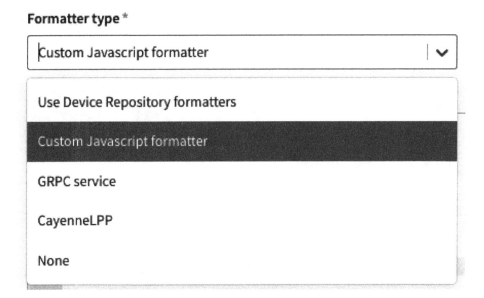

Figure 7.8 – Payload formatter

The **Integrations** menu link provides facilities for various configurations, including the following:

- **MQTT**: The TTN application can serve as an MQTT server such that you can connect a client such as the InfluxDB database to TTN to retrieve the data that was sent from end devices.

- **Webhooks**: A webhook is an API endpoint that you provide to an application, which it calls when an event occurs with relevant information. The TTN application can make an API call, similar to what our microcontroller was doing in a previous chapter. In this case, the REST endpoint will need to be exposed to the internet with either a public IP address or a domain name. There are a few webhooks that have been integrated, but you can create a custom one. The screen for creating a custom webhook looks like the following.

General settings

Webhook ID *

| my-new-webhook |

Webhook format *

| JSON | ∨ |

Base URL *

| https://example.com/webhooks |

Downlink API key

| |

The API key will be provided to the endpoint using the "X-Downlink-Apikey" header

Request authentication ⑦

☐ Use basic access authentication (basic auth)

Additional headers

| + Add header entry |

Filter event data ⑦

| + Add filter path |

Figure 7.9 – Custom webhook

- **AWS IoT** and **Azure IoT**: There are two separate integrations that make it possible to connect to two popular Cloud IoT platforms from Amazon Web Services and Microsoft Azure, respectively.

You can register end devices or nodes within applications. Let's discuss how you can purchase and set these up in the next section.

Purchasing and setting up radios and gateways

There is a multitude of device manufacturers; the quickest way of finding devices that are certified for LoRaWAN would be to visit the following URL: `https://lora-alliance.org/showcase/search/?_sfm_lorawan_certified_device=certified`. You will find various devices, both ready to use, as well as modules that you can integrate into your projects.

TTN sells a LoRa gateway device. You can find out all about it at the following URL: `https://www.thethingsnetwork.org/docs/gateways/gateway/`.

Since this is a book about Arduino, my examples are written using Arduino hardware. Let's consider these options.

Buying LoRaWAN-certified gateways

Arduino manufactures two LoRaWAN gateways, one for indoor use and a second for outdoor use. You can get more information about these gateways from the following URL: `https://www.arduino.cc/pro/lora-gateways/`.

I will be making use of the indoor gateway, called the **WisGate Edge Lite 2**. You can get more information about this gateway from the following URL: `https://store-usa.arduino.cc/products/wisgate-edge-lite2?selectedStore=us`.

You will need to purchase the gateway from the store in the region you are in so that you get the correct frequency options.

Once you have your gateway at hand, let's set it up. You will need to provide an Ethernet cable if one doesn't come in the box.

Setting up WisGate Edge Lite 2

Follow these steps to set up your new gateway device:

1. Remove the gateway and its accessories from its packaging.

2. Attach the antenna to the back of the gateway device.

3. Connect the network cable to the Ethernet port behind the gateway.

4. If you have an existing network, connect this cable to a switch or router. Check your network for the IP address that was assigned to the gateway and browse to it.

5. If you do not have an existing network, connect the cable to your computer and browse to `http://192.168.230.1`.

6. When you browse to the gateway for the first time, you will get a prompt asking you to set a password. Be sure to set a password that you will remember or use a password manager to store the password.

7. You will need to acknowledge the license agreement on the login screen, so go ahead and read it so you may proceed.

8. Click on the **Set password** button when you are done.

9. You will now be on the gateway dashboard.

Congratulations, you have successfully set up the gateway device. You can see the preceding steps in a video at the following URL: `https://packt.link/NsWYe`.

Next, let's register the gateway with TTN.

Connecting WisGate Edge Lite 2 to TTN

Follow these steps to connect the gateway to TTN:

1. Open a new browser and log in to TTN at the following URL: `https://console.cloud.thethings.network/`.

2. Go to the **Gateways** tab.

3. Click on the + **Register gateway** button.

4. A new page will pop up, asking you to provide a gateway EUI.

5. Return to the browser tab that is open to the gateway.

6. Navigate to the **Overview** tab. You should see a page similar to the following. Note that I have masked the important values.

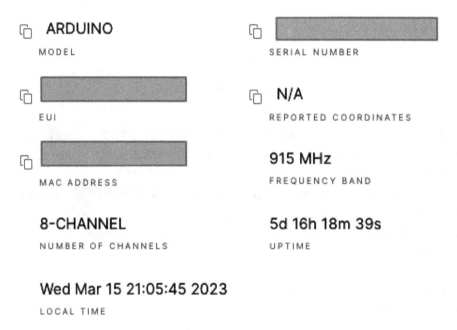

Figure 7.10 – WisGate Overview tab

7. Copy the EUI from the tab and return to TTN.

8. Paste the value into the **Gateway EUI** field.

9. Click on the **Confirm** button.

10. If this works, additional fields will appear on the page.

11. **Gateway ID** will be filled in automatically.

12. Fill in the **Gateway name** field.

13. Select a frequency plan from the dropdown. To be on the safe side, find the value with [**used by TTN**] and select that.

14. Scroll down to the bottom and click on the **Register gateway** button.

15. If this works, you will find yourself on the **Gateway Overview** page on TTN.

16. Find the menu on the left of the page.

17. Click on **API keys**.

18. Click on the + **Add API key** button.

19. Fill in the **Name** field.

20. Set an expiry date.

21. Under **Rights**, choose **Grant individual rights**.

22. Choose **Link as Gateway to a Gateway Server** for traffic exchange.

23. Scroll to the bottom and click on the **Create API key** button. A new popup will appear.

24. Click on the button with the image of an eye to view the API key that was generated.

25. Click on the *copy* button to copy the API key. It's a good idea to store this somewhere safe, such as in a password manager.

26. Return to the browser tab that is open to the **WisGate** device.

27. Navigate to the **Configuration** page.

28. Set **Work mode** to **Basics station**.

29. Set **Basics Station Server Type** to **LNS Server**.

30. Fill in the server URL. You can get this from the TTN gateway **Overview** page.

31. Set **Server Port** to **8887**.

32. Arduino has provided a trust certificate that you can download from the following URL: `https://letsencrypt.org/certs/isrgrootx1.pem`.

33. Upload the downloaded certificate into the **Trust (CA Certificate)** field.

34. Get the API key from earlier and paste it into the **Client Token** field after **Authorization: Bearer**. Be sure to put a space between the bearer and the API key.

35. Click on the **Save changes** button.

36. Return to the **TTN** browser tab.

37. Navigate to the **Overview** page of this gateway.

38. Observe that the page shows recent activity. It will look similar to the following figure.

↑ 0   ↓ 0   • Last activity 10 minutes ago ⑦

Figure 7.11 – Last gateway activity

Congratulations, you have successfully set up your gateway device and configured it to work with TTN! You can watch the preceding steps in a video at the following URL: `https://packt.link/NsWYe`.

Now that we have configured our gateway device, we are ready to purchase and set up an end device on TTN.

Buying LoRaWAN-certified microcontrollers

Arduino manufactures two microcontrollers with LoRa radios onboard – the MKR WAN 1300 and the MKR WAN 1310. Both of these microcontrollers are essentially the same as the MKR WiFi 1010 but with the WiFi and Bluetooth radio replaced with a LoRa radio. You can get additional information about the MKR WAN 1310 at the following URL: `https://docs.arduino.cc/hardware/mkr-wan-1310`. Because LoRaWAN operates on specific frequencies in different regions, you will need to pay special attention to where you purchase your microcontrollers. Ensure that you are in the right regional store when placing an order.

Arduino also manufactures a Vision Shield with an onboard LoRa radio for use with the Portenta family of microcontrollers. These shields do not make use of stacking headers. Instead, they make use of high-density connectors. There is a Vision Shield with Ethernet connectivity, so make sure you are placing an order for the version that has LoRa connectivity. You can get more information on the Vision Shield at the following URL: `https://docs.arduino.cc/hardware/portenta-vision-shield`.

If you have purchased and received your microcontroller, then it's time to set it up on TTN.

Before we set up our end device, we need its EUI. This isn't printed on the package. Let's get the device EUI.

Getting the microcontroller's EUI

Follow these steps to get the EUI of your microcontroller:

1. If you are using a Vision Shield – Lora, connect it to your Portenta.

2. Connect the microcontroller to your computer.

3. Launch the Arduino IDE.

4. Open the example sketch using the following menu: **File | Examples | MKRWAN | FirstConfiguration**.

5. Choose the right hardware from the drop-down menu.

6. Edit *line 27* to reflect the correct frequency for your region.

7. Upload the sketch to the microcontroller.

8. Wait for the upload to complete.

9. Open **Serial Monitor**.

10. Observe the output, which should be similar to the following figure.

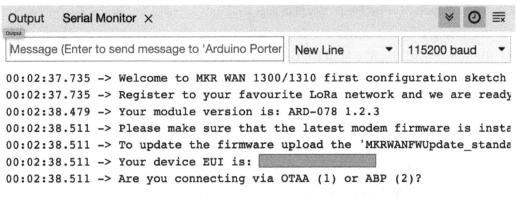

Figure 7.12 – The FirstConfiguration Serial Monitor output

11. Note the device EUI on the second-to-last line. I have masked the one in the screenshot.

Congratulations, you have successfully found the EUI of the microcontroller. The preceding steps are illustrated in a video available at the following URL: https://packt.link/NsWYe.

Now that we have an EUI, let's proceed to register this device on TTN.

Registering an end device on TTN

Follow these steps to register an end device on TTN:

1. Open a browser.

2. Browse to **TTN** at the following URL: https://console.cloud.thethings.network/.

3. Log in if you need to.

4. Navigate to the **Applications** tab.

5. Open an application. If you don't have one, go ahead and create one.

6. From the application overview page, click on the + **Register end device** button.

7. On the next page, choose **Arduino SA** from the **End device brand** dropdown.

8. A new dropdown called **Model** will appear.

9. Pick the right option for the model.

10. A dropdown called **Firmware Ver.** will appear.

11. The information you need is provided on the third line of the **Serial Monitor** output where we got the device EUI.

12. Fill in the correct information.

13. A new window called **Profile [Region]** appears.

14. Pick the correct information from the dropdown.

15. A new dropdown called **Frequency plan** appears.

16. Pick the right option from the dropdown. Make sure this frequency matches your gateway.

17. The next text field is called **JoinEUI**. This is *not* the device EUI.

18. You can put in any 16-digit value in this field. A lot of people use 0000000000000000.

19. Click on the **Confirm** button.

20. Next, in the text field called **DevEUI**, paste the device EUI value from **Serial Monitor**.

21. Click on the **Generate** button beside the **AppKey** field.

22. Scroll down and click on the **Register end device** button.

23. A new page will display the details of the newly registered device.

Congratulations, you have now registered the end device on TTN. You can watch the preceding steps in a video at the following URL: https://packt.link/NsWYe.

Now that our end device is registered with TTN, it is ready to communicate. You may test communication using the same example application, FirstConfiguration, that we used to get the device EUI. You can watch a video of that at the following URL: https://packt.link/NsWYe.

Our end device can only communicate with TTN using LoRaWAN. Communication over REST or MQQT will happen between TTN and any other platform that we set up. Let's write a sketch to send temperature and humidity data to TTN.

Project 3 – sending temperature and humidity data to TTN

Please follow these steps to send temperature and humidity data to TTN:

1. Attach your MKR ENV Shield to the MKR WAN.

2. Connect the microcontroller to your computer.

3. Launch the Arduino IDE.

4. Start a new sketch.

5. Create a new file and name it arduino_secrets.h.

6. Paste the following code snippet into it:

```
#define SECRET_APP_EUI ""
#define SECRET_APP_KEY ""
```

7. Put the correct values into the file.

8. Return to the sketch.ino file.

9. Add the required `include` files, as shown:

```
#include <Arduino_MKRENV.h>
#include <SPI.h>
#include <MKRWAN.h>
#include "arduino_secrets.h"
```

10. Define constants and variables, as shown:

```
unsigned long lastRead = millis();
const int myDelay = 60000;
float t,h;
const int stationId = 1;
LoRaModem modem;
String appEui = SECRET_APP_EUI;
String appKey = SECRET_APP_KEY;
```

11. Initialize the ENV Shield and connect to TTN in the `setup()` function:

```
void setup() {
  Serial.begin(115200);
  while (!ENV.begin()) {
    Serial.println("Failed to initialize ENV Shield, waiting
...");
    delay(10000);
  }
  Serial.println("Initialized ENV Shield");
  if (!modem.begin(US915)) {
    Serial.println("Failed to start module");
    while (true);
  };

  int connected = modem.joinOTAA(appEui, appKey);
  if (!connected) {
    Serial.println("Unable to initialize modem connection");
    while (true);
  }
  modem.minPollInterval(60);
}
```

12. Every minute, take the temperature and humidity readings, create a string representation, and send the string to TTN:

```
void loop() {
  // put your main code here, to run repeatedly:
  if (millis() - lastRead > myDelay) {
    lastRead = millis();
```

```
t = ENV.readTemperature();
h = ENV.readHumidity();
String msg = String(String(stationId) + "|" + String(t) + "|"
+ String(h));
Serial.println(msg);
for (unsigned int i=0; i<msg.length(); i++) {
  Serial.print(msg[i] >> 4, HEX);
  Serial.print(msg[i] & 0xF, HEX);
  Serial.print(" ");
}
Serial.println();

int err;
modem.beginPacket();
modem.print(msg);
err = modem.endPacket(true);
if (err > 0) {
  Serial.println("msg sent");
} else {
  Serial.println("Error while sending msg");
}
}
}
```

13. Upload the sketch to the microcontroller and wait a few minutes for it to send data to TTN.

Congratulations, you have successfully written a sketch to read temperature and humidity data from the ENV Shield and then send it to TTN! The preceding steps are illustrated in a code-in-action video at the following URL: `https://packt.link/NsWYe`.

You can view the end device activity on the TTN device overview page. The **Live data** section will show activity similar to the following screenshot.

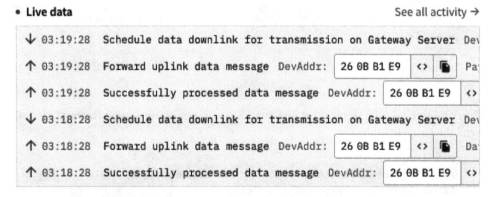

Figure 7.13 – The Live data section of the overview page

From the **Live data** section, you may click on **See all activity** -> to see additional details. From the new page, look for a message that shows a payload message. It looks similar to the following screenshot.

Figure 7.14: The TTN payload

What you are really interested in is the smaller section that holds the hex code. It looks like the following screenshot.

Figure 7.15 – The payload

The payload is what was sent from the end device to TTN. It is encoded. You may convert the payload into a human-readable format using the following hex code translator: `https://www.qbit.it/lab/hextext.php`.

You can paste the payload into the textbox in the hex code translator and click on the **Decode hex code to text** button. The result is similar to the following screenshot.

"317C32382E30307C35312E3336" decoded from Hex Code is:

1|28.00|51.36

Figure 7.16 – The decoded payload

This decoded payload shows exactly what was sent from the end device. The device sends the station ID, the temperature, and the humidity, all separated by a **pipe** (|) symbol.

The payload can be formatted by TTN and displayed directly. We need to do two things to accomplish this:

1. Set the end device to use the formatter configured at the application level.
2. Configure a formatter for the application.

Let's configure the end device to use a formatter at the application level.

Configuring the formatter on the end device

Follow these steps to configure a formatter on the end device:

1. Log in to your TTN console.
2. Navigate to **Applications**.
3. Click on the application ID.

4. Scroll down to the **Devices** section and click on the device ID.

5. Click on the **Payload formatters** tab, as shown in the following screenshot:

↑ 2   ↓ 1   ● Last activity 1 hour ago ⑦

| Overview | Live data | Messaging | Location | Payload formatters | Claiming | General settings |

Figure 7.17 – Device payload formatters

6. Click on **Uplink** to navigate to that page.

7. Set **Formatter type** to **Use application payload formatter**.

8. Scroll down and click on the **Save changes** button.

9. Click on **Downlink** to navigate to that page.

10. Set **Formatter type** to **Use application payload formatter**.

11. Scroll down and click on the **Save changes** button.

The preceding steps are illustrated in a video available at `https://packt.link/NsWYe`.

Let's configure the application payload formatter.

Configuring the application payload formatter

Follow these steps to configure a formatter on the end device:

1. Log into your TTN console.

2. Navigate to **Applications**.

3. Click on the application ID.

4. Expand the **Payload formatters** menu item.

5. Click on **Uplink**.

6. Set **Formatter type** to **Custom Javascript formatter**.

7. Paste the following code into the formatter code text that converts the payload from a hex into a string, then creates an array by splitting the string using the pipe (|) as a delimiter. It then returns a JSON object of the array content:

```
function decodeUplink(input) {
  var decoded = "";
  for (var i=0; i<input.bytes.length; i++) {
    decoded += String.fromCharCode(parseInt(input.bytes[i]));
  }
  const myArray = decoded.split("|");
```

```
    return {
      data: {
        stationID: myArray[0],
        temperature: myArray[1],
        humidity: myArray[2]
      },
      warnings: [],
      errors: []
    };
}
```

8. Scroll down and click on the **Save changes** button.

The preceding steps are shown in a video available at the following URL: https://packt.link/NsWYe.

The result of setting this formatter is shown in the following screenshot, which you can get by sending data from the end device to TTN after setting your payload formatter.

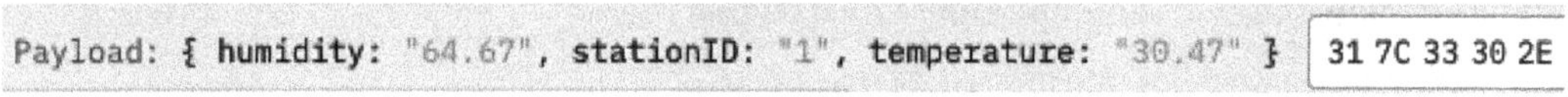

Payload: { humidity: "64.67", stationID: "1", temperature: "30.47" }   31 7C 33 30 2E

Figure 7.18 – The formatted payload

Let's consider how you can move the data from TTN to a database over REST. The database and the REST API will both need to either be hosted on the cloud or within a server that has a public IP or domain name.

Instead of setting up a server on the cloud, we will make use of a cloud endpoint to test our REST API callbacks.

Project 4 – communicating using RESTful APIs

Follow these steps to get data from TTN to a REST API:

1. Log in to your console on TTN.
2. Go to the **Applications** tab.
3. Click on your application ID to visit the application overview page.
4. Click on **Integrations** on the menu.
5. Click on **Webhooks**.
6. Click on the + **Add** webhook button.
7. Select **Custom webhook** on the next screen.

    We will make use of a free public service to test our webhook, but this would work the same way if you wanted to connect it to your REST API hosted on the cloud.

8. Visit `https://webhook.site/` from another browser tab.

9. The site will load and show you a unique URL.

10. Click on the **Copy to clipboard** button beside the unique URL.

11. Return to the **TTN** console.

12. Provide a webhook ID.

13. Paste the unique URL into the **Base URL** field.

14. Scroll down to the **Enabled event types** section.

15. Check the box beside **Uplink message**.

16. Leave the textbox blank. If you were using your REST API, you would put the name of the endpoint, such as `/readings`.

17. Scroll down and click on the **Add webhook** button.

18. Return to the **Live data** page.

19. Start sending payloads from the end device.

20. Wait for messages to show up on the **Live data** page.

21. Return to the webhook site to see data stream in.

Congratulations, you have successfully set up data transfer from TTN to a REST API. The steps are shown in a video available at the following URL: `https://packt.link/NsWYe`.

Let's send data from TTN over MQTT next. TTN serves as an MQTT server, and all you have to do is get the server credentials and configure your client, such as InfluxDB. Additional information about TTN as an MQTT server is available at the following URL: `https://www.thethingsindustries.com/docs/integrations/mqtt/`.

Project 5 – communicating using MQTT

Follow these steps to get data from TTN to a REST API:

1. Log in to your console on TTN.

2. Go to the **Applications** tab.

3. Click on your application ID to visit the application overview page.

4. Click on **Integrations** on the menu.

5. Click on **MQTT**.

6. Proceed to configure your client with the information available on TTN.

The preceding steps are illustrated in a video at the following URL: `https://packt.link/NsWYe`.

Summary

In this chapter, you learned how to set up an account on a public LoRaWAN server and configure a gateway and an end device to send data to the server. You also learned how to transmit data from the server using both REST and MQTT.

In the next chapter, you will learn how to work with SigFox, another LPWAN technology.

Further reading

To learn more about the topics covered in this chapter, you can visit the following links:

- *Arduino MKR WAN 1310*: https://docs.arduino.cc/hardware/mkr-wan-1310

- *Arduino WisGate Edge Lite 2*: https://www.arduino.cc/pro/lora-gateways/

- *Arduino Portenta H7*: https://www.arduino.cc/pro/hardware-product-portenta-h7/

- *Arduino Portenta Vision Shield – LoRA*: https://www.arduino.cc/pro/hardware-product-portenta-vision-shield/

- *The Things Network*: https://www.thethingsnetwork.org/

- *WisGate – getting started*: https://docs.arduino.cc/tutorials/wisgate-edge-lite-2/getting-started

- *LoRa 101*: https://docs.arduino.cc/learn/communication/lorawan-101

- *Hex code translator*: https://www.qbit.it/lab/hextext.php

8
Working with Ethernet

In this chapter, you will learn how to deploy Arduino solutions while making use of Ethernet technology. You will write a sketch that communicates with a weather service to get the current weather conditions in a city and then use that information to control the intensity of an onboard LED. You will learn how to work with a RESTful API endpoint and process the JSON response that is returned by that endpoint. This type of activity is useful for controlling devices based on environmental conditions, such as greenhouses and animal housing.

By the end of this chapter, you will have learned how to connect to a web service via Ethernet and process the response.

In this chapter, we are going to cover the following main topics:

- Introduction to Ethernet
- Communicating over Ethernet

Technical requirements

The code example in this chapter is available on GitHub at `https://github.com/securetorobert/Arduino-Data-Communications/tree/main/chapter-8`.

You will need to following to complete the example project in this chapter:

- Arduino Portenta H7 (or H7 Lite)
- Arduino Portenta Vision Shield – Ethernet
- A network switch with internet connectivity
- An Ethernet cable

Introduction to Ethernet

Ethernet is a wired communication technology. It is frequently used in both residential and commercial applications where a wireless network might be undesirable due to one or more of the following reasons:

- A need to implement communications without interfering with sensitive equipment, such as medical equipment

- A need to support much higher speeds than is possible over wireless networks

- A need to communicate through thick walls

- A need to provide power to devices while also communicating, using a technology called **Power-over-Ethernet** (**PoE**)

Ethernet networks comprise a switch or router and devices.

A network switch creates a dedicated network and enables communication between devices on the network. A switch might have a connection to the internet, in which case the switch will enable the devices to connect to the internet.

A network router enables connectivity between multiple networks. Routers might also serve as firewalls by preventing unauthorized access to networks and devices, and they might also make it possible to access one or more devices from outside the network using a technology called **Network Address Translation** (**NAT**).

Devices are connected to either the switch or router using cables. Two types of cables are used in Ethernet networks:

- **Shielded twisted pair cables**, called Cat5, Cat6, Cat6A, or Cat6E, have a maximum communication distance of 100 meters and are frequently used for connectivity between devices and switches or routers. These cables support communication speeds up to 10 Gbps. You can read up on the differences between these cables at the following URL: `https://www.blackbox.co.uk/gb-gb/page/43869/Resources/Technical-Resources/Black-Box-Explains/Copper-Cable/Category-5e-And-6`.

- **Fiber-optic cables** are frequently used for connectivity between switches and routers. These cables can transmit data up to a distance of 100 km. They also support speeds up to 40 Gbps.

Some Ethernet switches can transmit power over the same cable used for transmitting data. This is called PoE. This is useful in decluttering the setup because you will eliminate power cables where the network devices support this. One example application of this is in security cameras. When you utilize security cameras that support PoE, you eliminate the need to wire the building for power at every spot where you will have a camera. This cuts down the cost of setting up your infrastructure. You have to read the specification of any device you are working with to establish whether it supports PoE.

The Arduino MKR WiFi 1010 microcontroller development board doesn't have an Ethernet port. However, there are some shields and devices that have Ethernet boards.

Arduino devices that support Ethernet

The following devices support Ethernet communications:

- **Arduino Opta microPLC**: This comes in three variants. All three variants support Ethernet communication. The Opta is useful in industrial settings for controlling manufacturing equipment. You can learn more about the Arduino Opta at `https://www.arduino.cc/pro/hardware-arduino-opta/`.

- **Arduino Portenta Machine Control**: This is designed for upgrading legacy machinery. It is marketed as an industrial control unit. You can learn more about it at `https://www.arduino.cc/pro/portenta-machine-control/`.

The following carriers provide Ethernet connectivity:

- **Portenta Breakout**: This carrier has high-density connectors for interfacing with an Arduino Portenta and exposes all of the connectors so that headers can be soldered on. You can learn more about the Portenta Breakout at `https://www.arduino.cc/pro/hardware-product-portenta-breakout/`.

- **Portenta Max Carrier**: This is designed to convert your Portenta into a **Single Board Computer (SBC)**. You can learn more about the Max Carrier at `https://www.arduino.cc/pro/hardware-product-portenta-max-carrier/`.

The following shield provides Ethernet connectivity:

- **Portenta Vision Shield**: This shield provides a camera, a microphone, and an Ethernet port to a Portenta microcontroller. You can learn more about this shield at `https://docs.arduino.cc/hardware/portenta-vision-shield`.

In this chapter, we will be working with the Arduino Portenta H7 with the Portenta Vision Shield – Ethernet. If you can, get your hands on the Portenta Breakout; by doing so, you can prototype even better solutions. So, grab your equipment and head over to the next section.

Installing Arduino Portenta board drivers

If you have never worked with an Arduino Portenta, you must install the board drivers. Follow these steps to install the board drivers.

1. Launch the Arduino IDE.
2. Open **BOARDS MANAGER**.
3. Search for `portenta`.
4. Locate the entry for **Arduino Mbed OS Portenta Boards**. The result should be similar to the following:

Figure 8.1 – BOARDS MANAGER

5.   Click on the **INSTALL** button. If you have an older version of the driver, then the button will be labeled **UPDATE**.

Congratulations – you have successfully installed the Arduino Portenta board drivers!

Let's proceed and build solutions that communicate over Ethernet.

Communicating over Ethernet

Let's build a solution that will control the onboard LED based on the weather conditions in a particular location. We will make use of APIs from AccuWeather. You can sign up for free at `https://developer.accuweather.com/`.

Creating an AccuWeather app

Once you've created your account, you will need to create an app before you can get API keys to work with. Navigate to the **MY APPS** tab or go to `https://developer.accuweather.com/user/me/apps`. Follow these steps to create an app:

1.   Click on the + **Add a new App** button. This is shown here:

Figure 8.2 – AccuWeather developer portal

2. Specify a name for the app.

3. Under **Products**, choose **Core Weather Limited Trial**.

4. For **Where will the app be used?**, choose **Other**.

5. For **What will you be creating with this app?**, choose **Internal App**.

6. For **What is your app written in?**, choose **C++**.

7. For **Is this for Business to Business or Business to Consumer**, choose **Business to Consumer**.

8. For **Is this Worldwide or Country specific use?**, choose **Worldwide**.

9. Click on the **Create App** button.

Congratulations – you have created an AccuWeather app on the developer console! These steps are shown in a Code in Action video available at `https://packt.link/pwtsR`. Next, let's get your API key.

Getting your API key

Follow these steps to get your API key:

1. Navigate to the **My Apps** menu.

2. Click on the name of the app that you created. You should see a screen that looks similar to the following:

Figure 8.3 – Your API key

3.   Your API key is available for use at any time.

AccuWeather requires a location key before you can get any weather information. This requires just a little bit of work.

Getting your location key

The location key is a numeric identifier for any place for which you can get weather information. In this example, I will be getting the location key for a city called Jos in Nigeria. Follow these steps to get the location key:

1.   Open the command Terminal if you are on a Mac or Linux, or a CMD terminal on Windows.

2.   Paste the following cURL command but don't hit *Enter*:

```
curl -X GET "http://dataservice.accuweather.com/locations/v1/
cities/search?apikey=tA&q=jos&details=true"
```

3.   Edit the command and replace the `tA` value with your API key.

4.   Replace the `jos` value with any city that you are interested in.

5.   Hit *Enter* when you are done.

You will get a response similar to the following:

```
[{"Version":1,"Key":"255089","Type":"City","Rank":31,"LocalizedName":"Jos","EnglishN
e":"Africa"},"Country":{"ID":"NG","LocalizedName":"Nigeria","EnglishName":"Nigeria"},
```

Figure 8.4 – The location key

6.   Notice the value for `key` in the response. This value is what you need for the next step.

Congratulations – you now have a location key!

You can also get the location key programmatically once you know the structure of the response. One reason why you might not do this is that you will need to write additional code. Once again, here is the top of the response from the API call:

```
 1   [
 2       {
 3           "Version": 1,
 4           "Key": "255089",
 5           "Type": "City",
 6           "Rank": 31,
 7           "LocalizedName": "Jos",
 8           "EnglishName": "Jos",
 9           "PrimaryPostalCode": "",
10           "Region": {
11               "ID": "AFR",
12               "LocalizedName": "Africa",
13               "EnglishName": "Africa"
14           },
15           "Country": {
16               "ID": "NG",
```

Figure 8.5 – The response to the location key call

From line 4 of this response, you will see that the location key from the response is 255089. You are now ready to get the weather conditions at your chosen location.

Getting the weather conditions

Let's get the weather conditions manually before we program it into the Arduino Portenta. We will send a GET HTTP request to the following URL: http://dataservice.accuweather.com/ currentconditions/v1/255089.

The last part of the URL is the location key. Feel free to replace it with another location key. Just as you did in the previous call, you will need to append the API Key. Follow these steps to make a manual call to the API endpoint:

1. Open your command terminal.

2. Paste the following snippet, but don't hit *Enter*:

   ```
   curl -X GET 'http://dataservice.accuweather.com/
   currentconditions/v1/255089?apikey=tA&details=true'
   ```

3. Replace tA with your API key.

4. Replace 255089 with any other location key that you wish to use.

5. Hit *Enter*.

You will get an output similar to the following. I have formatted it for readability:

```
1    [
2        {
3            "LocalObservationDateTime": "2023-09-23T10:20:00+01:00",
4            "EpochTime": 1695460800,
5            "WeatherText": "Mostly sunny",
6            "WeatherIcon": 2,
7            "HasPrecipitation": false,
8            "PrecipitationType": null,
9            "IsDayTime": true,
10           "Temperature": {
11               "Metric": {
12                   "Value": 25.5,
13                   "Unit": "C",
14                   "UnitType": 17
15               },
16               "Imperial": {
```

Figure 8.6 – Weather conditions in JSON format

Congratulations – you have manually retrieved the weather conditions at a specified location!

Let's discuss the response. Consider the following screenshot. This is the response with the fields collapsed:

```
1    [
2  >      { ...
381        }
382  ]
```

Figure 8.7 – The response collapsed

The square brackets, [], show that the response is an array.

The { } property contained within the square brackets shows that the response contains an object.

Within the { } property of the object, we can see the **fields** (also called **keys**) and their **values**. Let's look at a snippet of the fields within the object:

```
 1  [
 2      {
 3          "LocalObservationDateTime": "2023-09-23T10:20:00+01:00",
 4          "EpochTime": 1695460800,
 5          "WeatherText": "Mostly sunny",
 6          "WeatherIcon": 2,
 7          "HasPrecipitation": false,
 8          "PrecipitationType": null,
 9          "IsDayTime": true,
10  >       "Temperature": {…
21          },
22  >       "RealFeelTemperature": {…
35          },
36  >       "RealFeelTemperatureShade": {…
49          },
50          "RelativeHumidity": 66,
51          "IndoorRelativeHumidity": 66,
52  >       "DewPoint": {…
63          },
64  >       "Wind": {…
82          },
```

Figure 8.8 – Weather conditions Eepanded

You will notice that the third entry (on line 5) is WeatherText and the value is Mostly Sunny. You will also notice another field on line 10 called Temperature. The value of this field is an object. Let's take a closer look at it:

```
10          "Temperature": {
11              "Metric": {
12                  "Value": 25.5,
13                  "Unit": "C",
14                  "UnitType": 17
15              },
16              "Imperial": {
17                  "Value": 78.0,
18                  "Unit": "F",
19                  "UnitType": 18
20              }
21          },
```

Figure 8.9 – The Temperature object

The `Temperature` object has two fields labeled `Metric` and `Imperial`. These fields are objects. Both fields have three values:

- `Value`: The numeric value of the temperature reading.

- `Unit`: The unit of measurement of the temperature reading. This is either C (Centigrade) or F (Fahrenheit).

- `UnitType`: A referential key that we will not be using in this example.

Knowing the structure of the response from this API call makes it possible for us to build our project. In this project, we will set the intensity of an onboard LED based on the temperature reading. In a real-world application, you could choose to activate a relay that opens or closes window blinds or shutters based on weather conditions.

Project 1 – Setting the onboard LED's intensity based on the temperature

The source code for this project is available at `https://github.com/PacktPublishing/ Arduino-Data-Communications/tree/main/chapter-8/weather-conditions/ weather`.

Follow these steps to build the project:

1. Launch the Arduino IDE.

2. Open a new sketch.

3. Begin by importing the necessary headers. We will need an extra header library for the Portenta to work with an Ethernet shield. We also need the JSON library to process our API responses. This is shown here:

```
#include <PortentaEthernet.h>
#include <Ethernet.h>
#include <SPI.h>
#include <Arduino_JSON.h>
```

4. We want to get these weather conditions hourly. Let's declare the variables that will let us keep track of how much time has passed since we did this:

```
unsigned long lastRead = millis();
const int myDelay = 3600000;
```

5. We need a character array to hold the value of the base URL of the service we will be working with:

```
char server[] = "dataservice.accuweather.com";
```

6. We need an instance of `EthernetClient` to communicate with the remote API service:

```
EthernetClient client;
```

7. We will do a few things within the `setup()` function. First, we will set the pin mode of the red onboard LED to OUTPUT so that we can control it. This code is shown here:

```
pinMode(LEDR, OUTPUT);
```

8. We would like to print some debugging output to the computer, so we will set up `Serial`:

```
Serial.begin(115200);
```

9. Whatever we try to do won't work if the Ethernet isn't working. Let's check for any errors that might occur when the device boots up but isn't able to get an IP address:

```
if (Ethernet.begin() == 0) {
    Serial.println("Unable to configure Ethernet via DHCP ...");
    if (Ethernet.hardwareStatus() == EthernetNoHardware) {
      Serial.println("Ethernet hardware missing. Aborting ...");
      while (true);
    }
    if (Ethernet.linkStatus() == LinkOFF) {
      Serial.println("Please connect an Ethernet cable and
reboot the MCU");
    }
  }
```

10. If there are no errors, then the Ethernet was properly configured, and the device got an IP address:

```
else {
    Serial.print("IP Address assigned: ");
    Serial.println(Ethernet.localIP());
    delay(1000);
    Serial.println("Ready ...");
  }
```

Let's move to the `loop()` function block.

11. Within the block, let's ensure we only fetch the weather conditions once every hour:

```
if (millis() - lastRead > myDelay) {
    lastRead = millis();
}
```

12. Next, let's ensure that `EthernetClient` isn't connected to any remote servers:

```
client.stop();
```

13. Next, let's attempt to connect to the API server:

```
if (client.connect(server, 80)) {

    }
```

14. If the server connection is successful, make a GET HTTP request to the relevant endpoint. We do this by sending a series of commands to the server using the `println()` method:

```
if (client.connect(server, 80)) {
        client.println("GET /currentconditions/
v1/255089?apikey=tA&details=true HTTP/1.1");
        client.println();
        client.println("Connection: close");
        client.println();



    }
```

15. We need to read the response from the server. We do this by declaring a `String` variable, then checking for a response from the server and reading one character at a time, placing it in the `String` variable:

```
String res = String("");
        while (client.available()) {
          res.concat(client.read());
        }
```

16. Next, let's convert the string into a JSON object so that we can extract the relevant fields:

```
JSONVar myArray = JSON.parse(res);
```

The rest of the code in this section checks for the existence of the fields we are interested in and then extracts the values of those fields. You can see this in action in this book's GitHub repository.

17. Finally, we want to log an error if we are unable to connect to the API server:

```
else {
        Serial.println("Unable to connect to the AccuWeather
server");
    }
```

Now, we are ready to upload the sketch to the microcontroller.

18. Connect the Vision Shield to the Arduino Portenta, making sure to align the connectors.

19. Connect one end of an Ethernet cable to a network switch.

20. Connect the other end of the Ethernet cable to the shield.

21. Connect a USB cable between the computer and the Portenta.

22. Upload the sketch.

23. Open **Serial Monitor** and wait for output.

Congratulations – you have successfully programmed the Portenta to read weather conditions from an API and set the intensity of an LED based on that value! These steps are available in a Code in Action video at `https://packt.link/pwtsR`.

Summary

In this chapter, you learned how to set up an account on a public API server, as well as how to fetch weather information from that server. You also learned how to send a HTTP GET request to the API server from an Arduino Portenta using Ethernet, and how to process the response from the server.

In the next chapter, you will learn how to work with cellular communication technologies.

9

Leveraging Cellular Communication Technology

Cellular communication technology is popular on mobile phones. It is popular across the world because it is deployed by large businesses that maintain the infrastructure. We will learn how to work with this technology by writing code that sends data, using **Simple Messaging Service** (**SMS**) and **General Packet Radio Services** (**GPRS**), so that we can deploy solutions that communicate using this technology.

In this chapter, we will cover the following main topics:

- Learning about cellular connectivity
- Choosing cellular radios
- Making phone calls
- Working with SMS
- Working with GPRS

By the end of this chapter, you will have learned how to send temperature and humidity data using cellular technology.

Technical requirements

We will make use of the following in this chapter:

- Arduino MKR GSM 1400
- Arduino MKR ENV Shield
- Antenna (this is bundled with the microcontroller if you purchase directly from the Arduino Store)
- The Arduino IDE

- A SIM card

- A 9V battery or similar source

- A 9V-to-5V buck converter

- The battery and buck converter can be replaced with a benchtop power supply if you have access to one

- Cables

The code snippets for this chapter are available at the following GitHub URL: `https://github.com/PacktPublishing/Arduino-Data-Communications/tree/main/chapter-9`

Learning about cellular connectivity

Cellular connectivity is provided by telecommunication networks. These networks are usually privately owned, although they can be publicly owned in some countries. These networks are licensed at a national level. As a result, even if a network has the same name as a network in another country, you can't use the other network unless the two networks have a roaming agreement.

In order to connect to a cellular network, you will need a device that is capable of communicating over the right frequency and a **Subscriber Identity Module** (**SIM**). A SIM can be either physical or virtual (or electronic). A physical SIM is also called a SIM card. Physical SIM cards have shrunk in size over the years, thus making it possible for device manufacturers to also make smaller devices. A SIM card with cutouts for three generations of sizes is shown in the following figure, with the card itself in the white area.

Figure 9.1 – A physical SIM card

The card itself holds a chip. This is visible on the opposite side of the card, as shown in the following figure.

Figure 9.2 – The chip on the SIM

The chip contains the subscriber information that makes it possible for a device to register on a network. The card (and the chip) is inserted into a device, which then registers on a cellular network. The device does this by communicating with a **cell site** that belongs to the network. The network maintains its presence by setting up a cell site.

Cellular technologies are currently in the fifth generation (5G), but the hardware we will work with supports the third generation (3G). Most telecommunication networks are backward-compatible from 5G to 3G, with a few still supporting 2G.

2G network technology introduced GPRS, SMS, and **Multimedia Messaging Service** (**MMS**). 1G network technology only supported voice communications.

SMS allowed for the transmission of 160 characters in a text format, while GPRS allowed for the transmission of data at a maximum of 5 **kilobytes** (**kB**) per second or 40 **kilobits per second** (**kbps**).

3G technology introduced better standards, with data transmission rates of at least 144 kbps. 3G technology introduced newer frequency bands and higher bandwidths.

You will have to use a SIM in order to connect to a network. This SIM is issued by the network and will not connect to another network provider unless that network provider has a roaming agreement with the issuer of the SIM. This is important to note for the following reasons:

- If you place a SIM into a device that is taken where the issuer doesn't have coverage, your device will be unable to connect

- If your device is used in a mobile (logistics) application, then you need to ensure that you have coverage in the areas that the vessels will be traveling to

Cellular communication technologies are typically not used in marine applications because international waters are not the jurisdiction of a single country, so licenses can't be obtained. Also, network providers simply don't implement such expensive infrastructure in places where it will be used sparingly.

Finally, cellular connectivity isn't free. You will need to either subscribe for a period or purchase units that will let you communicate. When debugging problems with cellular connectivity, this is one of the first things that you would want to check.

Let's discuss more tangible equipment.

Choosing cellular radios

There are two radios involved in cellular communications – one radio is mounted on the cell site and is outside of our control. The other radio is within our IoT device, and we can choose which radio to work with.

There are various cellular connectivity standards across the world. The choice of which one to use will be determined by the geographical location of the final deployment.

Deployments in North America

For deployments in North America, the available options are as follows:

- LTE Cat-1

- GSM (3G/4G/5G)

- NB-IoT

You can find various cellular connectivity modules at `https://sparkfun.com`.

Deployments in EMEA

For deployments in Europe, the Middle East, and Africa, the options are as follows:

- GSM (3G/4G/5G)
- LTE Cat-1

A great provider of modules is Blues Wireless (`https://blues.io/`). Let's discuss them in detail.

Blues Wireless

Blues Wireless is in the business of providing cellular connectivity modules and a platform to manage communications. They provide three distinct solutions:

- Notecards
- Notecarriers
- Notehub

Let's discuss these solutions.

Notecard

A notecard is described as "an integrated, low-power cellular data pump"; this device has an embedded SIM in it. It is widely classified as a **System-on-Module** (**SoM**). You can't make calls through this device, but you have access to data transmission. Subscription is managed by Blues Wireless, so you don't have to deal with any cellular carrier. All carriers are bundled with 10 years and 500 MB of cellular data coverage. They also come with integrated GPS and an accelerometer. All notecards expose M.2 key edge connectors. There are five notecards:

- An LTE Cat-M notecard for North America with an on-board SIM
- An LTE Cat-1 notecard for North America with an on-board SIM
- An LTE-M notecard with NB-IoT global coverage
- An LTE Cat-1 notecard for EMEA
- A Wi-Fi notecard

Notecards are designed to be used with **notecarriers**.

Notecarrier

A notecarrier is a "companion development board" that makes it possible to interface with a notecard, using an M.2 Key E edge connector port. A notecarrier can work with all notecards because notecards have the same interface. However, notecarriers have different form factors. There are four notecarriers:

- **Notecarrier-F**: This carrier hosts a notecard as well as a socket connector to house Adafruit Feather-based microcontrollers. It is designed for rapid prototyping.

- **Notecarrier Pi Hat**: This carrier is designed to be used with Raspberry Pi. It has a 40-pin header, so you can plug it directly into a Raspberry Pi. It also contains a slot for external (physical) SIM cards.

- **Notecarrier A**: This carrier provides female headers for use with DuPont cables, making it possible to prototype using a breadboard or directly with a microcontroller. It serves as a host for a notecard and also provides a slot for a SIM card.

- **Notecarrier B**: This comes with a small form factor for deployments, where you might choose to solder the carrier within a larger PCB. It provides a slot for a notecard but doesn't provide an external SIM slot. It also provides male headers, either pre-soldered or loose.

Your microcontroller communicates with the notecarrier, using either Serial or I2C, which in turn communicates with the notecard. The notecard sends its data to the Notehub.

Notehub

This is a hosted service that routes your data from a notecard to any cloud application of your choice. It also makes it possible to manage a fleet of devices, placing them into groups and routing data from different device groups to different applications and destinations.

Let's discuss our choices from the Arduino ecosystem.

Arduino cellular options

Arduino provides MKR boards with various connectivity options. We have already worked with a few of these, but there are three that we should highlight at this point:

- **Arduino MKR NB 1500**: This board provides **Narrowband-IoT** (**NB-IoT**) connectivity, while maintaining compatibility with the MKR ecosystem. Per Arduino's website, this board is designed to work on certain networks, including Vodafone, AT&T, T-Mobile, Telstra, and Verizon. This board communicates over LTE-M, NB-IoT, and EGPRS. It supports sending and receiving an SMS, sending data, and making calls. You can get the MKR NB 1500 at the following link: `https://store-usa.arduino.cc/products/arduino-mkr-nb-1500`.

- **Arduino MKR GSM 1400**: This board provides connectivity over a GSM/3G network. This board also supports sending and receiving an SMS, sending data, and making calls. This is the board that we will use for projects in this chapter. You can get the MKR GSM 1400 from the following link: `https://store-usa.arduino.cc/products/arduino-mkr-gsm-1400`.

- **Arduino Portenta CAT.M1/NBIOT GNSS Shield**: This shield will work with any Portenta to provide cellular connectivity. This shield is usable with MKR boards such as the Wi-Fi board. You will need to solder some headers on it though.

Arduino provides a global SIM that you can pick up for IoT purposes. This SIM is designed to roam on most global communication networks. This SIM only connects to the Arduino IoT Cloud. You can then forward the data using **webhooks**. You can learn about the SIM at the following link: `https://store-usa.arduino.cc/products/arduino-sim`.

Before writing your first sketch for cellular connectivity, there are two things you should be aware of

Cellular modems require more power than you can get from your computer USB port. Most of the modems require 5V and 2A. The solution to this is to make use of something that is called a *buck converter*. This will take power, something like a 9V battery, and output the desired voltage. Without the requisite power, the modem will not connect to the base station.

Cellular modems require an antenna. Be sure to attach your antenna; otherwise, you could spend a lot of time debugging unnecessary problems.

Let's look into the first capability of the MKR GSM 1400.

Making phone calls

Let's discuss the situation in which phone calls make sense by considering the alternatives.

SMS delivers messages as text. These messages can be delivered to any type of phone, even what is called a feature phone. However, SMS utilizes a methodology called store-and-forward. SMS is not an emergency service; the network will use a best-effort approach to deliver the message, but delivery could be delayed for many days.

GPRS delivers messages over the internet. This is immediate, but the message will end up on the cloud, from where a notification would need to be sent to a smartphone, or the end user would need to have a dashboard open in order to see the notification. In such a case, any device that doesn't have access to the internet, or that isn't smart, will be unable to get this information.

With the preceding information, how then could we implement an alarm? How might we implement a smoke alarm that would be guaranteed to notify the homeowner? A phone call might be useful. If you had a dedicated phone number for your fire alarm, you would be sure to respond accordingly whenever you got a call from it.

Let's set up our GSM board to make a call.

Project 1 – Making a call with the MKR GSM

Follow the following steps to make a call from the MKR GSM. The code illustrated here is available on GitHub (`https://github.com/PacktPublishing/Arduino-Data-Communications/tree/main/chapter-9/MKR-GSM-Simple-Phone-Call`):

1. Insert the SIM into the slot on the microcontroller.
2. Connect the **GND** pin on the microcontroller to the 5V negative terminal on the buck converter, using a DuPont cable.
3. Connect the **VIN** pin on the microcontroller to the 5V positive terminal on the buck converter, using a DuPont cable.
4. Connect the battery to the buck converter, using the appropriate cable(s).
5. Attach the **dipole** antenna to the microcontroller.
6. Connect the microcontroller to the computer.
7. Launch the Arduino IDE.
8. Confirm that the IDE has detected the microcontroller.
9. Turn on the power supply on the buck converter.
10. Create a new sketch.
11. Add a new tab, and save it as `arduino_secrets.h`.
12. Paste the following into the file:

    ```
    #define SECRET_PHONE        ""
    ```

13. Place a phone number to call between the quotes.
14. Return to the main sketch `.ino` file.
15. Open the **Libraries** tab.
16. Search for `MKRGSM`.
17. Install **MKRGSM by Arduino**. It should look similar to the following screenshot.

Figure 9.3 – The MKRGSM Library

18. Insert the following code to include the necessary header libraries:

```
#include <MKRGSM.h>
#include "arduino_secrets.h"
```

19. Declare a constant to get the phone number to call from the secrets file:

```
const char PHONE[] = SECRET_PHONE;
```

20. Declare variables to access the modem and make calls:

```
GSM gsmAccess;
GSMVoiceCall vcs;
```

21. Declare a function, callAndHangUp(), at the bottom of the file that calls the phone number we have specified and then hangs up three seconds after the call is answered:

```
void callAndHangUp() {
  Serial.print("Attempting to call: ");
  Serial.println(PHONE);

  if(vcs.voiceCall(PHONE)) {
    Serial.println("Call established, hanging up in 3
seconds.");
    delay(3000);
```

```
      vcs.hangCall();
    }
    Serial.println("Call ended");
}
```

22. Do the following within setup() {} – initialize the Serial port, wait for the Serial Monitor to open, initialize the modem, and then run the callAndHangUp() function. The code for all this is shown here:

```
void setup() {
  Serial.begin(115200);
  while (!Serial);
  bool connected = false;
  while (!connected) {
    if (gsmAccess.begin() == GSM_READY) {
      connected = true;
    } else {
      Serial.println("Error connecting, repeating attempt ...");
      delay(1000);
    }
  }

  Serial.println("GSM module initialized.");

  callAndHangUp();
}
```

23. We don't want to do anything repeatedly in this sketch, so we leave loop() {} empty.

24. Upload the sketch to the microcontroller.

25. Open the Serial Monitor.

26. Wait a few minutes for the module to establish communications with a base station. This isn't instantaneous.

27. Answer the call when your phone rings.

28. The call should terminate after a few seconds.

29. The output on your Serial Monitor should resemble the following.

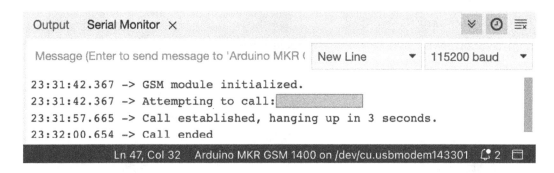

Figure 9.4 – The voice call output

Congratulations! You have successfully uploaded a sketch to the microcontroller that makes voice calls. You can watch the Code in Action video at the following link: https://packt.link/ZzDM1.

You can update the sketch so that the call isn't made in the setup but, instead, whenever an event is triggered from your sensors.

Let's work with SMS.

Working with SMS

SMS is a text-based two-way communication method. It is useful because it works well in the absence of internet connectivity, and it is used in a lot of applications where you want the microcontroller to do something, or where you want the microcontroller to report the status of something.

Let's consider the first instance where you would like a microcontroller to receive an SMS.

Project 2 – Receiving an SMS

Take the following steps to display the content of any SMS messages received on the microcontroller. The code for this section is available at GitHub (https://github.com/PacktPublishing/Arduino-Data-Communications/tree/main/chapter-9/MKR-GSM-Simple-Receive-SMS):

1. Connect the dipole antenna to the MKR GSM. This is the antenna that comes with the MKR GSM purchased from the Arduino Store.

2. Insert the SIM card into the holder.

3. Connect the negative pin of the 5V power supply to the GND pin of the microcontroller.

4. Connect the positive pin of the 5V power supply to the VIN pin of the microcontroller.

5. Connect the microcontroller to the computer.

6. Launch the Arduino IDE.

7. Create a new sketch.

8. Include the MKRGSM library so that the board can work with the GSM modem. This is shown in the following code snippet:

```
#include <MKRGSM.h>
```

9. Initialize variables to work with the modem and SMS, as shown here:

```
GSM gsmAccess;
GSM_SMS sms;
```

10. Create two character arrays to hold the number that sent the SMS, as well as the content of the message. The former is 20 characters long, while the latter is 180 characters long to account for the maximum length of a text message:

```
char fromNo[20];
char msg[180];
```

11. In the setup() {} function, initialize the serial interface, wait for the user to open up the Serial Monitor, and then initialize the GSM modem:

```
void setup() {
  Serial.begin(115200);
  while(!Serial);
  bool connected = false;
  while (!connected) {
    if (gsmAccess.begin() == GSM_READY) {
      connected = true;
    } else {
      Serial.println("Couldn't initialize modem, waiting ...");
      delay(1000);
    }
  }
  Serial.println("Modem initialized, waiting ...");
}
```

12. Within the loop() {} function, check whether any messages are available. If there are, get the sender number and store that in fromNo. Then, read each character of the message and store them in msg. Finally, output both to the Serial Monitor:

```
void loop() {
  if (sms.available()) {
    sms.remoteNumber(fromNo, 20);
    Serial.print("Message from: ");
    Serial.println(fromNo);
    int i = 0;
```

```
    int j;
    while ( (j = sms.read()) != -1) {
      msg[i++] = (char) j;
    }
    Serial.println(msg);
  }
}
```

13. Turn on the power supply to the microcontroller.

14. Upload the sketch to the microcontroller.

15. Open the Serial Monitor.

16. Send a message to the phone number registered to the SIM, and wait a few minutes to see the microcontroller print out any messages. The output should be similar to the following screenshot.

Output   Serial Monitor ×

Search
Message (Enter to send message to 'Arduino MKR GSM 1400' on '/de

```
02:31:48.037 -> Modem initialized, waiting ...
02:33:03.620 -> Message from: +2
02:33:03.620 -> Hold the door ...
```

Figure 9.5 – Showing received messages

Congratulations! You have programmed the microcontroller to read messages sent via text. The preceding steps are illustrated in a video, available at the following link: https://packt.link/ZzDM1.

You can program the microcontroller to carry out various tasks, based on the message received from one or more phone numbers. In the preceding example output, the sender's phone number is shown in an international format with a leading prefix.

Let's look at an example of sending temperature and humidity data from our microcontroller via an SMS.

Project 3 – Sending temperature and humidity data via SMS

Take the following steps to send temperature and humidity data via SMS. The code for this project is available on GitHub (https://github.com/PacktPublishing/Arduino-Data-Communications/tree/main/chapter-9/MKR-GSM-Simple-Send-T-H-SMS):

1. Attach the MKR ENV Shield to the top of the MKR GSM.

2. Connect the dipole antenna to the MKR GSM.

3. Insert the SIM card into the holder.

4. Connect the negative pin of the 5V power supply to the GND pin of the microcontroller.

5. Connect the positive pin of the 5V power supply to the VIN pin of the microcontroller.

6. Connect the microcontroller to the computer.

7. Launch the Arduino IDE.

8. Create a new sketch.

9. Create a new tab, and save it as `arduino_secrets.h`.

10. Paste the following code into the file:

```
#define SECRET_PHONE        ""
```

11. Enter the phone number that you want to send messages to.

12. Return to the `.ino` file.

13. Include the headers necessary to work with the ENV Shield and the GSM modem, using the following code snippet:

```
#include <Arduino_MKRENV.h>
#include <MKRGSM.h>
#include "arduino_secrets.h"
```

14. Declare variables to hold values for temperature and humidity, as well as help us iterate only once per our set delay. This is currently set to 60 seconds, so keep an eye on your microcontroller to ensure that it doesn't send out too many messages:

```
unsigned long lastRead = millis();
const int myDelay = 60000;
float t,h;
const int stationId = 1;
```

15. Declare a constant that holds the phone number that will receive messages. This phone number is declared in `arduino_secrets.h`:

```
const char PHONE[] = SECRET_PHONE;
```

16. Declare variables to work with the GSM modem and also with SMS:

```
GSM gsmAccess;
GSM_SMS sms;
```

17. Within the `setup()` `{}` function, initialize the ENV Shield and the GSM modem:

```
void setup() {
  Serial.begin(115200);
  while(!Serial);
```

```
  while (!ENV.begin()) {
    Serial.println("Failed to initialize ENV Shield, waiting
...");
    delay(10000);
  }
  Serial.println("Initialized ENV Shield");
  bool connected = false;
  while (!connected) {
    if (gsmAccess.begin() == GSM_READY) {
      connected = true;
    } else {
      Serial.println("Couldn't initialize modem, waiting ...");
      delay(1000);
    }
  }
  Serial.println("Modem initialized.");
  Serial.println("Ready ...");
}
```

18. Within `loop() {}`, once every 60 seconds, read the temperature and humidity, package the information into a string, and send it off as an SMS. Note the operations that happen with the sms object:

```
void loop() {
  if (millis() - lastRead > myDelay) {
    lastRead = millis();
    t = ENV.readTemperature();
    h = ENV.readHumidity();
    String msg = String(String(stationId) + "|" + String(t) +
"|" + String(h));
    Serial.println(msg);
    sms.beginSMS(PHONE);
    sms.print(msg);
    sms.endSMS();
    Serial.println("Sent SMS.");
  }
}
```

19. Turn on the power supply to the microcontroller.

20. Upload the sketch to the microcontroller.

21. Open the Serial Monitor.

22. Wait a minute for it to send a message. The Serial Monitor should output a message similar to the following.

```
03:17:25.991 -> Initialized ENV Shield
03:17:36.360 -> Modem initialized.
03:17:36.360 -> Ready ...
03:17:52.416 -> 1|29.80|56.92
03:17:54.242 -> Sent SMS.
```

Figure 9.6 – Sending an SMS

23. Turn off the microcontroller as soon as you see the confirmation to avoid sending messages endlessly.

Congratulations! You have successfully sent a message. Ensure that you don't leave the microcontroller running to avoid sending messages endlessly. Remember – messages might not be free. The preceding steps are illustrated in a video available at the following link: `https://packt.link/ZzDM1`.

Now, let's send data over the internet with GPRS.

Working with GPRS

You can make use of GPRS to access REST API endpoints, just as you did using Wi-Fi. However, there is one difference – you need to ensure that the SIM has an active data subscription. You will also need to find the **Access Point Name** (**APN**) of your telecom provider, as well as the credentials for connecting. This is normally published somewhere on the provider's website.

The SIM in our microcontroller can't communicate with the server in our local network. We will need to communicate with a server that is publicly hosted. Let's use `https://webhook.site` for this purpose. This will let us monitor the data we send from the Arduino without having to write a custom API to receive the data. This is useful to quickly debug what we send from our microcontrollers. Visit the site and search for the connection URL, which looks similar to the following.

Your unique URL (Please copy it from here, *not* from the address bar!)

`https://webhook.site/d347abf7-6079-4a2c-9048-72b606b6157`

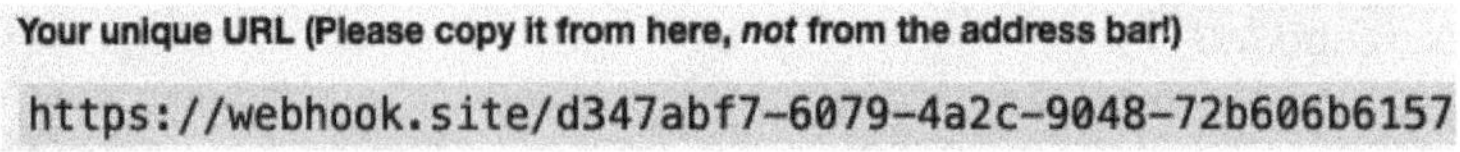

Figure 9.7 – The webhook.site unique URL

You will need to work with two parts:

- **The server**: This is `webhook.site`
- **The path**: This is the path from / to the end

In the following project, you will write a sketch that sends temperature and humidity data to the internet.

Project 4 – sending temperature and humidity data over GPRS

Take the following steps to read temperature and humidity data from the ENV Shield and send it to the internet, using GPRS. The code for this project is available on GitHub (`https://github.com/PacktPublishing/Arduino-Data-Communications/tree/main/chapter-9/MKR-GSM-GPRS`):

1. Attach the MKR ENV Shield to the top of the MKR GSM.
2. Connect the dipole antenna to the MKR GSM.
3. Insert the SIM card into the holder.
4. Connect the negative pin of the 5V power supply to the GND pin of the microcontroller.
5. Connect the positive pin of the 5V power supply to the VIN pin of the microcontroller.
6. Connect the microcontroller to the computer.
7. Launch the Arduino IDE.
8. Create a new sketch.
9. Create a new tab, and save it as `arduino_secrets.h`.
10. Paste the following code into the file:

    ```
    #define SECRET_APN "web.gprs.mtnnigeria.net"
    #define SECRET_USER "web"
    #define SECRET_PASS "web"
    #define SECRET_SERVER "webhook.site"
    #define SECRET_PATH "/7f5b8f0c-5f17-4639-aa81-64d0ea33d4b"
    ```

11. Replace all of the values accordingly.
12. Return to the `.ino` file.
13. Include the headers necessary to work with the ENV Shield and the GSM modem, using the following code snippet:

    ```
    #include <Arduino_MKRENV.h>
    #include <SPI.h>
    #include <Arduino_JSON.h>
    #include <MKRGSM.h>
    #include "arduino_secrets.h"
    ```

14. Declare variables to hold values for temperature and humidity, as well as help us iterate only once per outset delay. This is currently set to 60 seconds, so keep an eye on your microcontroller to ensure that it doesn't send out too many messages:

    ```
    unsigned long lastRead = millis();
    const int myDelay = 60000;
    ```

```
float temperature, humidity;
const int stationId = 1;
```

15. Declare constants that will let us connect over GPRS. These are declared in arduino_secrets.h:

```
char apn[] = SECRET_APN;
char user[] = SECRET_USER;
char pass[] = SECRET_PASS;
```

16. Declare variables to work with the GSM modem and also with GPRS:

```
GPRS gprs;
GSM gsmAccess;
GSMClient client;
char server[] = SECRET_SERVER;
char path[] = SECRET_PATH;
int port = 80;
```

17. Within the setup() {} function, initialize the ENV Shield and the GSM modem:

```
void setup() {
  Serial.begin(115200);
  while (!ENV.begin()) {
    Serial.println("Failed to initialive ENV Shield, waiting
...");
    delay(10000);
  }
  boolean connected = false;
  while (!connected) {
    if ( gsmAccess.begin() == GSM_READY) {
      if (gprs.attachGPRS(apn, user, pass) == GPRS_READY) {
        Serial.println("GPRS connected.");
        connected = true;
      }
    } else {
      Serial.println("Unable to initialize the modem");
      delay(1000);
    }
  }
  Serial.println("Ready ...");
}
```

18. Within `loop()  {}`, once every 60 seconds, read the temperature and humidity, package the information into a string, establish a connection to `webhook.site`, and then publish the payload. Note that our payload is in the JSON format:

```
void loop() {
  if (millis() - lastRead > myDelay) {
    lastRead = millis();
    temperature = ENV.readTemperature();
    humidity = ENV.readHumidity();
    Serial.print("T: ");
    Serial.println(temperature);
    Serial.print("H: ");
    Serial.println(humidity);


    if (client.connect(server, port)) {
      JSONVar payload;
      payload["stationid"] = stationId;
      payload["epochs"] = 1;
      payload["temperature"] = temperature;
      payload["humidity"] = humidity;

      String p = JSON.stringify(payload);

      Serial.println("Connected to server, posting data");

      client.print("POST ");
      client.print(path);
      client.println(" HTTP/1.1");
      client.print("HOST: ");
      client.println(server);
      client.println("Content-Type: application/json");
      client.print("Content-Length: ");
      client.println(p.length());
      client.println();
      client.println(p);
      client.println("Connection: close");
      client.println();

      Serial.println("Payload sent.");

      if (client.available()) {
        char c = client.read();
        Serial.print(c);
```

```
      }
      Serial.println();

      if(!client.available() && !client.connected()) {
        client.stop();
      }
    } else {
      Serial.println("Can't connect to server");
    }
  }
}
```

19. Turn on the power supply to the microcontroller.

20. Upload the sketch to the microcontroller.

21. Open the Serial Monitor.

22. Wait a minute for it to send a message. The Serial Monitor should output a message similar to the following.

```
05:58:41.464 ->
05:59:35.347 -> GPRS connected.
05:59:35.347 -> Ready ...
06:00:20.027 -> T: 31.24
06:00:20.027 -> H: 63.22
06:00:22.222 -> Connected to server, posting data
```

Figure 9.8 – The Serial Monitor output

23. Stop the microcontroller.

24. Return to the browser where webhook.site is open.

25. The left part of the screen should show a list of messages received, as shown in the following screenshot. The HTTP method used for communication with webhook.site is shown in a smaller box, before the message ID and date and time information in which the message was received.

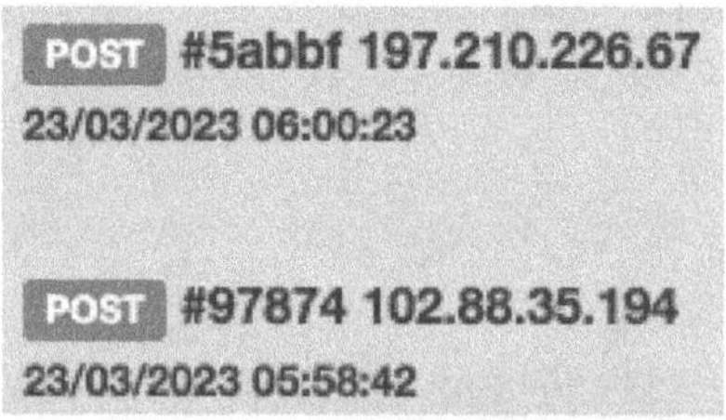

POST #5abbf 197.210.226.67
23/03/2023 06:00:23

POST #97874 102.88.35.194
23/03/2023 05:58:42

Figure 9.9 – The webhook messages received

26. Select any of the messages.

27. Look to the right for additional information about the message. This should be similar to the following screenshot.

Request Details   Permalink   Raw content   Export as ▾

POST   http://webhook.site/7f5b8f0c-5f17-4639-aa81-64d0ea33d4be

Host   197.210.226.67 whois

Date   23/03/2023 06:00:23 (11 minutes ago)

Size   89 bytes

ID   5abbfdfc-9c8c-4cc1-b20d-67143ad10a7d

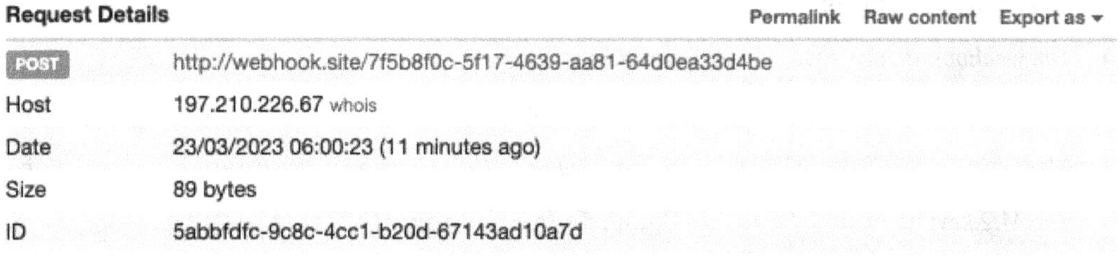

Figure 9.10 – The message details

28. Look to the bottom of the page for the payload that was sent from the microcontroller. This should be similar to the following screenshot.

Raw Content

```
{
    "stationid": 1,
    "epochs": 1,
    "temperature": 31.241058349609375,
    "humidity": 63.219230651855469
}
```

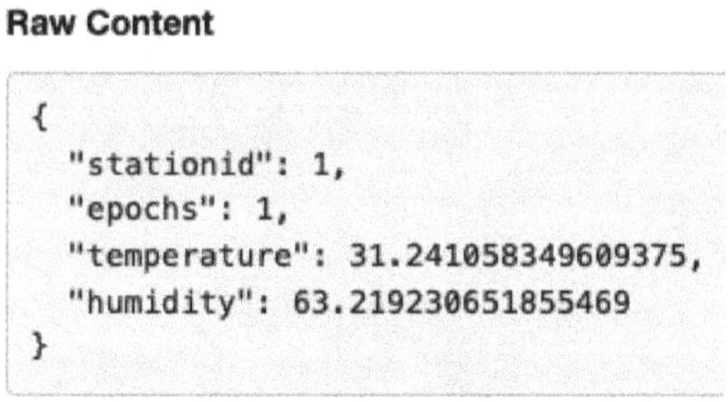

Figure 9.11 – The payload

Congratulations! You have successfully sent data to a REST endpoint over GPRS. The preceding steps are available in a video at the following link: https://packt.link/ZzDM1.

Summary

In this chapter, you learned about cellular connectivity options and also looked at some modules that you could make use of. You then worked with an MKR GSM board and made phone calls, sent and received an SMS, and sent data over GPRS to a REST endpoint.

In the following chapter, you will learn how to work with a communication technology that works over a peer-to-peer network.

Further reading

To learn more about the topics covered in this chapter, you can visit the following links:

- *Blues Wireless*: `https://blues.io/`
- *The webhook site*: `https://webhook.site`
- *GPRS*: `https://en.wikipedia.org/wiki/General_Packet_Radio_Service`
- *MMS*: `https://en.wikipedia.org/wiki/Multimedia_Messaging_Service`
- *The M.2 key*: `https://www.delock.de/infothek/M.2/M.2_e.html`
- *The Arduino SIM*: `https://store-usa.arduino.cc/products/arduino-sim`
- *The Arduino dipole antenna*: `https://store-usa.arduino.cc/products/dipole-pentaband-waterproof-antenna`

10
Communicating via HC-12

So far, we have learned about various communication technologies that require that we connect to a gateway to send and receive data over long distances. There are situations in which we don't have access to a gateway and are also not in a position to set one up. That is where HC-12 could come in handy. Using HC-12 modules, we can communicate at a distance of up to 1 km outdoors.

In this chapter, we are going to cover the following main topics:

- Learning about HC-12
- Acquiring HC-12 modules
- Setting up our hardware
- Sending and receiving data

Let's begin by listing what you will need to complete this chapter.

Technical requirements

You will need the following components to execute the labs in this chapter:

- Microcontroller: 2x Arduino MKR WiFi 1010
- 2x USB cables
- 2x breadboards
- 2x HC-12 modules
- 1x MKR ENV Shield
- Diodes: 2x 1N4007
- Capacitors: 2x (22uF to 1mF)
- Dupont cables

- 1x MKR ENV Shield

- 2x antennae

All the code for this chapter is available in this book's GitHub repository: `https://github.com/PacktPublishing/Arduino-Data-Communications/tree/main/chapter-10/`.

Let's proceed to learn about HC-12.

Learning about HC-12

HC-12 is a peer-to-peer broadcast technology and communication module that you can utilize to send and receive data between two or more devices. It is a low-cost, easy-to-use module that you can put into a variety of applications, such as robotics, automation, and industrial control.

HC-12 operates in the 433 MHz frequency band and has a maximum data rate of 100 kbps. It is a half-duplex module, which means that only one device can transmit at a time. However, you can use it to create a peer-to-peer network where multiple devices can communicate with each other.

HC-12 has several features that make it a versatile and reliable module. It has a built-in CRC checksum to ensure data integrity, and it can be configured to work with a variety of modulation schemes. It also has several power-saving features that allow it to operate for extended periods on a single battery.

HC-12 is a popular choice for a variety of applications. You can find it used in robotics and automation to control and monitor devices, as well as in industrial control systems to communicate between different components. In addition, it is used in a variety of other applications, such as asset tracking, telemetry, and security systems.

HC-12 modules are thumb-sized and come with a castellated design so that they can be easily integrated into a PCB design. It is also possible to solder headers onto the modules.

Some of the benefits of using HC-12 modules are as follows:

- Low cost

- Ease of use

- Versatility

- Reliability

- Energy efficiency

Let's discuss where you can purchase HC-12 modules.

Acquiring HC-12 modules

You can purchase HC-12 modules in generic form from several online stores, including Amazon, eBay, Banggood, and AliExpress. Simply put `HC-12` into the search bar and several options will appear. You can also purchase these modules from local electronics stores.

HC-12 modules don't carry a brand. As such, you should purchase them from a retailer that you trust, especially if it's an online vendor. Make sure you read the reviews from previous buyers so that you don't end up with a poor-quality knockoff.

The modules contain transmitters and receivers. As such, you might want to avoid importing them if you can purchase them locally. This is because you might be required to prove that the modules meet certain certification requirements for where you live. If you can pick these modules up locally, you will be sure that the importer has satisfied all requirements.

If you have to import these modules, try to check if there are any import restrictions with your customs office. You don't want to wait for your items only to find out that they have been confiscated. Also, if you are purchasing from China, note that a lot of places consider China to be a duty-free zone and will charge you the maximum duties. In a lot of cases, the cost of shipping and customs duties could exceed the cost of the module itself.

Setting up the hardware

The HC-12 module comes with five holes on one side. You can either mount it castellated or solver headers on it. Two of the connectors are meant for power (**VCC**) and ground (**GND**), while the other two are meant for serial communications (**TXD and RXD**). The final connector is labeled **SET** and is meant for reconfiguring the module. The opposite side of the module has an antenna connector (**ANT**) that is meant for RF input/output:

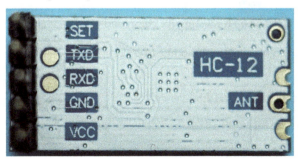

Figure 10.1 – The rear of the HC-12 module

You should ensure that your modules are physically apart by a distance of at least 2 meters. This prevents unusual behavior. This distance requirement exists because of how the modules transmit and receive data using radio waves.

The module works with voltages between 3.2 V and 5.5 V. The required current must exceed 200 mA. Similar to setups that utilize cellular radios, you can't power the setup via a USB cable. Instead, you will need to power it externally using either a battery or a bench-top power supply. You will also need to place a reservoir capacitor between 22 uF and 1 mF between the GND and VCC pins.

If the battery voltage is above 4.5 V, you will need to place a 1N4007 diode in series with the VCC pin.

The TXD and RXD pins can be connected to any digital pins on the microcontroller. Connect the RXD pin to digital pin 11 on the Arduino, and TXD to digital pin 10 on the Arduino.

Pulling the SET pin to GND will let you configure the HC-12 module. Let's look at how to do that.

Configuring the HC-12 module

The HC-12 module has a microcontroller on board. Instead of flashing firmware, you can send AT commands via serial to configure the microcontroller. The module supports various AT commands, as follows:

- **AT**: Test module communications.
- **AT+Bxxxx**: This sets the baud rate. The available options are 1,200, 2,400, 4,800, 9,600, 19,200, 38,400, 57,600, and 115,200. The default value is 9,600.
- **AT+Cxxx**: This sets the wireless communication channel. The values range from 001 up to 100. The default channel is 001.

The HC-12 module doesn't have an LED indicator. One way of testing whether the module works is using an AT command. We'll do that in the following exercise.

The AT test command

Follow these steps to flash firmware for testing AT commands:

1. Connect the SET pin of the HC-12 module to GND.
2. Create a new sketch.
3. Include the SoftwareSerial library:

   ```
   #include <SoftwareSerial.h>
   ```

4. Create an instance of SoftwareSerial using pins 10 and 11:

   ```
   SoftwareSerial HC12(10, 11);
   ```

5. Initialize both the computer serial port and the software serial:

```
void setup() {
  Serial.begin(9600);
  HC12.begin(9600);
}
```

6. Read any data coming from the serial port of the computer and send it to the HC-12 module, and read any data coming from the HC-12 module and send it to the computer's serial port:

```
void loop() {
  while(HC12.available()) {
    Serial.write(HC12.read());
  }
  while(Serial.available()) {
    HC12.write(Serial.read());
  }
}
```

7. Upload the sketch.

8. Open the serial port on your computer.

9. Type AT into the message field. This is shown in the following screenshot:

Figure 10.2 – Test module communication

10. Hit the *Enter* button.

11. Observe the output. It should be **OK**. You might need to do this two or three times because the module doesn't always respond to the first command. The output will look similar to the following:

$$00:24:49.391 \rightarrow OK$$

Figure 10.3 – The output of the AT command

Congratulations – you have successfully configured the HC-12 module to receive AT commands! You can pass in additional AT commands to change the channel or baud rate.

You can watch these steps in a video at https://packt.link/pCmIf.

Let's proceed to program the microcontroller so that it can send and receive data.

Sending and receiving data

You can configure a microcontroller to communicate with an HC-12 module using software serial, as we have seen previously. However, make sure that the SET pin is not pulled to the ground when in normal operation.

Let's consider a simple sketch that will output whatever the HC-12 module receives to the serial console of the computer to which the microcontroller is connected.

Exercise 10.1 – displaying whatever the HC-12 module receives

Follow these steps to read whatever the HC-12 module receives and print it out on the serial monitor on your computer:

1. Begin by importing SoftwareSerial:

    ```
    #include <SoftwareSerial.h>
    ```

2. Create an instance of SoftwareSerial called HC12. This takes two parameters, the first being the pin that TX is connected to, and the second being the pin that RX is connected to:

    ```
    SoftwareSerial HC12(10, 11);
    ```

3. Initialize the serial port on the microcontroller to a baud rate of 9600. Do the same for the software serial port:

    ```
    void setup() {
      Serial.begin(9600);
      HC12.begin(9600);
    }
    ```

4. Use the .available() method of the software serial port to check for incoming data, and then read it and write it out to the serial port of the computer:

    ```
    void loop() {
      while(HC12.available()) {
        Serial.write(HC12.read());
      }
    }
    ```

5. Upload the sketch to the microcontroller.

6. Open the serial monitor on the Arduino IDE.

You will need to connect an antenna to the HC-12 module. You can refer to the following Code in Action video to see the entire process: https://packt.link/pCmIf.

The serial monitor will only output something if there are transmissions within range. We haven't programmed a microcontroller to transmit any data yet, but don't worry – we will do that next.

Sending temperature and humidity over HC-12

Follow these steps to read temperature and humidity from an ENV shield and send it over to the HC-12 module:

1. Begin by including the necessary header files:

    ```
    #include <SoftwareSerial.h>
    #include <Arduino_MKRENV.h>
    ```

2. Declare variables and constants to hold values such as the last time you read the temperature, the current millisecond, and the temperature and humidity:

    ```
    SoftwareSerial HC12(10, 11); //TX, RX

    unsigned long lastRead = millis();
    const int myDelay = 60000;
    float t,h;
    const int stationId = 1;
    ```

3. Initialize serial ports and the MKR ENV shield:

    ```
    void setup() {
      Serial.begin(9600);
      HC12.begin(9600);

      while (!ENV.begin()) {
        Serial.println("Failed to initialize ENV Shield, waiting
    ...");
        delay(10000);
      }
      Serial.println("Initialized ENV Shield");
      Serial.println("Ready ...");
    }
    ```

4. Within `loop()`, we will set up code to read any data received from either the computer or the HC-12. We will also read temperature and humidity data, create a message, and send it out via the HC-12 module:

    ```
    void loop() {
      while(HC12.available()) {
        Serial.write(HC12.read());
      }
    ```

```
  while(Serial.available()) {
    HC12.write(Serial.read());
  }

  if (millis() - lastRead > myDelay) {
    lastRead = millis();
    t = ENV.readTemperature();
    h = ENV.readHumidity();
    String msg = String(String(stationId) + "|" + String(t) +
"|" + String(h));
    HC12.println(msg);
    Serial.println("Sent MSG.");
  }
}
```

5.   Upload the sketch to the second MKR board. Wait a few seconds and observe the first microcontroller for any incoming messages.

Congratulations – you have successfully programmed a microcontroller to send out data over HC-12! These steps are shown in a Code in Action video at `https://packt.link/pCmIf`.

Summary

In this chapter, you learned about HC-12 and how to use it to send and receive data. You can now implement peer-to-peer networks out in the field when using a technology such as cellular or LoRaWAN is not suitable.

In the next chapter, we will look at how to communicate when radio signals are not convenient and would constitute interference to other equipment nearby.

Further reading

To learn more about AT commands, you can visit `https://1ot.mobi/resources/blog/beginners-guide-to-at-commands`.

11
Managing Communication with RS-485

In the previous chapters, we learned how to communicate using various wireless technologies and hardware. However, there are times when communicating over wireless isn't suitable because it would cause interference with critical hardware in the vicinity. In this chapter, we will learn about a communication technology that isn't wireless and is popular in industrial settings.

In this chapter, we're going to cover the following main topics:

- Introducing RS-485
- Introducing Modbus
- Communicating using RS-485 hardware

Let's consider what we will need to complete the projects in this chapter.

Technical requirements

You will need the following items to complete the exercises in this chapter:

- MKR WiFi 1010
- MKR 485 Shield
- MKR ENV Shield
- Jumper wires

The code snippets for this chapter are available in this book's GitHub repository: https://github.com/PacktPublishing/Arduino-Data-Communications/tree/main/chapter-11.

Introducing RS-485

RS-485 is a standard for serial communication that allows multiple devices to communicate on the same bus. It is a differential voltage signaling standard, which means that it uses two wires to transmit data. This makes it less susceptible to noise than other serial communication standards, such as RS-232.

RS-485 is a half-duplex communication method, so, as such, only one device can transmit at a time. You can still use it to create a multi-drop network where multiple devices can share the same bus. You can utilize it in the following settings:

- **Industrial automation**: RS-485 is used in industrial automation and control systems to communicate between devices such as **Programmable Logic Controllers** (**PLCs**), sensors, and actuators

- **Building automation**: RS-485 is used to control **Humidity Ventilation and Air Conditioning** (**HVAC**) systems, as well as lights, security, and access control

- **Medical equipment**: RS-485 is used to communicate between devices such as patient monitors, infusion pumps, and imaging devices

- **Transportation systems**: RS-485 is used to communicate between devices such as traffic lights, parking meters, and train control systems

RS-485 supports communications between devices that are up to 1 km apart. You can utilize a twisted-pair cable, such as the one used in telephony, to accomplish this.

Benefits of RS-485

The RS-485 standard has certain benefits:

- **Robust**: RS-485 is a very robust communication standard. It is less susceptible to noise than other serial communication standards, such as RS-232.

- **Long distance**: RS-485 can support long distances. The maximum distance between two devices on an RS-485 bus is 1,200 meters.

- **Multi-drop**: RS-485 can support multiple devices on the same bus. This makes it ideal for applications where a central controller needs to communicate with a large number of devices.

- **Low cost**: RS-485 is a relatively low-cost communication standard. This makes it a good choice for budget-conscious applications.

Cons of RS-485

RS-485 has a few constraints or limitations that you should be aware of.

- **Slow**: RS-485 is a relatively slow communication standard. The maximum data rate for RS-485 is 100 kbps.

- **Not suitable for all applications**: RS-485 is not suitable for all applications. For example, it is not suitable for applications where real-time data communication is required.

Communicating over RS-485 requires hardware that supports RS-485, with one controller and one or more peripherals. Let's consider these next.

RS-485 hardware

You can purchase a shield for working with the Arduino MKR and Arduino Portenta families of microcontrollers. This shield is called the **Arduino MKR 485 Shield**. You can purchase this shield at `https://store-usa.arduino.cc/products/arduino-mkr-485-shield`.

This shield works with the MKR boards we have been using. As a result, we will be utilizing it for the exercises in this chapter.

MKR 485 Shield

The MKR 485 Shield looks similar to the following:

Figure 11.1 – Arduino MKR 485 Shield

The block on the right-hand side of the preceding figure allows for connections. There are six terminals, labeled as follows:

- **ISO GND**: Connect this from the terminal of the peripheral device to the GND pin of the controller

- **A**: Leave this vacant on the peripheral

- **B**: Leave this vacant on the peripheral

- **Y**: Connect a cable from this block on the peripheral to A on the controller
- **Z**: Connect a cable from this block on the peripheral to B on the controller
- **ISO VCC**: Leave this vacant

There are three switches next to the block that need to be configured on the shield, depending on whether it's being used as a controller or a peripheral. The switches are labeled 1, 2, and 3, and they can be on or off.

For peripherals (or senders), the switches should be set as follows:

- **1**: Set to OFF
- **2**: Set to ON
- **3**: Set to ON

For controllers (or receivers), the switches need to be set as follows:

- **1**: Set to ON
- **2**: Set to ON
- **3**: Set to OFF

You will need the ArduinoRS485 library to program the microcontrollers. Follow the steps provided in the following sub-section to install the library.

Installing the RS485 library

Follow these steps to install the RS-485 library from Arduino:

1. Launch the Arduino IDE.
2. Open the library manager.
3. Search for `rs485`.
4. Locate the entry for **ArduinoRS485 by Arduino**.
5. Install this entry.

You can watch a video showing how to install this library at `https://packt.link/Axyff`.

With this library installed, you are ready to program the peripheral device to take temperature and humidity readings from the MKR ENV Shield and send them across. We'll do that next.

Sending temperature and humidity data using RS-485

Follow these steps to send temperature and humidity data over RS-485:

1. Connect the MKR ENV Shield on top of the MRK WiFi 1010.

2. Connect the MKR 485 Shield on top of the MKR ENV Shield.

3. Attach a black male-male Dupont cable or jumper wire to the ISO GND terminal.

4. Attach a blue male-male Dupont cable or jumper wire to the Y terminal.

5. Attach an orange male-male Dupont cable or jumper wire to the Z terminal.

6. Connect a micro-USB cable between the microcontroller and your computer.

7. Launch the Arduino IDE.

8. Start a new sketch.

9. #include the necessary header files:

    ```
    #include <Arduino_MKRENV.h>
    #include <ArduinoRS485.h>
    ```

10. Declare constants and variables to aid with tracking the environment variables and the last time that they were read:

    ```
    unsigned long lastRead = millis();
    const int myDelay = 60000;
    float t,h;
    const int stationId = 1;
    ```

11. Within the setup() function, we initialize the MKR ENV Shield and the MKR 485 Shield. We set the transmission baud rate of the MRK 485 to 9600:

    ```
    void setup() {
      while (!ENV.begin()) {
        Serial.println("Failed to initialize ENV Shield, waiting
    ...");
        delay(10000);
      }
      RS485.begin(9600);
    }
    ```

12. Next, within the loop() function, read the temperature and humidity periodically and send that data over RS-485:

    ```
    void loop() {
      if (millis() - lastRead > myDelay) {
        lastRead = millis();
    ```

```
    t = ENV.readTemperature();
    h = ENV.readHumidity();
    String msg = String(String(stationId) + "|" + String(t) +
"|" + String(h));

    RS485.beginTransmission();
    RS485.println(msg);
    RS485.endTransmission();
  }
}
```

13. Upload the sketch to the microcontroller.

Congratulations – you have successfully programmed the microcontroller to send out temperature and humidity readings over RS-485! These steps are illustrated in a video available at `https://packt.link/Axyff`.

Now, we need to receive what has been sent out. Let's program a controller to do that.

Receiving data over RS-485

Follow these steps to set up a controller:

1. Connect the second MKR 485 Shield to the top of the second MRK WiFi 1010 microcontroller.

2. Connect the black cable from the `ISO GND` terminal on the peripheral to the GND pin on the controller.

3. Connect the blue cable from the Y terminal on the peripheral to the A terminal on the controller.

4. Connect the orange cable from the Z terminal on the peripheral to the B terminal on the controller.

5. Connect a micro-USB cable between the microcontroller and a computer.

6. Launch the Arduino IDE.

7. Start a new sketch.

8. `#include` the required header file so that you can make use of the MKR 485 Shield:

```
#include <ArduinoRS485.h>
```

9. Initialize the MKR 485 Shield and set it to receive mode. We can do this in the `setup()` function:

```
void setup() {
  Serial.begin(9600);
  while (!Serial) {
    //
  }
  RS485.begin(9600);
```

```
    // enable reception, can be disabled with: RS485.noReceive();
    RS485.receive();
}
```

10. Next, we simply listen for any available data within the `loop()` function and print it out to the computer serial:

```
void loop() {
  if (RS485.available()) {
    Serial.write(RS485.read());
  }
}
```

11. Upload the sketch to the microcontroller.

12. Open **Serial Monitor** and set the baud rate to 9600.

13. Ensure that the peripheral we programmed in the previous section is powered.

14. Wait a few seconds for data to start streaming into **Serial Monitor**. You should see something similar to the following:

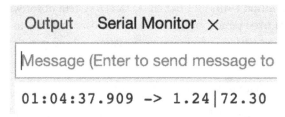

Figure 11.2 – The data received via MK0485

Congratulations – you have successfully programmed a controller to receive data over RS-485! You can watch these steps in a video at https://packt.link/Axyff.

There is an Arduino device with embedded capabilities for RS-485. We'll look at this next.

Arduino Opta

Arduino has a new micro PLC with industrial IoT capabilities called Arduino Opta. This micro PLC comes in three variants:

- **Opta Lite**: With onboard Ethernet

- **Opta RS485**: With onboard Ethernet and RS485

- **Opta WiFi**: With onboard Ethernet, RS485, and Wi-Fi/BLE

You can use the Opta RS485 and Opta WiFi in projects that require RS-485, although we won't be making use of them in this book. The Opta is powered by the STM32H747XI dual-core processor. You can read about it at `https://www.arduino.cc/pro/hardware-arduino-opta`.

While we might communicate directly over RS-485, there is a protocol that was introduced a while back that we should be aware of.

Introducing Modbus

Modbus was designed for use with PLCs by *Schneider Electric*, at that time the PLCs were manufactured by a company called **Modicon**. Modbus is commonly used for communications between industrial electronic devices, often transmitting data sensors, instrumentation, and control devices back to a main controller. It is royalty-free and published openly. Compared to other standards for industrial communication, Modbus is easy to deploy and maintain. It also places a few restrictions on the format of the data to be transmitted.

Modbus uses character serial communications, Ethernet, or **Internet Protocol** (**IP**) as a transport layer. It supports communication to and from multiple devices on the same cable or Ethernet network. Modbus is used in **Supervisory Control and Data Acquisition** (**SCADA**) to connect supervisory computers to **Remote Terminal Units** (**RTUs**). SCADA is a system of software and hardware that collects and monitors data from remote or field devices and uses that data to control other devices. SCADA is used in several industries, including transportation, oil and gas, elevators, manufacturing equipment, water, and energy. SCADA systems consist of three components:

- **Sensors**: The devices that measure physical conditions
- **Actuators**: The devices that control physical devices, such as valves and pumps
- **Communication network**: This connects the sensors and actuators of the master station

The master station is a computer that collects data from the sensors, displays them on a **Human-Machine Interface** (**HMI**), and sends commands to the actuators. The HMI allows a human operator to control the system.

There are several versions of the Modbus protocol, such as Modbus RTU, Modbus TCP, Modbus Plus, and Modbus ASCII. Nodes communicate using send request messages and read response messages. At the physical layer, Modbus can take advantage of the same two-wire communication that RS-485 utilizes.

If you choose to communicate using the RS-485 infrastructure, the entire network will be dedicated to only Modbus communication. If you need to send other types of messages to other devices on the network, you will have to utilize an Ethernet network.

Modbus communication is primarily peer-to-peer, but it supports point-to-point and multidrop networks.

Only one device can initiate transactions on a Modbus network. This device is the controller.

Modbus pros

Modbus has several advantages.

- **Openly published and royalty-free**: Modbus is an open standard, which means that anyone can use it without paying royalties. This makes it a cost-effective solution for many applications.

- **Reliable**: Modbus is a reliable protocol that has been used in industrial environments for many years. It is well-suited for applications where data integrity is critical.

- **Versatile**: Modbus can be used to communicate with a wide variety of devices. This makes it a flexible solution for many applications.

- **Easy to implement**: Modbus is relatively easy to implement. There are many available implementations for different platforms, making it a quick and easy solution for many applications.

Modbus cons

However, Modbus has its weaknesses:

- **Slow**: Modbus is a relatively slow protocol. The maximum data rate for Modbus is 100 kbps. This may be a limitation for applications that require high-speed data transfer.

- **Not suitable for all applications**: Modbus is not suitable for all applications. For example, it is not suitable for applications where real-time data communication is required.

- **Security**: Modbus is not a secure protocol. It does not provide any encryption or authentication, which means that data can be easily intercepted and modified.

Modbus communication can take place over both RS-485 and Ethernet. As such, there are more Arduino shields and devices that support communicating over Modbus.

Modbus hardware

The following shields are compatible with Modbus:

- MKR 485 Shield
- MKR ETH Shield
- Portenta Vision Shield – Ethernet
- Ethernet Shield Rev 2

The following carriers are compatible with Modbus:

- Portenta Machine Control
- Portenta Max Carrier

The following device is compatible with Modbus:

- Arduino Opta

When setting up your Arduino device as a controller for devices that communicate over a Modbus interface, you will need to be mindful of the labels on the peripherals.

Connecting peripherals

Peripherals have three terminals that are frequently labeled as follows:

- **A**: This could also be labeled as TX-/RX- or D-. Connect this to the **Y** terminal on the MKR 485 Shield.

- **B**: This could also be labeled as TX+/RX+ or D+. Connect this to the **Z** terminal on the MKR 485 Shield.

- **COM**: Connect this to **ISO GND** on the MKR 485 Shield.

You will also need to set the switches on the MKR 485 Shield to the following:

- **1**: Set to OFF

- **2**: Set to OFF

- **3**: Set to ON

Unlike RS-485, where you just broadcast messages, Modbus has a bit of methodology that you will need to be aware of.

Modbus messaging

Modbus messaging is centered around reading and writing to device registers on the peripheral. Messages are made up of four components and this never changes. The controller initiates the conversation, and the peripheral responds. The message structure is as follows:

- **Device address**: This is the address of the peripheral. Peripherals will only respond to messages sent to their address.

- **Function code**: This instructs the peripheral to either read a device register or write to it.

- **Data**: This contains either the data requested, or the data being sent.

- **CRC error check**: This is a checksum that makes it easy to detect accidental changes in the message that was sent.

Let's read the current energy consumption, as recorded by an energy meter, as an example.

Industrial devices might communicate information that you read using Modbus. Let's consider the example of reading electrical energy generation or consumption using a Modbus-compatible energy meter. You can purchase these meters from Amazon or any store that sells these types of products. The specific meter that I will be using for this example is available at `https://www.amazon.co.uk/gp/product/B098QGZ4KG/ref=ppx_yo_dt_b_asin_title_o01_s00?ie=UTF8&psc=1`.

Because this meter is rated for 100A, you might be able to use it to monitor the consumption of an entire phase, but you could choose to install it in a cabinet or distribution box and use it to monitor the energy consumption of a room or a few appliances.

> **Warning**
>
> You must exercise extreme caution when working with alternating currents because of the danger that this poses. The best approach might be to have an electrician install this meter.

Reading data from a peripheral

The code for this exercise is available at `https://github.com/PacktPublishing/Arduino-Data-Communications/tree/main/chapter-11/modbus-meter-reading`.

Follow these steps to connect your microcontroller to the smart meter:

1. Connect a wire from the 4 terminal on the meter to the Z terminal on the MKR 485 Shield.
2. Connect a wire from the 5 terminal on the meter to the Y terminal on the MKR 485 Shield.
3. Connect a wire from the 6 terminal on the meter to the ISO GND terminal on the MKR 485 Shield.
4. Set switch 1 to OFF on the MKR 485 Shield.
5. Set switch 2 to OFF on the MKR 485 Shield.
6. Set switch 3 to ON on the MKR 485 Shield.
7. Connect the MKR 485 Shield to the Arduino MKR WiFi microcontroller board.
8. Launch the Arduino IDE.
9. Open **Library Manager**.
10. Search for `Arduino Modbus`.
11. The result should look similar to the following:

Figure 11.3 – The Arduino Modbus library

12. Click on the **INSTALL** button to install the library.

13. You might get a prompt similar to the following:

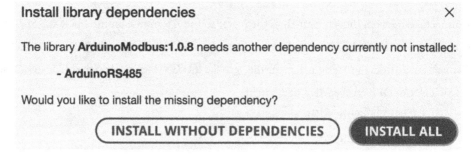

Figure 11.4 – A prompt asking you to install library dependencies

14. If you get this prompt, click on the **INSTALL ALL** button to install the necessary dependencies.

15. Start a new sketch, if you don't have one open already.

16. You will need two libraries, so include them, as shown here:

```
#include <ArduinoRS485.h>
#include <ArduinoModbus.h>
```

17. Let's define the variables that will make it possible to read the meter registers every minute:

```
unsigned long lastRead = millis();
const int myDelay = 60000;
```

18. Let's start the serial port and the Modbus RTU client in the setup () function:

```
void setup() {
  //initialize the serial port
  Serial.begin(115200);
  delay(1500);
  //start the modbus RTU client
  if (!ModbusRTUClient.begin(9600)) {
    Serial.println("Unable to initialize Modbus RTU Client"); //
there was an error
  }
}
```

19. Let's define a function that gets the energy consumption from the buffer register of the meter. We must also define a variable, kWh, that holds the consumption value:

```
double getEnergy() {
  double kWh = 0.;

  return kWh;
}
```

20. Within the getEnergy() function, we need to read the holding register of the meter using the requestFrom() method of the Modbus RTU client. This method takes four parameters: the ID of the target, the location to read, the start address, and the number of values. We will be reading three values from the start address, which is documented for energy readings:

```
double getEnergy() {
  double kWh = 0.;

  if (!ModbusRTUClient.requestFrom(0x01, HOLDING_REGISTERS,
0x0109, 3)) {

  }
  else {

  }
  return kWh;
}
```

21. If we get an error while attempting to read the register, we will need to print out a notification:

```
double getEnergy() {
  double kWh = 0.;
  if (!ModbusRTUClient.requestFrom(0x01, HOLDING_REGISTERS,
0x0109, 3)) {
```

```
        Serial.print("Error reading energy consumption: ");
        Serial.println(ModbusRTUClient.lastError());
    }
    else {

    }
    return kWh;
}
```

22. If we were successful in reading the register, we will need to read three successive words from the register and concatenate them by carrying out a binary shift:

```
double getEnergy() {
    double kWh = 0.;
    if (!ModbusRTUClient.requestFrom(0x01, HOLDING_REGISTERS,
0x0109, 3)) {
    }
    else {
        uint16_t w1 = ModbusRTUClient.read();
        uint16_t w2 = ModbusRTUClient.read();
        uint16_t w3 = ModbusRTUClient.read();
        uint32_t dw = w1 << 32 | w2 << 16 | w3;
        kWh = dw / 1000.0;
    }
    return kWh;
}
```

23. With the function definition complete, we can call it from the `loop()` function once every minute:

```
void loop() {
    if (millis() - lastRead > myDelay) {
        lastRead = millis();
        float consumption = getEnergy();
        Serial.print("kWh: ");
        Serial.println(consumption);
    }
}
```

24. You may now upload the sketch.

Congratulations – you have successfully communicated with a meter using Modbus!

Summary

In this chapter, you learned about the RS-485 serial communication standard and Modbus.

In the next chapter, you will learn about some of the security risks that the data you transmit is exposed to and some approaches to mitigating those risks.

Further reading

To learn more about the topics that were covered in this chapter, take a look at the following resources:

- *MKR 485 Shield*: `https://store-usa.arduino.cc/products/arduino-mkr-485-shield`

- *MKR ETH Shield*: `https://store-usa.arduino.cc/products/arduino-ethernet-shield-2`

- *Portenta Vision Shield – Ethernet*: `https://store-usa.arduino.cc/products/arduino-portenta-vision-shield-ethernet`

- *Arduino Opta*: `https://www.arduino.cc/pro/hardware-arduino-opta`

- *RS-485*: `https://docs.arduino.cc/hardware/mkr-485-shield`

- *Modbus*: `https://docs.arduino.cc/learn/communication/modbus`

- *Arduino Modbus library*: `https://www.arduino.cc/reference/en/libraries/arduinomodbus/`

- *Modbus protocols*: `https://realpars.com/modbus/`

Part 3:
Miscellaneous Topics

In this section, you will learn about some considerations you will need to make when going from an idea to an early-stage start-up, including the risks that exist when you collect, transmit, and store data, and the requirements for any infrastructure that you are setting up to collect and store data.

This section has the following chapters:

- *Chapter 12, Enhancing Security for Reducing Risk*
- *Chapter 13, Scaling for High Availability*
- *Chapter 14, Building and Manufacturing Hardware*

12
Enhancing Security for Reducing Risk

Security is something that you need to consider before you place any new product on a shelf. By the end of this chapter, you will have learned about some of the threats that devices are exposed to when they send data over a network. You will have also learned how to reduce some of those risks.

In this chapter, we will cover the following topics:

- Learning about the threat landscape
- Embracing cloud security
- Enforcing edge security
- Learning about certificate authorities

We will not make use of any hardware in this chapter.

Learning about the threat landscape

The **Internet of Things (IoT)** is all about data. You have hardware in the mix, but the hardware collects and transmits data.

The importance of data in this era has been compared to the importance of oil in the industrial era. Data is considered to be a valuable resource by most people. Data can be used for making predictions, such as the data collected from weather stations being used to forecast weather patterns.

Data collected from a smart home system can be used to understand user behavior, such as what appliances are being used at certain times leading you to understand room occupancy. A positive application of user behavior is targeted advertising. However, it is also possible to utilize data negatively. Knowing when a room is occupied implies that bad actors know when the room isn't occupied.

Another example is with fitness trackers that collect location information. If this information falls into the wrong hands, it becomes possible for bad actors to tell when an individual works out and what route they take if they do this outdoors.

There are significant benefits to effectively collecting, storing, and analyzing data. This leads to better service delivery and even new product development. However, most businesses tend to have some security lapses when it comes to securing their data systems. Reports of data breaches are common. There is a thriving black market where data that has been stolen is sold for all sorts of nefarious purposes.

There is also something called **ransomware**. This is a situation in which your data is encrypted and held ransom until you have paid out a certain amount of money, usually in untraceable digital assets.

Humans are the weakest link in most security systems. Bad actors target humans to get either their security credentials or to get some information about them that might make it easy to guess their credentials. This is called **social engineering**. It isn't a coincidence that social engineering and social networks share a common name. That is because a lot of social engineering happens on social media networks. Some password recovery questions are just horrible. Consider some of these questions:

- What was your first dog's name?

- In what city did you attend high school?

- What is your mother's maiden name?

While those look like good recovery prompts because they are things that you should remember easily, they are terrible because it's easy for a lot of people to find out. People who love their pets tend to post them on social media. Your high school information tends to be part of your profile. And your mother's maiden name? People just need to find all of your cousins who don't share your surname.

Humans also have another problem. Most humans can't create or remember strong passwords. Most passwords are either generic, dictionary words, or they tie back to something obvious on the social media profile. A report from a 2021 survey on the website Statista shows that about 80% of Americans have a password that is, at most, 11 characters long (`https://www.statista.com/statistics/1305713/average-character-length-of-a-password-us/`).

There is a website called KeepSolid that is available at `https://www.keepsolid.com/passwarden/help/use-cases/how-long-to-crack-a-password`. It shows that most passwords that are only 10 characters long and are in all lowercase can be cracked instantly! This is assuming a brute-force attack occurs where the bad actor uses a list of "potentially known credential matches." Passwords that have more than 12 characters and that also have special characters and numbers, and utilize both lowercase and uppercase characters, are progressively more difficult to guess or crack. This all assumes that the password is being guessed. If your password was obtained via a data breach, then there won't be any need to guess it!

We made use of certain services on the internet in previous chapters. Services that are hosted on the internet are prone to **Denial-of-Service (DoS)** attacks. These attacks attempt to overwhelm a service with requests, thus making it unavailable to its users.

There are many other security threats that we will not attempt to exhaust in this section. Instead, let's discuss some common solutions to these threats.

Encryption algorithms

One way to ensure that any of your data that is stolen is not used against you is by employing data encryption. Encryption employs a key to scramble data such that only a system or person with the corresponding decryption key can unscramble it. This makes it difficult for any bad actor to utilize the data if they can steal it.

Encryption is an advanced field with ongoing research. There are functions in a lot of programming languages, as well as applications that make it easy to implement encryption. However, not all encryption algorithms are equally effective. There are different types of encryption that you should be aware of to make the right choice. Some of these are as follows:

- **Symmetric encryption**: This uses the same key for encryption and decryption, requiring both the sender and receiver (either human or computer) to have the same key. It is used in applications where speed is important. A compromised key leaves the system open to attack. As a result, the keys that are used must be stored securely. One approach to securely storing your keys is by utilizing Google Cloud Secret Manager. You can learn more at `https://cloud.google.com/secret-manager`. The symmetric key encryption method is relatively cheap and easy to implement.

- **Asymmetric encryption**: This uses two different keys and is commonly known as public-private key cryptography. The public key is required to encrypt the data, while the private key is required to decrypt the data. The set of keys can only be used to encrypt data in one direction. You will need a second set of keys to send data in the opposite direction. This encryption method is secure and extremely difficult to break, but it is also much slower and more difficult to implement than symmetric encryption.

- **Hybrid encryption**: This uses symmetric encryption to encrypt the data using a randomly generated key. The key is then encrypted using asymmetric key encryption. Both the data and the key are then sent to the recipient. This approach uses the much faster option of symmetric encryption on larger data that needs to be encrypted. However, because the key isn't reused, the risk of compromise is minimized. Also, because the key is encrypted asymmetrically, only the intended recipient can decrypt the key, and thus the message.

Encryption can be applied to data that is on a storage medium, such as the flat files that we worked with in *Chapter 4*. This type of data is called data at rest.

Exercise 1 – symmetric key encryption

In this exercise, you will learn how to encrypt and decrypt text using symmetric key encryption. You can expand your APIs to encrypt sensitive data before storing the data in a database. That way, if the database is compromised and data is stolen, the sensitive data will be encrypted and difficult to read. The code for this exercise is available at `https://github.com/PacktPublishing/Arduino-Data-Communications/tree/main/chapter-12/symmetric-key-encryption`.

Follow these steps to complete this exercise:

1. Open your terminal.

2. Confirm that you have Python installed by typing the following into the terminal:

    ```
    python
    ```

3. Hit *Enter*.

    The output should look similar to the following:

```
Python 3.7.1 (default, Dec 14 2018, 13:28:58)
[Clang 4.0.1 (tags/RELEASE_401/final)] :: Anaconda, Inc. on darwin
Type "help", "copyright", "credits" or "license" for more information.
>>> █
```

Figure 12.1 – The Python command-line interface

4. Type the following command at the prompt to quit the Python interface:

    ```
    exit()
    ```

5. Hit *Enter*.

6. Type the following command to install the required cryptographic library:

    ```
    pip install cryptography
    ```

7. Hit *Enter*.

8. Wait for the operation to complete.

9. Open any Python editor.

10. Create a new file and save it as `main.py`.

11. Begin by importing the `Fernet` class from the cryptography module, as shown in the following line:

    ```
    from cryptography.fernet import Fernet
    ```

12. Define a Python function that will take a key and a piece of text to encrypt and that will return the encrypted text. The function will do this by creating an instance of `Fernet` and then using the `encrypt()` function to encrypt the text. This is shown here:

```
def my_encrypt(key, text):
    f = Fernet(key)
    t = f.encrypt(text)
    return t
```

13. Define a Python function that will take a key and some text and that will decrypt the encrypted text:

```
def my_decrypt(key, text):
    f = Fernet(key)
    t = f.decrypt(text)
    return t
```

14. Create the function that will run when this file is executed. Let's generate some text and output it to the console:

```
if __name__ == '__main__':
    my_text = b'0.0, 0.0, 21.6, 56'
    print(f'Text to encrypt: {my_text}\n')
```

15. Let's generate our cryptographic key within this function. We will make use of the `generate_key()` function for this. We have to store the generated key in a variable within our code:

```
key = Fernet.generate_key()
```

16. Let's encrypt our text using the key we just generated:

```
my_encrypted_text = my_encrypt(key, my_text)
```

17. Let's print this out to confirm that our encryption worked:

```
print(f'Encrypted text: {my_encrypted_text}\n')
```

18. Let's decrypt the encrypted text:

```
my_decrypted_text = my_decrypt(key, my_encrypted_text)
```

19. Let's print the decrypted text out to confirm that the decryption works:

```
print(f'Decrypted tex: {my_decrypted_text}\n')
```

20. Let's find out what the data type of the key we generated is:

```
key_type = type(key)
print(f'TypeOf Key: {key_type}\n')
```

21. Let's see what our key was:

```
print(f'Key: {key}\n')
```

Congratulations – you have successfully encrypted and decrypted text using symmetric key cryptography! You can see the Code in Action at `https://packt.link/Yaqqe`.

The step in this exercise where we generated a key in our code can be replaced with Google Cloud Secret Manager. The key can be generated and maintained by Secret Manager, while we programmatically access this key from our code. You can read about this at `https://cloud.google.com/secret-manager/docs/create-secret-quickstart#secretmanager-quickstart-python`.

Encryption can also be applied to data as it is being transmitted. This type of data is called data in transit. This type of encryption protects data from being intercepted. Let's look at two common approaches to encrypting data in transit:

- Using a secure communication protocol such as **Secure Sockets Layer** (**SSL**) or **Transport Layer Security** (**TLS**). They encrypt the data before it is sent over the network, and decrypt it when it reaches the destination. These protocols are implemented at the level of the application server with the help of security certificates that are issued by a **Certificate Authority** (**CA**). It is also possible to issue certificates locally for development purposes.

- Using a **virtual private network** (**VPN**). This creates a secure tunnel between two devices. Data is sent via this tunnel and only devices that are a part of this tunnel can read this data.

Encryption prevents bad actors from making use of your data if it falls into the wrong hands. However, it doesn't do anything for you if you are locked out of your system. This is called ransomware. You need backups of your data if you are going to recover from a ransomware attack.

Data backup

A backup of your data will give you peace of mind in the event of a disaster. You might be required to have a **disaster recovery** (**DR**) strategy or plan in place if you operate in certain industries.

Separate from a DR strategy, you might also need to have an archival policy in place. This policy states how long you need to keep data and to make it available when requested by regulators or other authorities. Data that you have archived is not available for regular access but is available to be restored for operational purposes.

When you create a backup of your data, you can store it in various locations:

- **Local storage**: You can copy the data to devices or storage media such as external drives, DVD drives, optical drives, and others.

- **Cloud storage**: You can copy your data to a storage bucket, such as **Simple Storage Service (S3)** on **Amazon Web Services (AWS)**, or **Google Cloud Storage (GCS)** on **Google Cloud Platform (GCP)**. When you work with cloud storage, you should learn about the storage classes that exist and choose the appropriate one. This will help you save money on storage.

- **Hybrid storage**: You can copy your data to a mix of the previously mentioned locations.

It is important to note that the backup cannot exist on the same storage medium as the original. That is not a backup.

You must test out your DR strategy periodically. Here, you must check that the backups can be restored and that they work when restored. This way, you will have a clear idea of how long it takes to restore a backup and recover from a disaster. Here is a possible checklist for a DR plan:

- **Identify data**: You need to know what data needs to be backed up. If you generate a lot of data, then perhaps not everything needs to be backed up.

- **Choose storage**: You will need to choose the storage medium that meets your needs. If you have a lot of data in the cloud, local storage might not be a viable option because of the amount of time it would take to transfer the data. Where possible, choose to utilize various methods and ensure that they are kept in a safe location. Also, do not forget to encrypt your backups (data at rest).

- **Create a schedule**: How frequently do you need to create backups to minimize loss? Some businesses are fine with daily backups, while others require hourly backups.

- **Test your backups**: You need a second schedule for testing your backups. There is no point in having backups that you can't utilize.

Now, let's move on to something that has to do with passwords and logins.

Multi-factor authentication

On any system where you make use of a password to log in, there is the risk of your password falling into the wrong hands due to a data breach. When that happens, there is nothing you can do to prevent someone else from logging in using your credentials. That is where **multi-factor authentication (MFA)** comes into play. It is sometimes called **two-factor authentication (2FA)**.

MFA relies on using something you know (the password) as well as something you have (a device) before you can log in. There are various approaches to MFA:

- **One-time passwords (OTPs)**: In this approach, the system you are trying to access will generate a single-use code and send it via voice, SMS, or email to an address that you own. You will then need to provide this OTP on the site before you can gain access. This approach is secure, so long as your phone and email have not been compromised. However, you need to know that in a sophisticated attack, bad actors tend to try to take over email addresses (using password recovery) and phone numbers (by calling the networks and pretending that they lost their phone).

- **Authenticators**: In this implementation, a piece of software is synchronized with the account. This authenticator generates a new OTP periodically. This approach is considered to be more secure than the previous approach because the OTP doesn't get sent to the person trying to sign in, thus minimizing the risk of interception. Some of these authenticators are available as a piece of hardware with a button. These are usually handed out by financial institutions to their customers.

- **Hardware keys**: Some software platforms are compatible with a security standard that lets you enroll a hardware key. This key is something that you need to have with you before you can complete your authentication on the system. This is considered to be one of the best authentication methods. You can purchase these keys from various vendors, such as Yubico (`https://www.yubico.com/`) and Titan Security Key (`https://cloud.google.com/titan-security-key`).

While MFA is important, we can't overstate the importance of unique passwords. The question becomes, how can anyone remember a strong, unique password for every individual site or service? That is where password managers come into play.

Password managers

A password manager is a piece of software that helps you store your passwords. A lot of password managers do more, such as the following:

- Integrate an OTP generator so that you don't have to make use of a separate authenticator
- Securely store recovery codes, which you will need for each platform where you have enabled MFA
- Track password breaches for websites where you have stored credentials, thus notifying you to change your credentials
- Keep a history of credentials so that you know if you are reusing an old password
- Generate strong, random passwords
- Notify you if you share credentials between platforms
- Send credentials securely, for a certain period, to enable third-party logins

The importance of password managers can't be overstated.

Having set a foundation, let's consider security from the perspective of the cloud, where a lot of services are hosted.

Embracing cloud security

There are various providers of cloud computing both at the platform level and at the infrastructure level. All providers have security features native to them that might appear to be overwhelming at first. You only need to do a bit of studying to get up to speed.

Multi-factor authentication

We already discussed MFA in the previous section, but repeating it here will only reinforce its importance. Every cloud provider worth using will have MFA baked in. Ensure that all of your users utilize MFA.

Identity and access management

Identity and Access Management (**IAM**) is how you control access to what a user can do on your cloud platform. On a cloud platform, users aren't limited to humans. They could also be services. When it comes to controlling or granting permissions, apply the principle of least privilege. This simply means that you grant privileges or permissions that let the user do only what they need to do. For example, on GCP, you can grant a user access to GCS. However, if the user only needs to read objects, you shouldn't grant *Creator* privileges. This is shown in the following screenshot:

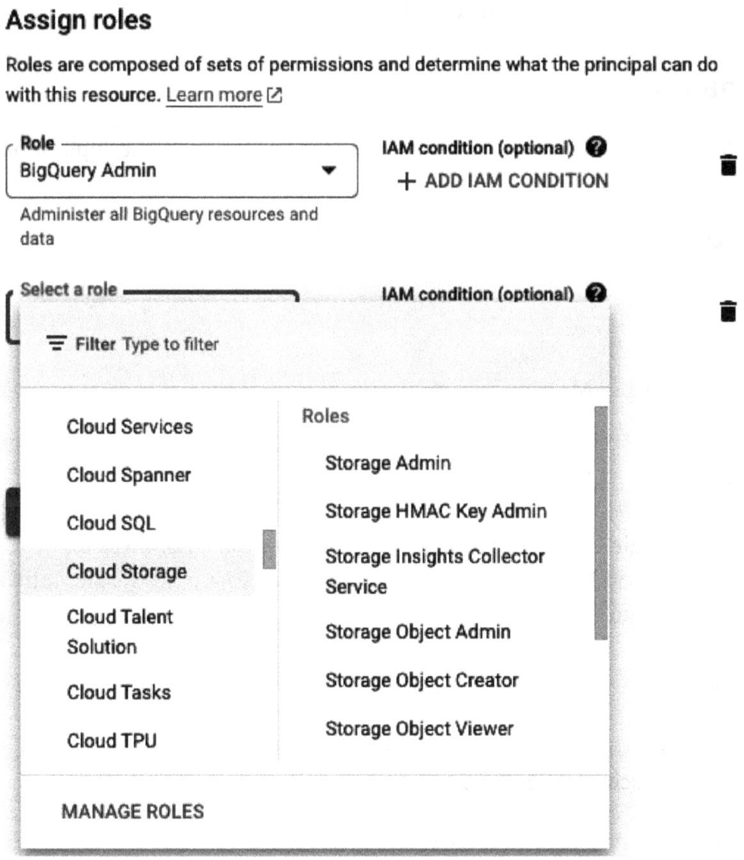

Figure 12.2 – IAM on GCP

Next is KMS.

Key Management Service

Keeping your cryptographic keys safe is of utmost importance. But how do you do that? Should you place them in a storage bucket? How about versioning? This is where **Key Management Service** (**KMS**) comes in. Most KMSs have the following features:

- **Key generation**: This makes it easy to generate new encryption keys.

- **Key backup**: The last thing you want is to lose your encryption/decryption keys. KMS will let you back up and restore your keys.

- **Key rotation**: Keys need to be changed regularly, just like passwords. Think of your KMS as a password manager for encryption keys.

While we're on the topic of passwords, password managers work for humans, but what happens when your applications need to make use of security credentials? That's where the next feature comes in handy.

Secrets Manager

Secrets Manager lets you store and manage secrets (credentials) for use at the application level. It lets you do the following:

- Create secrets

- Version secrets

- Encrypt secrets

- Manage access using IAM

- Set expiration for secrets

- Rotate secrets

You can make use of Google Cloud Secret Manager to accomplish all of these aspects. It's available at `https://cloud.google.com/secret-manager`. Now, let's consider infrastructure for backing up data on the cloud.

Storage buckets

Storage buckets are called different things, such as S3 on AWS and GCS on GCP. Storage buckets provide several benefits, such as the following:

- **Security**: The cloud providers provide industry-grade security features to protect data

- **High availability**: Storage buckets ensure that data is always available within the specified domain location

- **Global availability**: Storage buckets tend to be globally distributed so that you can find a location with minimal latency from where you are operating

Storage buckets support access policies and encryption of data at rest. They also make it possible to make your data publicly accessible using special **Universal Resource Identifiers (URIs)**. These URIs could be designed to expire after a certain period. You can make use of Google Cloud Storage to gain all of these benefits. It's available at `https://cloud.google.com/storage`.

Managed databases

Cloud providers provide managed databases. When they do this, they take care of certain aspects of keeping the database running, while giving you complete control over the setup. For example, GCP has a managed database called Cloud SQL that will let you set up a database instance of MySQL, PostgreSQL, or Microsoft SQL Server. You can specify your memory, processors, and storage. However, GCP takes care of and enforces security and replication (high availability). Cloud SQL provides both a public and private network interface. Services running within your project on GCP can access database instances via the private interface. However, anything outside of the project that wants to access the database instance must utilize a proxy service that is governed by IAM policies. This ensures maximum security for database instances. One managed database service that you can get started with is Google Cloud SQL: `https://cloud.google.com/sql`.

Virtual machines

We made use of small, physical computers while prototyping in this book. These are great for use on the edge. When you need to run certain services that need to be accessed from various locations, you will need to set up a computer on the internet. These computers are called **virtual machines (VMs)**. VMs are fully customizable:

- You can choose the number and type of processors you want
- You can choose the number and type of storage devices you want
- You can choose the operating system and version that you run on it

You can choose to run VMs continuously or start them periodically. You can even choose to boot up additional VMs to handle traffic surges. You can get started with VMs at `https://cloud.google.com/compute`.

You can't have too much security, so some cloud providers have something called a shielded VM.

Shielded VMs

Shielded VMs offer verifiable integrity for VMs. They do this so that you can be sure that your VMs haven't been compromised by malware or rootkits at the boot level or the kernel level. They do this using the following:

- **Secure boot**: The VM only boots up after verifying the authenticity of all boot components by checking that they are signed using certificates that are issued by a trusted CA

- **Virtual Trusted Platform Module**: This is hardware that performs comparisons between subsequent startups of the VM to ensure that nothing has changed
- **Measured boot**: This keeps track of changes in the boot order of components in the operating system

You may set up everything right internally, but that won't stop you from being targeted, so long as your domain name or IP address is known. Have you read about service outages caused by DoS attacks? Let's consider some tools that could help with this.

DoS protection

GCP provides a service called **Cloud Armor**. It is described as a *"fully managed, enterprise-grade DDoS protection service that helps you defend your web applications and APIs from a wide range of attacks."* It helps protect against commonly exploited vulnerabilities in web applications. It inspects all traffic to your applications and APIs. It can handle requests from known, malicious IP addresses, and redirect these elsewhere, thus leaving your services available to legitimate users. You can get started with Cloud Armor at `https://cloud.google.com/armor`.

Virtual private networks

Cloud service providers will give you the necessary tools to set up secure tunnels between your physical infrastructure and the cloud. The data that travels via the VPN tunnel is encrypted between the source and the destination, even when it travels over the public internet. You can get started with VPNs at `https://cloud.google.com/network-connectivity/docs/vpn/concepts/overview`.

There are more advanced connectivity options, although we won't go over them in this book. However, I would like to mention something called a bastion host.

Bastion hosts

A bastion host is a single VM with both a public and private network interface. This is the only VM that allows login from outside the network. You can only log in to the other VMs within the network from the bastion host or another VM within the network. This way, the bastion host is configured for maximum security, and there is only one point of failure. Your bastion host should use an extremely strong password, and where possible, you should use a security certificate for logging in and disable password login.

Firewalls

Firewalls let you control traffic going into and out of your network. Firewalls protect your network from unauthorized access, malicious activity, and unwanted intrusions. They do this by reading a set of rules to determine whether or not to allow or block traffic. You can learn more about firewalls at `https://cloud.google.com/firewall?hl=en`.

There is a whole lot more to cloud infrastructure, but let's move on to edge devices.

Enforcing edge security

Your edge devices are computers. A lot of the things that apply to VMs apply to the computers that you will be setting up and deploying. However, you will not have the support of the cloud providers when you set up your edge devices, so you need to take care of everything yourself.

Operating system

The choice of the operating system that you install on your edge device is critical. You will want to avoid bleeding-edge and beta software. If possible, go for **long-term support** (**LTS**) variants of any operating system. Also, consider operating systems that will only run signed software. This will ensure that the computer will not run malicious software. One example of this is Ubuntu Core, which is designed for embedded applications and optimized for security.

Login and access control

Your computer can be accessed physically, so you want to ensure that bad actors can't brute-force their way onto the computer. The way to avoid this is by disabling password login and utilizing only security certificates. Any user who wishes to access the computer will need to do that from a computer with the necessary certificates.

If you do not have physical access to your edge device, you should consider remote access. If the device is on a network with access to the internet, then you can provision it for remote access. For example, Ubuntu Core will let you connect installations to your Ubuntu Cloud account and manage security certificates on Ubuntu Cloud. The certificates uploaded to Ubuntu Cloud will let you establish a remote connection to your instance of Ubuntu Core.

Over-the-air updates

Operating systems are constantly getting patched or maintained to respond to any security flaws that have been discovered. On a phone or PC, you will normally either perform the updates manually or set it to check for updates automatically.

With an embedded system, the operating system needs to check for updates periodically. The apps need to utilize a private store or repository to where you push your app updates.

Backups

If you are storing data in flat files, then you will need to back these up to a storage bucket in the cloud. You can utilize APIs and shell scripts to accomplish this. Every cloud provider provides resources to accomplish this.

If you are storing data in a database, you should set up replication to a cloud instance. You can then extract backups from your replicas. Each database has documentation on how to accomplish this.

Physical ports

There are devices that bad actors utilize to help them break into a computer system. These devices need to be connected to a port. Ensure that you disable any USB or other ports on your embedded computer. Lock this down from the BIOS. You might think that you need the ports but you don't, since you only connect remotely. Besides, you can enable anything that you need later on.

Firewalls

Bad actors utilize software that helps them scan all the ports on a computer network for vulnerabilities. You should lock down all ports that aren't required. Make use of a firewall within the operating system to accomplish this. You may also redirect ports. For example, if a database uses port 3306 by default, you may block this port and open a different one instead. That way, bad actors can't tell that you are using that particular database because the port is blocked.

We have discussed digital certificates a few times. Now, let's discuss CAs, which are required for generating certificates that are globally acceptable.

Learning about certificate authorities

A CA is a trusted third party that issues certificates. These certificates are used to verify the identity of a computer or a website, as well as for encrypting and decrypting data.

While you can issue your own certificates, these are only for your private use. When you consider a website that you access using HTTPS, the web server uses a digital certificate that is globally recognized. The essence of the certificate is to confirm to others that the site they are visiting is what it claims to be.

The certificate contains the identity information of the entity that it is issued to, along with the entity's public encryption key. This key is used by browsers to encrypt and decrypt data that is passed along between web/application servers and browsers/clients.

But how can you get a globally acceptable digital certificate?

Let's Encrypt

Let's Encrypt is a non-profit that makes obtaining certificates relatively easy and, of course, free. The certificates are only valid for three months at a time, but it is easy to set up a renewal schedule. You can learn more at `https://letsencrypt.org/`.

Let's Encrypt is one example of a public CA. What if you want a CA that isn't public or global so that you can control who is accessing your resources? That is when you need a private CA.

Certificate Authority Service

Certificate Authority Service (CAS) is a service on GCP that lets you issue and manage both CAs and certificates. As is the case with the cloud, CAS makes use of industrial-grade security to protect certificates and is also easy to get started with. One advantage of using CAS is that you can determine the length of validity of the certificates that you issue.

Summary

In this chapter, you learned about various security topics to consider when your product idea is about to go live, including what sort of security flaws you might be exposing and how to go about reducing them. In the next chapter, we will look at what you need to take care of when the demand exceeds your expectations and you have more than a handful of users – that is, how to go about creating systems with high availability.

13
Scaling for High Availability

When you go from the prototype stage to a full-fledged release of your hardware, you will be faced with demands on your computing infrastructure. In this chapter, you will learn about the various demands that are placed on computing resources as you scale, and the various options for meeting this demand as your users continue to grow.

In this chapter, we will cover the following topics:

- Understanding high availability
- Understanding load balancing
- Implementing high availability for databases
- Implementing high availability for RESTful servers

Let's begin!

Understanding high availability

High availability (**HA**) refers to a characteristic of a computing system that aims to provide an agreed level of performance. This normally refers to the proportion of time that the system is available and is given in terms of a percentage. You can convert this percentage into the number of days in a year that the system is guaranteed to be available, or conversely, the maximum number of days in a year during which the system can be down or unavailable.

For example, if the availability of a system is given as 95%, then the system is guaranteed to be available for approximately 347 days in a year and could be unavailable for up to 18 days in a year. Does that sound good?

The answer to that question, like everything, is "*It depends.*" A continuous 18-day outage could lose you customers, but when you look at it from a monthly perspective, that would translate to an average outage of 1.5 days every month. Does that sound acceptable? That is a 36-hour outage every month.

We might start this conversation by asking why the system might be unavailable in the first place. If you consider a server that is running somewhere, there are several reasons why it might become unavailable:

- Power outages
- Network outages
- Hardware failure
- Downtime for upgrades
- Increased demand

This list isn't exhaustive.

Let's revisit the question of whether 95% is good enough. We won't answer that question. Rather, we will look at what other availability options exist. These are normally called service levels and are represented in a **service-level agreement (SLA)** that the IT vendor (this could be you) provides to the customer.

99% availability guarantees that the system will have a maximum downtime of 3.65 days in a year. This sounds much better. That is an outage of, at most, 87.6 hours in the entire year or an average of 7.3 hours in a month. This SLA is commonly called "two nines" but isn't considered HA.

Commonly acceptable provisions of HA are "three nines," "four nines," and "five nines." Three nines availability is 99.9%, while four nines is 99.99% availability.

99.9% availability assures availability 364.635 days in a year, with a maximum outage of 0.365 days, or 8.76 hours in a year.

A service provider that promises a maximum outage of 8.76 hours in a year is likely to be taken more seriously than another that promises a maximum outage of 87.6 hours in the same year. Clients in the automotive, industrial, and healthcare sectors expect to have as little downtime as possible.

The benefits of HA include the following:

- **Improved reliability**: These systems are less liable to fail, and as a result, users can place more trust in them
- **Increased availability**: These systems are more likely to be available and can be relied on as a critical component
- **Reduced downtime**: These systems help reduce the impact of system failures on components that rely on their availability

Let's take a closer look at some reasons why system outages occur.

Power outage

Consider a desktop computer. It will not come on unless it is connected to a power source. What happens when the power source is interrupted? The computer goes off. Can you guarantee that the power source will never be interrupted? Not really, because all sorts of natural disasters could affect the power station at a distance from you. We have identified one cause.

How easily can we fix this problem that we have identified? We could introduce battery storage between the power station and our computer. This is a common solution. However, batteries can only operate for a certain period. This introduces the concept of "days of autonomy," which asks how many days the battery bank can keep your system operating before the battery itself goes out. 2 days of autonomy implies that the battery bank will provide at least 48 hours of power before the batteries are depleted.

So, the next question to ask is how long it takes the power station to come back online in the event of an outage. This sounds like asking what the SLA of your power provider is.

We could go on and add a second power provider to the battery bank so that the batteries can be charged before they get depleted in the event of an outage. This is also common practice in data centers. The second power provider could be a second power station, or it could be a generator or solar panels – whatever it is that can generate electricity.

At this point, we can take a step back and consider the cost of doing this. Is the cost worth it? If not, what can we cut down on? Should we reduce the number of days of autonomy of the system? Should we go for half a day? Can we guarantee to provide a power backup up in 12 hours? What if the system goes down in the middle of a holiday?

We could also ask whether the batteries provide a 100% guarantee. Is there such a thing? Could the system fail us when we least expect it? Can we introduce some redundancy to our power system?

Some servers have what is called a **redundant power supply**. They let you connect to two independent power supplies so that the system keeps running if one supply experiences an outage. However, this would imply duplicating your power backup system.

At this point, you can start to see that greater availability means spending more money. Let's consider another type of problem.

Network outages

Communication between computers takes place over networks. For a server, this is normally over a wired connection that goes to a switch or router (network device). The network device is subject to the same power problems as the server so that problem needs to be solved.

However, the network device could experience a hardware failure. Introducing redundancy at this level requires having a second hardware device. You could see this as having two routes between your origin and your destination. This introduces additional costs to your setup.

But how do you make your server communicate over two separate networks? You will need to have two independent network interfaces on the server. This is a small additional expense.

Hardware failure

Various components can fail on a server. One example is the network interface card. If you have two network interfaces, then you have already addressed such a failure. However, the server itself could fail.

The obvious solution to this is having a second server that can handle the load. There are two ways of looking at this problem.

One approach involves having a replica of your server sitting in a box. In the event of a failure, you can swap out your server with the replica. This approach assumes that someone is always on duty to swap out the servers. It also assumes that you can quickly move data between the two servers within your allowable downtime. In reality, you could take the hard drives from the first server and place them into the second server. This should work, so long as the two servers are identical. Let's call this approach a cold backup.

Another approach is one in which the backup is constantly running and is ready to start work the moment the primary server becomes unavailable. This approach is a warm backup. This approach requires a bit more work to ensure that the data is available to both servers at the same time, but it is worth it because you don't need to wait for an engineer to go in and swap out servers.

Please take note of this warm backup solution because we will discuss it some more when we address the problem of increased demand.

Let's consider a downtime that isn't the result of a system failure.

Hardware upgrades

There are times when the server is running, either optimally or sub-optimally, but you need to replace something. This could be memory, storage, or even some interface cards. In a lot of these scenarios, you will need to shut down the server and take it offline. This is where having a backup, whether cold or warm, saves the day.

Increased demand

Every server has limited capacity. When the server reaches its limit, it stops responding to new requests and starts dropping connections. The simplest solution to this situation is to upgrade the server or replace it with one that has a higher specification. This is called scaling up.

A preferable solution is to scale out. This involves adding one or more servers with identical specifications. There is just one problem: multiple servers can't share the same server address. So, how can you take the traffic and distribute it between multiple servers? That is where load balancing comes in. We will take a look at this solution in a short while.

To summarize, the reasons why a system outage might occur can be addressed using various approaches, including the following:

- **Redundancy**: Having multiple copies of servers and components can help ensure that if one server or component fails, another one can take its place

- **Load balancing**: Distributing traffic across multiple servers can help prevent any one server from becoming overloaded

- **Failover**: Automatically switching to a backup system can help keep systems running, even in the event of a failure

- **Fault tolerance**: Designing systems to continue operating in the event of a failure can help minimize the impact of outages

These approaches can be used in combination to create a more robust and reliable system.

Now, let's discuss load balancing.

Understanding load balancing

You can set up load balancing using a compute cluster. This is a collection of identical servers, called nodes, that run the same operating system and software. The load balancer is a server that sits in front of the cluster and directs traffic to individual nodes. An example is illustrated in the following diagram:

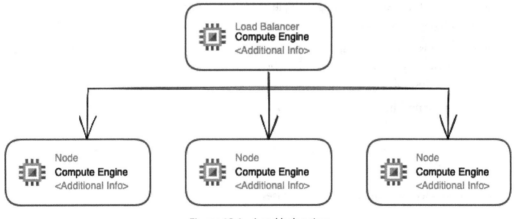

Figure 13.1 – Load balancing

The nodes are connected on a single high-speed network that they use for communication and sharing resources. The load balancer keeps track of which nodes are available and sends traffic to them.

In some situations, you can make use of load balancing to provide redundancy and failover while also minimizing expenses.

You can minimize expenses by shutting down nodes when you don't need them and starting them up when you do. There are two reasons why you would want to take this approach:

- In a physical data center, more nodes running means higher energy and cooling requirements. Shutting down nodes that you don't need ensures that you consume less power and run fewer coolers.

- In a virtual data center or on the cloud, nodes cost money. You can save money by shutting down nodes you don't need.

Similarly, spinning up nodes when you need them ensures that your system is highly available. There are various approaches to doing this, with one approach being that you monitor the resource utilization across your entire cluster and spin up nodes when the resource utilization is above a certain threshold, such as your CPU utilization going above 75% on all nodes. Similarly, you would shut down one node if CPU utilization went down below a certain threshold, such as 35%.

Let's consider the specific case of HA for a database.

Implementing HA for databases

HA for databases is the ability of a database system to continue operating even if one or more of its components fail. This is critical for databases that are used for essential applications. There are various ways of accomplishing this:

- **Replication**: This involves creating multiple copies of the database and storing them on different servers. If one server fails, the other servers can continue to provide access to the database.

- **Failover**: This involves having a standby server that is ready to take over if the primary server fails. The standby server can be kept in sync with the primary server in real time, or it can be updated periodically.

- **Load balancing**: This involves distributing the workload across multiple servers. This can help improve performance and availability as it reduces the load on any single server.

- **Clustering**: This involves grouping several servers so that they work together as a single system. This can help improve performance, availability, and scalability.

Replication introduces several benefits to databases:

- **Scalability**: Replication makes it possible to spread the load across multiple servers, ensuring that your solution is scalable. You can write new data to the source, while all reads take place on the replicas.

- **Data security**: Replicas make it possible to back up data without impacting the source database. This minimizes data corruption on the source, while also ensuring that new replicas can be spun up in the event of corruption on an existing replica.

- **Analytics**: Replicas are the best place to run analytics workloads. This is because those workloads are heavy and shouldn't be run on the source; otherwise, you could have resources lock up on you.

If you are running InfluxDB on the edge, you can set up replication to a remote server from multiple edge instances. You can also reduce or aggregate the amount of data you have on the edge before replication. This is a perfect way of getting high, low, and average temperatures, for example, while collecting hourly or even more granular data on the edge.

There are links to replication guides in the *Further reading* section of this chapter.

Database replication is the process of copying data from one database to another. This can be done for a variety of reasons, such as to improve performance, to provide redundancy, or to create a backup. However, database replication also introduces certain challenges.

One challenge is cost. Every additional replica costs money, both to acquire the server and to keep it running. This can be a significant expense, especially for large databases.

Another challenge is complexity. Setting up database replication can be complex, and it is important to choose the right replication method for your needs. There are a variety of different replication methods available, each with its advantages and disadvantages.

A third challenge is consistency. When data is replicated, there is always the possibility that it will become out of sync. This is known as replication lag. It is important to monitor replication lag and to take steps to mitigate it. Otherwise, your data could become corrupted or inaccurate.

Finally, security is a concern with any database, and it is especially important with multiple database instances. It is important to carefully control access to each database and use appropriate security measures to protect your data.

Overall, database replication is a powerful tool that can provide several benefits. However, it is important to be aware of the challenges involved before implementing it.

Next, let's take a look at HA for your application servers.

Implementing HA for RESTful servers

A RESTful server is a web server that makes API endpoints available for consumption. There are various web servers, such as Apache and NGINX, and configuring each one is different.

To implement HA for a web server, you must implement a proxy server in front of the web servers that you will be setting up. In this scenario, the web servers will all make use of the same static files and assets, which will be deployed in a central location. If there is a need for a database connection, then the database server will be hosted separately. Rather than connecting to individual web servers, all traffic is directed to the load balancer, which then distributes traffic. That is how all major websites function.

One of the considerations for a load balancer is how to distribute traffic to the nodes within your cluster. Some common methods in use are as follows:

- **Round-robin**: In this approach, traffic is distributed evenly. For example, if you have three nodes, traffic is sent to the first node, then the second node, and finally the third node. This is done sequentially and the traffic wraps around.

- **Least connections**: In this approach, the node with the least number of active connections is sent a new request. This ensures that the duration of a session is taken into consideration to avoid overloading a specific server.

Check out the *Further reading* section of this chapter for links to additional resources if you are going to be setting up and managing your servers yourself.

If you are making use of the cloud, you can leverage something such as GCP to set up load balancing easily. One benefit of using cloud services for load balancing and HA is that you can distribute your workload across different regions to guard against natural disasters:

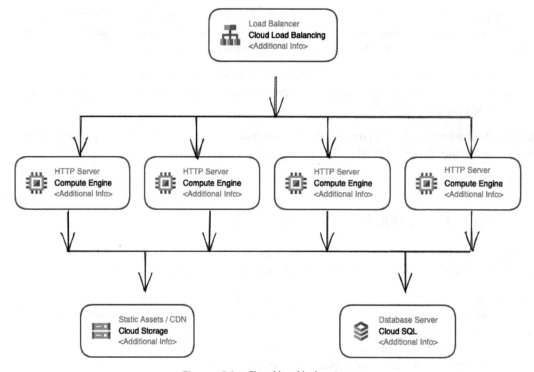

Figure 13.2 – Cloud load balancing

Follow these steps to configure web servers:

1. Create Compute Engine instances.

2. Open port 80 on each instance.

3. Install Apache on each instance.

4. Create a firewall rule to allow external traffic to the instances.

5. Get the IP address of each instance and browse to it.

The previous step gives you various nodes. However, you need to configure a load balancer. You can do that using these steps:

1. Create a network load balancer.

2. Add a legacy health check resource.

3. Add a target pool in the same region as your instances.

4. Add the instances to the pool.

5. Add a forwarding rule.

6. Get the external IP address of the forwarding rule from the previous step.

7. Browse to the external IP address.

You can get specific instructions for these steps in the *Further reading* section. If you are using a different cloud provider, you can read the documentation to find out how to create a similar setup.

Summary

In this chapter, you learned about the need to have a setup that is going to be available when the demand for your services increases. You learned about HA and load balancing, and you learned how to make your database and web application servers more redundant and highly available.

In the next chapter, you will learn how you can take your breadboard circuits and manufacture them.

Further reading

To learn more about the topics that were covered in this chapter, take a look at the following resources:

- *Implementing HTTP load balancing with NGINX*: `https://docs.nginx.com/nginx/admin-guide/load-balancer/http-load-balancer/`

- *Implementing HTTP load balancing with Apache*: `https://httpd.apache.org/docs/2.4/mod/mod_proxy_balancer.html`

- *GCP cloud load balancing*: `https://cloud.google.com/load-balancing/docs/load-balancing-overview#a_closer_look_at_cloud_load_balancers`

- *GCP – creating a Compute Engine instance*: `https://cloud.google.com/compute/docs/instances/create-start-instance`

- *GCP – creating firewall rules*: `https://cloud.google.com/firewall/docs/using-firewalls`

- *Installing Apache on GCP*: `https://cloud.google.com/compute/docs/tutorials/basic-webserver-apache`

- *GCP – configuring a network load balancer*: `https://cloud.google.com/load-balancing/docs/network`

- *MySQL replication*: `https://dev.mysql.com/doc/refman/8.0/en/replication.html`

- *InfluxDB replication*: `https://docs.influxdata.com/influxdb/cloud/write-data/replication/`

14
Building and Manufacturing Hardware

Congratulations on making it to the final chapter of this book. The previous two chapters focused on considerations for when your hardware or IoT start-up scales and you have to manage many customers. This chapter will focus on what you need to consider when you want to move from breadboard-based designs to prototypes that can be deployed in the real world, and considerations for getting your final hardware product certified.

By the end of this chapter, you will have learned about building hardware from prototypes, getting them manufactured, and the need for certification.

In this chapter, we will cover the following topics:

- Designing more compact hardware
- Designing printed circuit boards
- Manufacturing hardware
- Understanding the need for certification

Designing more compact hardware

We used development boards throughout this book, and we specifically chose Arduino boards because they are designed to a high standard. While you might find a few of the Arduino MKR boards being used in real-world applications, the majority of real-world applications do not make use of a development board. But let's begin with our development boards.

Proof-of-concept (PoC) prototypes

If you are done with your design and find that you have pins to spare, then there is an opportunity for a smaller setup. Even if you don't have pins to spare, if you made use of a breadboard, then there could be an opportunity for a smaller design. You certainly can't ship a solderless breadboard into the field. The DuPont cables frequently used in solderless breadboards are likely to shake and come off.

This is where protoboards come in handy. These let you position your components and solder them together using wires. At this point, you will have a design that you can test within a controlled environment. In a lot of cases, you might be able to run tests without actually creating a case at this stage. Just find a box that is large enough and place your components inside. Then, place the box in the desired location and begin testing.

Testing goes hand-in-hand with updating your PoC prototype. If you find that something doesn't work as expected, you will need to update or replace it. This applies to both the electronic components and the firmware.

When the PoC prototype works, it's time to move to the next step, which is understanding the microcontroller. We have been working with the development board and have outsourced the worry of the particular microcontroller to Arduino up to this point.

Microcontrollers

We made extensive use of the Arduino MKR WiFi 1010 microcontroller development board in this book. The board itself costs a little under $40 if you purchase it from the USA store. However, it might come with several components that you don't need in your project.

By checking the technical specifications of this board, you will see that the microcontroller is a 32-bit SAMD21 Cortex-M0+. There are typically four questions that you might want to ask at this point:

- Does it get the job done?
- Is it available?
- Is it affordable?
- Is there a smaller or less powerful alternative?

Let's consider each of these questions in detail.

Does it get the job done?

At this point, the response should be affirmative. You have already run a bunch of tests on your PoC prototype and you shouldn't be at this point if things didn't work out.

Is it available?

This question is more important than it might first appear to be. The COVID-19 pandemic led to lockdowns that affected logistics and manufacturing and resulted in shortages in electronic components. You can check for their availability on sites such as Mouser Electronics (`https://mouser.com`):

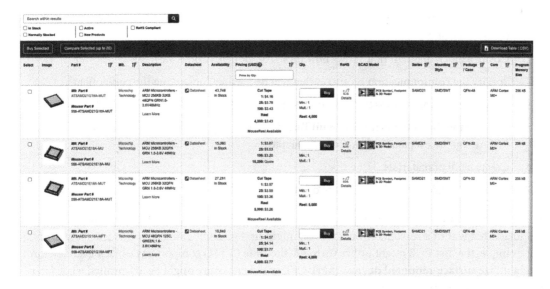

Figure 14.1 – Finding microcontrollers

Is it affordable?

If the microcontroller you are looking for is available, the next question to answer is that of cost. The prices go down if you purchase in bulk, but for now, you are interested in the unit cost. You can get the unit cost from the site where you found the microcontroller.

Is there a less powerful alternative?

This is related to not overengineering a solution while simultaneously saving money. Is there a microcontroller with fewer pins and resources that can get the job done? If it's cheaper, you could find yourself saving money. If you identify such a microcontroller, then you might want to go back to the list and answer the questions all over again.

You can use a similar approach to identify the other components that you made use of in your PoC prototype. It's important to bear in mind that you will need to factor in several components that you didn't think about during the early prototypes. For example, the MKR WiFi 1010 has an onboard LED that you might have utilized as a status indicator. You will need to factor this into your design. Let's look at the design phase.

Preliminary production design

Preliminary production design is a high-level product overview before final details are worked out. This step helps you avoid costly mistakes and identify potential problems early on. You may perform the following steps for this stage:

1. Identify the core components. These should include the controller, inputs, outputs, transceivers, connectors, and power.

2. Create a block diagram that shows how these components come together.

3. Specify the communication protocols that will be used in connecting the components.

4. Select the best microchips to use in this design. You did this in the *Microcontrollers* section.

5. Estimate the size of the **Printed Circuit Board** (**PCB**) and the number of layers. We will discuss PCB design in a separate section of this chapter.

6. Create a bill of materials.

7. Determine and design the enclosure or casing.

These steps will provide clarity on just how complex the design is, and whether or not it can be manufactured within a reasonable budget. You might find yourself going over this list a few times. For example, the first PCB might utilize **through-the-hole** (**TTH**) components while a later version might utilize **surface-mounted devices** (**SMDs**). The first enclosure might be 3D-printed while later ones will have to utilize injection molding.

At this point, you may choose to manufacture a PCB prototype just to see what your product looks like as a single unit. This unit will be larger than the final product because you might not get to customize the PCB layout. Alternatively, you might proceed with the traditional schematic and PCB design process. Let's look at how the first approach might work.

PCB prototyping

Since you already know all of the components that go into your product, you could opt for a manufacturer that provides rapid prototyping services. One such manufacturer is SparkFun Electronics, with the **A La Carte** (**ALC**) service: `https://alc.sparkfun.com/`.

The ALC service provides an online interface with a three-step process:

1. **Select your controller**: This is where you select the particular microcontroller that you would like to work with. You might not find a wide range of microcontrollers here, but you should be able to find something to start with.

2. **Add components**: All you have to do is pick the components you need. ALC will keep track of the number of pins and the total power consumption.

3. **Check out**: When you are done, simply check out and pay for your design, and wait for it to arrive in the mail.

At the time of writing this book, ALC doesn't let you choose where your components are placed on the final PCB.

When you receive the PCB, you may either test it out as-is or design an enclosure for it. This is where 3D printing comes in handy for enclosures. Do note that most 3D-printed enclosures aren't extremely durable. They are simply functional. It is possible to get durable enclosures using 3D printing, but the cost might not be justifiable.

At this point, you have another prototype that is more suitable for field tests. You might want to start by ordering only one unit just to confirm that everything works as expected. When you confirm this, you may proceed to order a few additional units for testing purposes. Note that this manufacturing approach is more expensive, so you don't necessarily want to go to market with these prototypes.

Another prototyping service you might want to consider is the Fusion service from Seeed Studios (https://www.seeedstudio.com/fusion.html).

The result of this phase is a prototype that works as it should but doesn't necessarily look the way you want.

Next, you need to design your schematic to bring your components together.

Schematic design

This is the point at which things start to get serious. The schematic is a circuit diagram. It is based on your preliminary production design, which you are sure works because you have a working PCB.

The schematic diagram is about all of the little details. This is where you connect all of the pins and ensure that your power supply is accurate and flowing in the right direction. You should utilize **Electronic Design Automation** (**EDA**) software for this phase. A popular choice of software is DipTrace (https://diptrace.com/diptrace-software/).

Any time you invest in learning this software will not go to waste because you can also utilize it for your PCB design at a later stage.

You may also research a free EDA software called KiCAD: https://www.kicad.org/.

You will need to verify your schematics using **Electrical Rule Check** (**ERC**). ERC verifies the robustness of your design and ensures that the circuit will work as intended. It checks that all the connections are acceptable and that there are no floating or unconnected signal lines, or other common errors.

If this phase feels a little too much for you to carry out yourself, several manufacturers provide design services.

After your schematic design comes your PCB design.

PCB design

We will discuss PCB design in greater detail in the next major section. After the PCB design comes your **Bill of Materials (BoM)**, similar to how you would prepare a BoM after your architectural design and renderings in construction.

Bill of Materials

This is the final BoM and will factor in all of the components that you will be utilizing. It's a good idea to have this even if you don't know the prices of some of the components on the list. The BoM is useful for your business plans.

Designing printed circuit boards

PCBs are designed using EDA software, similar to, and in a lot of cases the same as, the ones used for schematic design. The primary difference here is that you need to place the components and connect them using circuits. All of this has to fit within the dimensions of your chosen board, so PCBs have layers. The board itself is non-conductive, with the circuits etched on using copper. The connections between components are called traces.

The copper traces are thinner than the wires that you worked with during the prototyping phase. Since traces are electrical conductors, they mustn't cross each other. This is called a collision. You may notice from electrical schematic diagrams that wires jump over each other. That is the same principle that applies here. However, since traces are etched onto the PCB, they can't jump over each other on the same plane or layer. Instead, they jump to a different plane and then continue their journey. The jump to a new layer is made using a *via*. You will frequently see these as holes on a PCB.

Certain manufacturers support PCB designs with more than two layers. These two layers are the ones on the outside. In a situation where you need more space to route traces, you may introduce additional layers. Some manufacturers support as many as 14 layers. The other layers are hidden from you and connected using vias.

Electronic circuits generate heat. Copper traces need to be wide enough to dissipate heat, without being so wide as to waste space. On the other hand, if the traces are too narrow, then the circuit will fail at some point.

A lot of EDA software will integrate your schematic design with your PCB design and will let you update one from the other. They will also have a library of components so that you can pick the specific component that goes into your design. You will need to read the documentation for each of the components that you choose to use. This is because you might have to factor in certain requirements, such as maximum trace distance between components, pins that need to be pulled to ground, pins that require capacitors, and more.

There are quite a few software out there for PCB design. Some that you might want to consider are as follows:

- EasyEDA
- KiCAD
- DipTrace
- Altium Designer

EasyEDA is particularly interesting because it integrates the component library from two other companies:

- LCSC Electronics, a vendor of electronic components with over 2 million parts listed from over 2,000 manufacturers
- JLCPCB, a PCB and SMT manufacturer

EasyEDA lists as many as 800,000 components from these two partners and updates pricing and stock levels in real time. It gives users the ability to search by part numbers, thus speeding up the design process.

Make sure you get an engineering review for each of your designs before you send them off for manufacturing. This is important because you need someone else to verify the work that you have done. You might be too excited to pick out some design errors.

Manufacturing hardware

There are two parts that you will need to manufacture:

- The PCB
- The Enclosure

Let's consider these in detail.

PCB fabrication

There are a large number of PCB fabrication providers and you can pick any one, depending on where you live. If there are none within your geography, then you may look to Asia. You will need to send the fabricator a file that it will use to print out the PCB. Most fabricators accept Gerber files.

Most PCB fabricators will only manufacture the PCB. This will require you to solder the components yourself. This could be a problem if you make use of tiny SMD components. Some fabricators can solder these components for you and send you the finished board. This is called PCB assembly.

You can find PCB manufacturers online. Here is a list of a few that might interest you:

- JLC PCB
- PCB Way
- Seeed Studios
- Sparkfun Electronics

With your PCB done, let's consider enclosures.

Enclosures

The only time you want to make use of a PCB without an enclosure is when it's on your desk. There are various sources of enclosures:

- **Repurposing**: There are all sorts of enclosures that you could choose to use. These might have been designed for generic use, and all you have to do is find one that has the closest size to what you want and repurpose it. This might entail cutting out some sections. This approach is best for early prototypes.

- **3D printing**: Cheap 3D printers will let you manufacture an enclosure that fits the PCB pretty well. However, you will need to design the enclosure using software such as Fusion 360. The enclosures that you print this way will not last very long but will provide some protection during field tests.

- **Injection molding**: This is how most enclosures you see on finished products are made. The actual manufacturing process involves injecting plastic under high pressure into a mold. This process is expensive and is normally left for last. The major investment is in the mold. As you might imagine, these molds can't be shared between projects but can be reused for several enclosures before the mold itself becomes unusable. The cost of the mold is dependent on the number of enclosures that will be made, among other things. You can design your enclosure with Fusion 360, or outsource the design to an industrial designer.

With all of the manufacturing done, you are almost set to hit the market.

Understanding the need for certification

Every electrical product must undergo certification. The specific certification required depends on the country in which the product will be sold. Just as you design with manufacturing in mind, you must also design with certification in mind.

You need to wait until your product is ready for market before you certify it. Any changes to the product, including the enclosure, will normally require recertification.

While certification will be done at the end, it is important to consult a certification expert at the point of preliminary production design.

Here are some certification bodies to be aware of:

- **Federal Communications Commission**: This US-based regulator certifies all electronic products, making sure that the electromagnetic radiation from those products is within acceptable levels and doesn't interfere with the operation of other wireless communication devices.

- **Underwriters Laboratories (UL) or Canadian Standards Association (CSA)**: These bodies certify electrical appliances that connect to an AC outlet.

- **Conformité Européene**: This certification is required in the EU and is similar to the FCC and UL.

- **RoHS certification**: This certification is required to prove that a product does not contain lead. This certification is required in both the EU and the USA.

And, it's a wrap. We have gone over the key things you should know when you decide to manufacture your electronic products.

Summary

You have made it to the end of this chapter, and also the end of this book. In this chapter, you learned how you can take what you have built using Arduino and maybe some breadboards and convert it into a prototype that you can test. After initial testing, you learned about the various phases that your prototype needs to go through before you can manufacture it for sale.

Congratulations, you have made it to the end! I hope you build something awesome.

Further reading

To learn more about the topics that were covered in this chapter, take a look at the following resources:

- *Learn to design PCBs*: https://predictabledesigns.com/academy/

- *EasyEDA*: https://easyeda.com/

- *KiCAD*: https://www.kicad.org/

- *Altium Designer*: https://www.altium.com/altium-designer

- *DipTrace*: https://diptrace.com/diptrace-software/

- *Fusion 360*: https://www.autodesk.co.uk/products/fusion-360/overview

Index

M

`Packtpub.com`

Subscribe to our online digital library for full access to over 7,000 books and videos, as well as industry leading tools to help you plan your personal development and advance your career. For more information, please visit our website.

Why subscribe?

- Spend less time learning and more time coding with practical eBooks and Videos from over 4,000 industry professionals

- Improve your learning with Skill Plans built especially for you

- Get a free eBook or video every month

- Fully searchable for easy access to vital information

- Copy and paste, print, and bookmark content

Did you know that Packt offers eBook versions of every book published, with PDF and ePub files available? You can upgrade to the eBook version at `packtpub.com` and as a print book customer, you are entitled to a discount on the eBook copy. Get in touch with us at `customercare@packtpub.com` for more details.

At `www.packtpub.com`, you can also read a collection of free technical articles, sign up for a range of free newsletters, and receive exclusive discounts and offers on Packt books and eBooks.

Other Books You May Enjoy

If you enjoyed this book, you may be interested in these other books by Packt:

Mastering PLC Programming

M. T. White

ISBN: 978-1-80461-288-0

- Find out how to write PLC programs using advanced programming techniques
- Explore OOP concepts for PLC programming
- Delve into software engineering topics such as libraries and SOLID programming
- Explore HMIs, HMI controls, HMI layouts, and alarms
- Create an HMI project and attach it to a PLC in CODESYS
- Gain hands-on experience by building simulated PLC and HMI projects

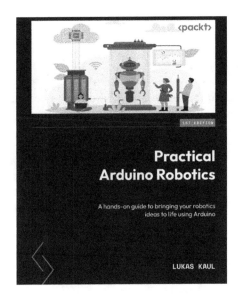

Practical Arduino Robotics

Lukas Kaul

ISBN: 978-1-80461-317-7

- Understand and use the various interfaces of an Arduino board
- Write the code to communicate with your sensors and motors
- Implement and tune methods for sensor signal processing
- Understand and implement state machines that control your robot
- Implement feedback control to create impressive robot capabilities
- Integrate hardware and software components into a reliable robotic system
- Tune, debug, and improve Arduino-based robots systematically

Packt is searching for authors like you

If you're interested in becoming an author for Packt, please visit `authors.packtpub.com` and apply today. We have worked with thousands of developers and tech professionals, just like you, to help them share their insight with the global tech community. You can make a general application, apply for a specific hot topic that we are recruiting an author for, or submit your own idea.

Share Your Thoughts

Now you've finished *Arduino Data Communications*, we'd love to hear your thoughts! Scan the QR code below to go straight to the Amazon review page for this book and share your feedback or leave a review on the site that you purchased it from.

`https://packt.link/r/1837632618`

Your review is important to us and the tech community and will help us make sure we're delivering excellent quality content.

Download a free PDF copy of this book

Thanks for purchasing this book!

Do you like to read on the go but are unable to carry your print books everywhere?

Is your eBook purchase not compatible with the device of your choice?

Don't worry, now with every Packt book you get a DRM-free PDF version of that book at no cost.

Read anywhere, any place, on any device. Search, copy, and paste code from your favorite technical books directly into your application.

The perks don't stop there, you can get exclusive access to discounts, newsletters, and great free content in your inbox daily

Follow these simple steps to get the benefits:

1. Scan the QR code or visit the link below

https://packt.link/free-ebook/9781837632619

2. Submit your proof of purchase
3. That's it! We'll send your free PDF and other benefits to your email directly